WHAT BREXIT MEANS

What Brexit Means explores the rise of populism in Britain. Drawing on several years of ethnographic fieldwork amongst ideologically committed Brexit activists, it examines the discourse of populism across language, culture, politics, psychology, and cognition. It explains how populism is expressed in terms of ritually renewing social order and solidarity. Rejecting the notion that the territory of populism studies belongs to political science, this book shows how it is in the realm of anthropology – myth, ritual, alterity, consciousness, selfhood – that we witness the most compelling examples of how a phenomenon as modern as populism depends upon the same symbolic logics that we find in the premodern world. *What Brexit Means* is a demonstration of the power of anthropology to explain momentous and poorly predicted transformations in the global order. It will become a benchmark text for those eager for anthropology's contribution to understanding the political turbulence that is rocking the stability of Western democracies.

Max Horder is a cognitive anthropologist working on issues of belief, trust, and identity in modern Europe. He completed his MPhil from the University of Cambridge and a BSc from the London School of Economics. Max Horder received his PhD in Anthropology at Princeton University for his work on populism in Britain. He is also a Fellow of the Royal Society of Arts.

ANTHROPOLOGY OF NOW
Series Editor: Jack David Eller

The Anthropology of Donald Trump
Culture and the Exceptional Moment
Edited by Jack David Eller

Love and Technology
An Ethnography of Dating App Users in Berlin
Fabian Broeker

Dispossession
Anthropological Perspectives on Russia's War Against Ukraine
Edited by Catherine Wanner

Gun Rights Activism and the US Culture War
Embodied Fantasies of the Ethical Warrior in Contemporary Gun Culture
Joe Anderson

Anthropology of Ascendant China
Histories, Attainments, and Tribulations
Edited by Mayfair Yang

Culture and Diversity in the United States
So Many Ways to Be American
2nd Edition
Jack David Eller

What Brexit Means
An Anthropology of Polarization and Cultural Change in Britain
Max Horder

https://www.routledge.com/Anthropology-of-Now/book-series/ANTHNOW

WHAT BREXIT MEANS

An Anthropology of Polarization and Cultural Change in Britain

Max Horder

Routledge
Taylor & Francis Group
NEW YORK AND LONDON

Designed cover image: extravagantni

First published 2025
by Routledge
605 Third Avenue, New York, NY 10158

and by Routledge
4 Park Square, Milton Park, Abingdon, Oxon OX14 4RN

Routledge is an imprint of the Taylor & Francis Group, an informa business

Library of Congress Cataloging-in-Publication Data
A catalog record for this title has been requested

ISBN: 978-1-032-60296-7 (hbk)
ISBN: 978-1-032-60293-6 (pbk)
ISBN: 978-1-003-45851-7 (ebk)

DOI: 10.4324/9781003458517

Typeset in Sabon
by Taylor & Francis Books

CONTENTS

ACKNOWLEDGEMENTS

I owe an enormous debt of gratitude to the many that made this project possible. I owe a particular debt to my supervisors at Princeton, John Borneman and David Cannadine, for their years of guidance and advice turning this from an idea in 2017 to a fully published manuscript. I also am profoundly grateful to my editor, David Eller, for giving me both the opportunity and the encouragement to develop my PhD into a book for this series.

I am indebted to my wonderful committee of Carolyn Rouse and Laurence Ralph. So too to innumerable mentors and teachers at Princeton; Julia Elyachar, Lauren Coyle Rosen, Rena Lederman, and João Biehl, as well as James Van Wyck, Miqueias Mugge, Bentzi Brook, Carol Zanca, and many others. Neither would this have been without previous guides at Cambridge and the LSE; Graham Denyer Willis, Nick Long, Tom Grisaffi, Jason Hickel, Harry Walker, and Laura Bear, to name only a few.

For many conversations that helped me make sense of the project itself, I am grateful in particular to Tony Winston and EM West London.

Colleagues and friends, too, made the experience of writing a PhD a profoundly gratifying (if not always easy) experience. Special thanks to Mai Alkhamissi, Jagat Sohail, Jack Williams, Aderayo Sanusi, Brandon Hunter, Wei Gan, Max Cohen, Luke Forrester, Aleksander Kostić, Eliav Grossman, Gabby Lovett, Joshua Picard, Joel Finkelstein, Mochi Liu, Will Freeman, Ipsita Dey, Donald Della Pietra and Abigail Levner.

The journey to completion was long, and there were many whose presence made it special. In particular, Daniel and Miri Gellert-Shemtov, Sam Lessons, Abbie Williams, Nick Kling, Ben Shaps, Sebastian Damberg-Ott, Evelien Lemmens, Andrew Bax, Rebecca Reid, James Kusher, Jeremy Neumark-Jones, Rowan Roberts, Tom Montagu-Harrison, Morgan Lockyer, David

Gluckstein, Sarah Kilkenny, Fred Warshaw, Hugh and Hannah Style, Luke Valori, Alec Scragg, Will Bywater, Daniel Lichman, Alan Gluckman, Maurice Amaranatho Robey, Martin Dives, Edwin Chomer, Matthew Rosen-Marsh, Val Uvarov, Michael Dean, Ilai Schechter, Yossi Koffler, Ben and Charlotte Leon, Maya Raphael, Nigel Canin, David Hirsh, Amit Kahana, Hadas Haimov, Nurit Starborg, and Anthony Martin. For Ollie, Ellie, and Jane, Shirley and Howard, as well as Vardit, Roni, Shay, and Sagi, my gratitude is immense.

The most thanks to my parents, for the innumerable sacrifices it took getting me here. I will be forever unable to articulate my gratitude.

Finally, for Shachar, this book is dedicated to you.

INTRODUCTION

"Brexit Means Brexit"

Theresa May, Prime Minister of the UK, 2016

In 2016 the United Kingdom held a nationwide referendum to determine whether or not to stay within the European Union (EU). The vote to leave won a narrow victory, with an overall split of 52 per cent/48 per cent. These latter voters who wanted continued membership identified as 'Remainers'; those who wanted an exit, 'Leavers' or 'Brexiters'.[1] The emergence of these novel political categories transformed the contours of British life, rapidly overcoming the traditional affiliation with mass political parties that broadly characterised the voting cleavages of the 20th century (Sobolewska and Ford 2020). This book's central concern is understanding how politically engaged individuals made sense of, fought for, grieved over, and ultimately tried to move on from one of the most important transformations for Britain since the Second World War.

The results of the referendum sharply diverged from the predicted outcome, both among specialists and the wider population (Jennings and Fisher 2016). Folk theories of varying complexity and sophistication quickly became a household explanation for this unprecedented result. Many of these themes indulged in the same conspiracy fantasy about Russian interference or 'dark money' that mirrored accusations of Donald Trump's 2016 election in the United States (Rutland 2017). In addition, media representations of the 'forces' behind Brexit varied wildly in relationship to different audience expectation. What for some was a triumph of democracy in the face of technocratic federalism was for others a tragic regress into the pre-war world of xenophobia, isolation, and reactionary politics. These interpretations reflect the underlying

DOI: 10.4324/9781003458517-1

structural changes that increasingly characterise Western democracies, such as a decline of trust towards mass-media, politicians, or indeed any state capacity to pursue meaningful economic change (Ford and Jennings 2020; Mair 2013).

The academic field emerging in relation to the vote remains a contentious arena for debate and disagreement. This chapter will provide an anthropological perspective to much of the current literature on the topic which remains broadly within the realm of sociology and political science. Certainly, the most widely cited explanation for the referendum result fits within the broader question of 'right-wing populism'. Yet despite the prevalence of this term across a host of academic disciplines, a great deal of consternation remains around its precise meaning. Few other subjects match the sheer number of texts addressing how to either measure or define 'populism'; whether we can see it as a 'thin ideology', a style or aesthetic, the shadow of representative democracy, a political logic, or others (Laclau 2005; Moffitt 2016; Müller 2017; Stanley 2008).

Prefiguring the debates that will feature in the rest of this book, my introduction will adopt the most viable definition or populism as:

> "an ideology that considers society to be ultimately separated into two homogeneous and antagonistic groups, 'the pure people' versus 'the corrupt elite', and which argues that politics should be an expression of the *volonté générale* (general will) of the people".
>
> *(Mudde 2004, p. 543)*

This definition succinctly captures both the anti-pluralist makeup of populism with the philosophical underpinning of a forgotten, silent majority who feel unrepresented by the 'business as usual' of technocratic, liberal policymakers, and elites (Eatwell and Goodwin 2018; Müller 2017).

The central question to this introduction is how other scholars have accounted for the emergence of populism in Britain, expressed in the decision to leave the EU in 2016. Like almost all contemporary populist phenomena, it is the consequence of both global and local conditions, linking long-term social-structural changes in modern societies with the contingent actions of conscious agents (Ford and Jennings 2020). In the case of Brexit, this specific context is defined by the presence of long-term Euroscepticism that has pervaded British history since the Second World War (Hawkins 2021; FitzGibbon et al. 2016; Forster 2002). Similarly, the fact that the UK is an island nation off the coast of the European continent – one that has not been truly conquered by any European power since 1066 – likely also contributed to the weak legitimacy of continental political influence (Carol et al. 2019). Yet, these abstract factors are difficult to account for empirically, and their resonance may rest more on methodological assumptions or disciplinary conventions than any epistemological reality.

Altogether, making sense of Brexit in the categories of empirical social science remains a tremendous challenge. From a structural point of view, there is an almost uncountable array of factors which influenced the 2016 referendum. Methodologically, there is clearly a role for studying the long-term, macroscale sociodemographic trends that can be measured with economic indices, attitude surveys, social questionaires, and in-depth ethnographic research. Yet such attempts to broadly account for Brexit are likely to miss both the contingent nature of infighting among political elites and the effects of the pre-vote campaign itself. One illustrative example of this problem is Shipman's (2016) journalistic account of the days around the referendum, a narrative which speaks to how the competencies of a small group of political elites can alter the destiny of entire continents. While these descriptions have trouble accounting for large-scale voting patterns and political or cultural context, they provide an important perspective on the contingency of individual actors that cannot be easily captured by other social-scientific disciplinary paradigms.

However, caution is always necessary for data-thin narratives, whether ethnographic, statistical, or others. There is little shortage of scholarship promoting outlandish explanations for the Brexit vote with little evidence beyond academic folk-theory. And while the empirical bar for what counts as evidence may be varied across disciplines (Lambert 2009), evidence for theories of Brexit range from anecdotal accusations, systematic survey data and grounded, in-depth participant observation. Each provides a unique perspective into a topic so vast that, only a few years on, millions of words have been spilt trying to adequately capture why it happened and for what purpose.

I have to a large extent avoided several important frameworks in this overview. One is the more peripheral explanations that rest on psychological (Zala et al. 2017) and psychoanalytic (Covington 2018; Mandelbaum 2020) terminology. This is in large part because I address them from a more ethnographic perspective later on in the book. It is worth noting that I am certainly sensitive to the drawbacks of psychologising political choices. Such a framing is often theoretically unsound, empirically questionable, and motivationally suspect (Müller 2017). Yet, as I hope to show throughout the text, psychoanalytic anthropology is very often a highly generative framework for making sense of the mental dynamics that lead to supporting populist political candidates. Ensuring balance between these two poles is a real challenge, and one that I hope I have addressed adequately throughout. Indeed, one of my principal motivations for conducting this research was to bring an empathetic lens more fully to the Brexiter point of view – one that did not dismiss the vote as a psychological pathology. As I try to steer a path between the Scylla and Charybdis of these two framings, one cannot help but fall back on the widely shared sense there was indeed something deeply irrational about the vote to leave the EU, given how little membership impacts daily life of the average UK citizen. Making sense of that is at the heart of this text.

The second omission is the role of social media and the growth of populist support. Wide explorations in the literature between social media and polarisation have demonstrated that there are considerable correlations between the two (Engesser et al. 2017; Faulkner et al. 2021). This is especially relevant for the 2016 referendum: there is little doubt that Facebook advertising contributed in no small degree towards the result. However, this chapter is simply unable to account empirically for the relationship between the two, given that it is almost completely an ethnographic research project. Although Twitter data has been cited as occasional examples of public-facing emotional content, I shall merely bracket a literature which can speak for itself.

Why An Anthropology of Brexit?

In some ways, it is a slight misnomer to designate this ethnographic project as one focused centrally on Brexit. It is true this populist moment stretching from 2016 until 2022 forms the principal object of investigation, but we cannot hope to understand any such phenomena in such narrow terms. The very nature of ethnographic research over a long period of time necessarily brings in a great variety of other questions, issues, problems, themes, and topics. This is true not only for the researcher himself, but of the great many interlocutors who formed the bedrock of the ethnography. For even though Brexit was the main process under investigation, the truth is that many events came and went during this period – notably the Coronavirus pandemic, the *Black Lives Matter* protests, and the 2019 election – which all in some way folded and unfolded themselves along the contours of the British culture in fascinating and complicated ways. As I will shortly demonstrate, we can thus perhaps think of Brexit not as unique moment in modern British history, but rather simply one iteration of an underlying social cleavage between, depending on one's viewpoint: 'upper' and 'lower' classes, 'cosmopolitans' and 'communitarians', 'Anywheres' and 'Somewheres', 'winners' and 'losers' of globalisation, or those with 'materialist' and 'post-materialist' values, for example.

Indeed, the dominant concern of this book is the relationship between such underlying structural dynamics and the psychological, cultural, or cognitive expressions of them. Sociologists are apt at understanding such macro-scale changes, but this is much less the realm of anthropological speciality. A lack of survey data, a distaste for generalisations, and a methodological inability to create anything resembling a 'big' data set precludes us from answering too many questions about the nature of modern social structure itself. Our discipline can thus never truly ask *why* Brexit happened in the sense of understanding the long-term trends of voting mobilisation. Nor would we want to: demographic and national issues are simply too large a cluster of phenomena for anthropology to make accurate assertions on. But this is not to our detriment. It is not that we should feel the need to answer such questions: they are not the right questions for us to be asking in the first place. Our focus as anthropologists is on the minute, the particular, the unique, the qualitative, the singular event, and in many senses the psychic or cognitive aspects to cultural change – not macro-scale demographic or electoral trends. When approaching Brexit from an anthropological point of view, what both our discipline and our ethnographic methodology open up are the *personal* reflections on a process of tremendous cultural instability. With the exception of Chapter Three, which quite consciously puts Brexit under the lens of structural-functionalism, this book's principal concern will be on the individual lifeworlds and personal experiences of those many individuals who were involved in the tumult of the past six years.

The research questions thus inevitably focus on their thoughts, feelings, and sensations towards both Brexit and the general sentiments that have defined Britain since the referendum result. When I began this research, my specific questions were still somewhat hazy. Why did people feel such an attachment to Brexit? How did they narrativise their journey towards adopting a 'populist' position on Europe? To what extent did racism and xenophobia emerge as salient attributes of their political worldviews? This latter issue was a common piece of collective wisdom which seemed to be both true and false at the same time. I felt that it was too politically expedient to condemn Brexiters for a kind of moral degeneracy. So too did I personally know Brexiters who really in no way fit the pattern. Indeed, some of time key interlocutors throughout this book – many of whom were taken from the Brexit Party – were themselves not ethnically White British. However, it is clear to anyone in Britain that Brexit had at least something to do with immigration and ethnic change. Something about much of the academic literature was not convincing – and I was determined to understand what that was.

In the end, the research questions which really drove this ethnography were not about why people did or did not like the EU, Donald Tusk, the European Court of Justice, Schengen arrangements, or any of the other institutional, cultural or political facets of post-war continental integration. They were fundamentally about *change*. Why do things change? How people feel about it? What makes some change better, and some worse? Why do some things stay the same, and others do not? If change is inevitable, why do we still find it so frustrating? Does anyone *cause* it? What is about empirical transformations in demography, political sovereignty, communication or myth, which we sometimes find compelling and other times revolting?

Britain has changed remarkably in the past several decades, notably in its adoption of Thatcherite economics, mass-immigration, decline in religiosity, and overall collapse in global political influence. For Brexiters and Remainers, these are things either to greatly celebrate or greatly mourn. Why some people felt such an affinity to changed past – as opposed to those who longed for a different future – remained a key concern throughout almost all of the ethnographic research I conducted. Rather than focusing solely on the classic issues like race, gender, or class, then, I looked to find what it was about people's personality and lifeworld which encouraged them to feel so strongly about what they felt Britain was becoming.

Choosing former Brexit Party candidates for much of the empirical research, I purposefully looked for some of the most ideologically committed members of the anti-EU faction. The party itself was formed in 2018 in response to European elections, and has since the 2019 election merged into the Reform Party. The details of such institutional relationships will unfold in the following chapters: the point is merely to emphasise that my research questions centered on those individuals who were committed to Brexit regardless of social, ethnic, or cultural characteristics. Indeed, one of the curious features of all of these activists is the sheer range of cultural diversity between them: some were rich, others quite poor; some white, others not, and a few were my age, while many were spread across generational cohorts. The stereotype of 'male, pale, and stale' which defines much popular liberal discourse on Brexiters was something I purposefully avoided, not always to great success. In taking a diverse set of interlocutors for my ethnographic research, I am thus unable to answer questions about certain correlations, other than that these were dedicated Brexiters. But this by no means impacts the central questions of this book: which are to understand how my small but diverse sample of ideological activists experienced, reflected upon, believed in, fought for, and ultimately felt vindicated by their support for the populist victory of the second decade of the 21st century.

Finally, I believe that such questions put me in the best of anthropological company. Cultural change has been one of the most fundamental (and vexing) questions in the discipline over the past several decades. Indeed, the question of how and why society changes can be traced all the way through early Marxist (2008) approaches to the interaction between base and superstructure, as well as between the means and mode of production. Many such debates interlink with more specific anthropological concerns: how myth and (sometimes violent) ritual stabilises social relations, for instance, by foreclosing some cultural change and opening up other spaces for transformation. More specifically disciplinary theories like structuralism (Lévi-Strauss 1974) implicitly recognise that cultural change is in a perpetual flux of *bricolage* – but perhaps remains more ambivalent about whether cultural contents are infinite in either variety or form.

However, scholars like Sahlins (1987) were ultimately unsatisfied with structuralism's ability to truly understand the nature of cultural change. He sought to understand it in terms of structure and history, or what he called structure and 'event'. This latter concept refers to the connection between a historical moment and an overall symbolic ecosystem with pre-given ways of interpreting phenomena. In his example of Captain Cook's voyages to Hawaii, the collision between an old system of cultural categories and a new one provides the opening moment for a new process of cultural reproduction. Not unlike a dialectical idea of synthesis, these moments create an opening for transformation and innovation. Cultural change emerges in the space between a set structure and its reproduction via novel historical events. Neither fully fixed nor totally open, such an approach is sensitive to the complex manner by which human's grasp of symbols oscillate between mutually shared categories and systems of thought, and the radically open-ended possibilities for their transformation.

In many ways, we can see the Brexit 'event' as a similar example of such a process. Before the 2016 referendum, there was a relatively stable sense of how politics worked in terms of the traditional left-right political cleavage. Afterwards, British political culture – if we can speak in such general terms – necessarily began to reproduce itself through the incorporation of the Remainer-Leaver symbolic binary. These were two entirely novel cultural categories which even until now index diverse forms of identity, affiliation, and belonging. The events *after* the 2016 referendum – such as the pandemic and the 2019 election – also split along these lines much more than they did alongside previous ones. But now people were *conscious* of this reality, whereas before the referendum such value divides were, as Ronald Inglehart (1977) says, mostly 'silent'. In many ways, then, understanding how people managed such a new reality at the level of the reproduction of culture is one of the key framings of this book. How did these new ways of making sense transform the way people thought about each other? To what extent was polarisation in Britain a symptom of these changes in cultural values, one which created an entirely new way of making sense of things? How much destabilisation was caused simply by an inability for us to co-ordinate across traditional social divides?

These are classically anthropological questions, and ones which I will explore in the following chapters of this book. In outlining the state of play, however, this introduction will distinguish between five major analytical frameworks for making sense of Brexit. I provide such an overview to give a sense of how other scholars have so far tackled the problem, and encourage readers to see where my analysis fits into a pre-existent cultural system of its own. These broad theories are (a) economic grievance; (b) cultural backlash; (c) ethnoracial tension; (d) the British Empire; (e) neo-nationalism; and (f) anti-politics. And while such perspectives are not exhaustive, they represent some of the fundamental mainstream approaches to understanding the trends that led up to the referendum result. In order to make sense of the conversation around populism, and by extension the broader context in which this book is based, it is also worthwhile briefly summarising some of the principal approaches to understanding Brexit in the literature.

Previous Approaches to Brexit Populism

Economic Grievance

Perhaps the most widespread theory of Brexit draws on what could be called an 'economic grievance' thesis. This approach turns on the framework that the neoliberalisation of the global economy, rapid and destabilising technological change, increasing inequality and uneven development have together produced widespread economic deprivation of huge swathes of the Western world. Populism can be viewed as a reaction to this process. In the Brexit context, the 2016 referendum result could be seen as the consequence of the 'have-nots' or 'left behinds' delivering a protest vote against a technocratic government which has promoted these policies for several decades (Koch 2017).

Typically, scholars who concur with this idea will cite the pernicious and corroding effects of neoliberal transformation of society since the 1980s. Populism occurs then as a "reaction to a neoliberal political and economic order" (Gusterson 2017, p. 210). Others see Brexit as a backlash to globalisation more broadly, especially as between the 'winners' and 'losers' of this process in relation to poverty, education, and achievement (Hobolt 2016; O'Rourke 2019). Many of these frameworks emphasise the social consequences of the uneven impact of capitalist development across the country (Coyle 2016), an approach which draws heavily on scholarship on the 'unevenness' of capitalist development (Hudson 1988).

Within this paradigm, the key question remains how to measure who these 'losers' or 'left-behinds' might be. It is certainly not immediately clear what these voting groups consist of, especially in the age of general class decomposition particularly in urban centres (Wacquant 2007, 2009). More specifically, the risk in this approach involves assumptions about where precarity in the contemporary neoliberal economy can be located: a problem which does not concern only scholars of populism (Butler 2004, 2010; Molé 2010; Neilson and Rossiter 2008; Standing 2011). Neoliberalism is a complex and variegated process with wide-ranging effects on different professions. The imagery of 20th-century proletarian politics may hardly converge with the reality of precarity of labour today: among delivery drivers, supermarket workers, or academic adjuncts, for example.

Nevertheless, it is a reasonable assumption that we can locate the 'losers' of globalisation in areas of post-industrial decline, given that much of the neoliberalisation process in the West erodes the strength of organised labour through the offshoring process to East Asia (Harvey 2007). It follows that that exploring the effects of Chinese import substitution could be an appropriate sphere of investigation. Indeed, the economic theory proposed by Autor et al. (2013), suggests that the export-orientation of the Chinese economy has had measurably pernicious consequences on labour markets in the United States. By virtue of their industrial specialisation, these markets have been extremely vulnerable to being undercut by East Asian competition. The systematic hollowing out of the American manufacturing base and its transfer across the Pacific, they suggest, may have been profoundly negative economic consequences. This may have turned to the isolationist politics of Trump in 2016 (Autor et al. 2017).

This approach can be applied to the UK, locating the 'left-behinds' as those same industrial workers who would have been dislocated by the identical process of Chinese import substitution in the former manufacturing centres of Northeast England and Wales. Colantone and Stanig (2018) demonstrate a clear and reasonable link to Brexit within these industrial areas that suffer from greater import substitution than those without. Although this is a small study with little insight into why wealthier post-industrial regions in the Southeast also voted for Brexit, it provides a generative example of how industrial decline and a populist message of bringing back manufacturing, halting immigration and restoring national greatness may find a great deal of sympathy in economically 'left-behind' areas.

All these perspectives converge in their vision of a legitimate resentment against the inequalities caused by Thatcher's neoliberal restructuring of the economy. Financial deprivation, cultural abandonment, and geographical isolation have together produced a social antipathy which, rather than being correctly channelled through appropriate social democratic vehicles, leads instead to a kind of 'false consciousness' and misguided political reaction (Lewy 1982). This framing is shared Calhoun (2016), who sees anger specifically against London by the 'left-behinds' one of the key drivers of Brexit. In this case, the resentment flows towards those 'winners' of globalisation who have managed to successfully adopt to changing economic and cultural realities of the wealthy metropole. Although the EU did not cause this economic decline, it may function symbolically as a useful scapegoat for the globalising and technocratic tendencies of neoliberal capitalism.

Regardless of which metric can be used to frame the empirics of this approach, the overall theory of 'economic grievance' has had a tremendous amount of public, journalistic, and academic support. Certainly, it is apparent to many people studying Brexit ethnographically that there is at least some element of class or economic deprivation which strongly correlates to supporting Leave (Evans 2020; Koch 2017; Ringel 2020). At the same time, there is also a risk that these insights are the consequence of selection bias. If scholars – especially those with a historical materialist worldview – already assume that Brexit was a reaction to neoliberalism, it is not difficult to find people who provide evidence of this connection. By choosing to do fieldwork about Brexit in post-industrial regions of the UK, finding concrete examples of how people rationalise their political choices in relation to their day-to-day life may provide interesting insights Koch 2017. But they may have trouble extrapolating their findings across the whole UK. The considerable percentage of wealthier individuals who voted for Brexit is a solid illustration of a complex challenge to this problem (Dorling and Tomlinson 2019).

More fundamentally, however, the argument that political decisions represent translated concerns from economic relationships is itself dubious. This questionable assumption was already something associated with a Marxist theory of a class 'in itself' versus a class 'for itself' (Andrew 1983; Bourdieu 1987). Class identity – and the political action that may or may not flow from this self-understanding – is by no means a natural consequence of either proletarianisation or embourgeoisement. A political position does not necessarily mature from an economic one, something which has remained a persistent challenge for socialist intellectuals. Rather, there must be concrete shifts in consciousness for this to happen, a situation noted in the historical context by E.P. Thompson (1975). There is no straightforward translation between the two.

Another general problem with 'economic grievance' theory – although one that can be applied to all of these frameworks – is that any single, all-encompassing explanation for the Brexit 'type' is likely to be reductive, simplistic and erroneous (Eatwell and Goodwin 2018). For an explanation as mainstream as the theory of economic grievance, this must be roundly emphasised. Demographic data demonstrates that there is in fact a complex coalition who voted in favour of Brexit (Curtice 2016, 2017). It is far from clear whether poverty, or even economic variables in general, can be said to really define who these 'left-behinds' are. Age and education are demonstrably bigger factors than income or property ownership (Norris and Inglehart 2019; Sobolewska and Ford 2020). Narratives and imagery which prize a post-Marxist framing of the importance of the industrial proletariat may distort the genuine empirical relationship between capital, property, work, and voting for Brexit.

A concrete illustration of this problem is a tremendous generational divide in the Brexit vote. Any purely economic focus is likely to obscure the relationship between voting, age, and wealth. In the post-2008 era, the old are often more financially secure than those younger than them. The popular image of a misled angry, older working-class 'left behind' in a dilapidated seaside town may be a reassuring image for those with a Remain-voting disposition but may little reflect the economic reality of the Brexit-voting population. Younger generations tend to be living in a far more economically precarious situation than their parents were. A great many have little hope of ever owning a home of their own, especially in the south-east of England. Yet, they are the least likely to have voted for Brexit, despite also being in such an economically precarious position (Sobolewska and Ford 2020). It is thus unclear, even on an anecdotal level, how to tease out any causal relationship between financial marginalisation and desire to leave the EU. Some of the strongest support for Brexit came from asset-wealthy older individuals, and this complicates any simple economic narrative.

A third grounds for scepticism about economic grievance theory is simply the lack of solid empirical data to support it. Norris and Inglehart (2019, p. 397), for instance, argue with great statistical evidence that "support for Brexit was not significantly stronger among unskilled workers, among the unemployed, and among those with left-wing economic values". A similar note is argued by Dorling and Tomlinson (2019), who demonstrate that most people who voted Leave were not from post-industrial towns but wealthier southern England. Around 60 per cent of them were middle-class, and only 41 per cent were working-class (ibid., p. 36). The Brexit vote was thus decided much more by the middle-incomed group rather than the poor. And it was, they claim, much more about *feelings* about one's income than it was about the numerical amount of that income itself (ibid., p. 37). Such an interpretation of this empirical data does not easily lend itself to the notion that Brexit was a type of working-class revolt, although it does of course support the notion that economic sentiment probably had a role to play in the vote.

A fourth criticism of scholars who link neoliberalism to Brexit is in making an error of reasoning in attributing causation to correlation. While certain data may suggest that lower economic classes tend to vote more pro-Brexit, this fact does not necessarily imply a causal link. As Dorling and Tomlinson (2019) note in relation to this problem, obesity also appears to correlate strongly with voting Leave. However, it is patently untrue that there is something about being overweight that makes one vote in favour of leaving the EU. Evidently a cluster of factors, including poor health, low wages and unhealthy food choices all connect to economic inequality – but they do not cause it. There are thus many other correlations which also exist which provide alternative – but just as compelling – explanations for the vote. It remains up to the scholars to provide a strong narrative justification which supports any concrete relationship between the two.

The final major problem of economic grievance theory is that it conceptually muddles the distinct sociological categories of status and class, a thorny theoretical point that has concerned social scientists since at least Weber (2010). While both categories considerably overlap, they are never quite the same, and much of the confusion around the economic grievance theory may be distilled through a focus on this point. One theoretical example of this distinction emerges with Weberian critiques of Marx's thoughts on political economy. The latter's framework which pits the proletariat against the bourgeoisie presents, from a Weberian perspective, a reductive approach to understanding social hierarchy (Bendix 1974; Jones 1975). Status and party affiliation are also tremendously important in the context of modern power relations. Position in relation to the sphere of production and exchange are not necessarily the chief factors for the organisation of social life, nor are they the most psychologically influential when it comes to voting on national priorities.

An empirical example of this problem in practice is the context of Brexit is demonstrated by a status-based criticism of the economic grievance theory. Drawing on the Weberian (1958) distinction of status as between *commensality* and *connubium*, Chan et al. (2020) argues that class has only a rough relationship to voting for Brexit. This structure of inequality based in relations of production, must be contrasted with status understood as the "level of social respect or esteem people believe is accorded them within the social order" (Gidron and Hall 2017, p. 5). Using evidence from the Subjective Social Status measure, they argue that social status anxiety may well be one of the most important factors which predict support for populism. Such a view overlaps with both Norris and Inglehart's (2019) and Dorling and Tomlinson's (2019) argument that *feeling* about income is more important than its quantitative financial reality. And although there is wide overlap between the two categories, foregrounding sentiment around position in a social hierarchy (without necessarily directly linking it to the material signifiers of class like wages or house prices) remains a compellingly holistic approach.

Ethnoracial Antagonism

The second principal framework for explaining the Brexit vote focuses on the extent to which the result was driven by an underlying sentiment or predilection towards racism and xenophobia. Within this sub-literature, it is useful to distinguish between clusters of texts which directly label Brexit a racist endeavour, and those which avoid such stark and morally condemnatory terms. Both types of argument foreground the consequences of ethnoracial turbulence – especially concerning mass-immigration – as pivotal in deciding the vote.

For the former authors, the vote to leave the EU was an unequivocally racist one. And while there is a degree of conceptual conflation between racism and xenophobia, the overarching framing of the issue concerns anxieties over the presence of ethnic 'others'. Pitcher (2018, p. 2) sums up this imperative by insisting that scholars "recognise the centrality of racism in the Brexit vote". The evidence for this assertion he takes from the *Breaking Point* poster during the 2016 campaign – an image unveiled by Nigel Farage which portrays hundreds of darker-skinned migrants heading (presumably) to the UK. This picture is also evidence for many of the other texts in this section as demonstrable sign that leaving the EU was motivated by fear and hatred of non-white immigrants.

For Virdee and McGeever (2018, p. 1), the foundation of racism that mobilised the Leave campaign is comprised of two integrated visions. The first one is that of a "longing to restore Britain's place in the world as a first among pairs that occludes any coming to terms with the corrosive legacies of colonial conquest and racist subjugation". The second is an "insular, Powellite narrative of an island retreat from a 'globalising' world' – one that is no longer recognisably British". Drawing attention to the "presence of 'internal others'" – notably immigrants and racialised minorities – this perspective centres how Britain had to define itself historically, suggesting that Britain still needs to exclude certain ethnic groups to maintain its own identity. They concur not only in lamenting the politicisation of Englishness but in marshalling the common academic trope that Brexit is an episode of 'postcolonial melancholia' as noted by Paul Gilroy (2020).

Martin Shaw (2020, p. 347) posits a similar argument: that "right-wing populism produced the country's exit from the EU, increases in racial abuse, prolonged constitutional conflict and the election of an authoritarian Conservative government under Boris Johnson". Moreover, he argues that academics like Eatwell and Goodwin (2018) and Kaufmann (2018), despite composing highly acclaimed scholarship on populism, purposefully and demonstrably "obscure the role of racism in the political science literature" for their own ideological ends (ibid p. 348). This *ad hominem* attack is a lamentable discoloration on an otherwise interesting foray into the standpoint epistemology of Brexit scholarship: a perspective which has so far been neglected despite over 90 per cent of university staff being pro-Remain (Times Higher Education, 2016). However, it certainly does not negate the possibility that racism was indeed pivotal in the events of the past five years.

Another example is deduced from "over one hundred incidents of racial violence since the referendum" (Burnett 2017, p. 85). Making sense of how "Brexit certainly means racism" is predicated not only "in terms of the racist climate not just during a clearly nativist debate, but also in the divisive politics preceding it" (ibid). The 2016 referendum was, from this perspective, merely a pretext for many people to 'get their country back' and to right the wrong of decades worth of mass-immigration. And while some studies have confirmed that there may be a statistically significant (15–20 per cent) rise in hate-crime after the referendum (Carr et al. 2020), it is yet unclear the extent to which this was caused by an anti-immigration campaign for Brexit. Certainly, however, any straightforward assertion that Brexit is perfectly equivalent to racism in the abstract is a provocative simplification of a complex sociological issue.

More nuanced views on the perspective of ethnoracial hostility have been provided by several authors. Patel and Connelly (2019, p. 969), for instance, argue that racial aggrievement evades the classic discursive forms of the past but continues unabated in novel ways. Drawing from thirteen interviews with Leave voters in Manchester, the authors argue that their interlocutors reject accusations of racism as a motivating factor in the vote. Rather, they couched their views "in seemingly non-racial ways" and "framed their concerns about immigration as a 'legitimate' response to a victimised whiteness" (ibid). The conclusion, the authors suggest, is that the British do not live in a post-racial epoch, and that racisms "continue to thrive through new modes of articulation" (ibid).

While it is certainly true that racism can be rationalised through the adoption of anti-immigration views (Banton 1996), it is yet unclear how, under the framework set out by these scholars, any alternative claim could pass the falsification test (Popper 2002). If denial of racism simply means the circulation of racism in 'new ways', it becomes near impossible to escape accusation of guilt. Not only can these interlocutors ever escape the accusation of racism 'thriving in new modes', but they are also handicapped from expressing discomfort with the rapid ethnocultural dislocation that accompanies much higher immigration than the historical average (Kaufmann 2018). The risk of this situation is in creating a destructive feedback loop which only promotes more extreme growth in right-wing populism (Eatwell and Goodwin 2018).

Other scholars highlight the role of epistemic misrecognition when analysing the relationship between race and the vote to leave the EU. Indeed, racism as a form of systematic misrecognition has a detailed history as part of critical understandings of human diversity (Thompson and Yar 2019). In this case, however, a focus on racial antagonism can serve as a misrecognition of the reality of class (Mondon and Winter 2019, p. 510). Interlinking with the argument from economic grievance, these authors argue that the "populist racialisation of the working class as white and left-behind" only served to make race central, occlude the class makeup of the vote, and allow "for the re-assertion of white identity as a legitimate political category" (ibid). This resulted in the normalisation of racism and the far right. In doing so, it also delegitimised working class voters who were not white. Although problematic for arguing on the strength of working-class support for populism, the authors still make the strong case that occluding racial and gender dynamics will reify the narrative of a white working-class revolt.

A similar attention to the politics of misrecognition is put forth by Bhambra (2017, p. 214), who sees both Brexit and Trump supporters longing for a "White" conception of the past into which "racialized others had insinuated themselves and gained disproportionate advantage". This pervasive "methodological whiteness" has distorted scholarly accounts of Brexit; one which foregrounds the economic grievance account and creates a synonymous coupling of white and working-class. The consequence of this euphemistic language, she claims, is to obscure the fact that class itself is not a racially neutral category but tends to signify white; in doing so, it "puts all [working-class] others outside the operation of history and social processes" (ibid, p. 227).

Overall, then, scholars have differed on the degree to which racism played a pivotal role in the Brexit vote. But few have paid sufficient attention to racism as a discursive phenomenon in addition to a sociomaterial one: something "tied within a cycle of contestations, denials and affirmations" (Mintchev 2020, p. 123). The idea of Brexit as either racist or not does not converge with the complex, messy reality experience of people themselves. Yet this binary way of organising political life has become, since 2016, the "central organising principle of political experience" (Mintchev 2020, p. 125). And although Mintchev skirts over the possibly that binary oppositions form the conceptual organising principles of *all* social life, as Durkheim (2008) suggested, the point stands: that framing the issue along a simplistic racist/not-racist binary caricatures each side and renders nuanced discussion on the relationship between ethnicity and Brexit impossible.

Finally, perhaps the most significant intervention in the debate about Brexit and populism comes from Kaufmann (2018), whose book *Whiteshift* presents an argument about the relationship between whiteness and populism with much less of the ideological derision and epistemological certitude than has been provided by the other scholars. Euro-American society is amid what he terms a "whiteshift" – the social process by which majority white populations have absorbed many different peoples through immigration and intermarriage, yet remain coupled with existing myths of descent, symbols, and traditions. In demographic terms, the once overwhelming percentage of these countries as white Caucasian is undergoing an unprecedented decline. A major consequence of this change is a weakening of cultural self-confidence in addition to a profound sense of existential insecurity. In such a context, flashpoints like immigration provoke voters into supporting increasingly extreme populist positions. Unlike economic grievance theory, however, Kaufmann argues that the rise of populism is the result of concerns over *cultural identity*, rather than material or economic deprivation (although there is a clear dovetailing of the two).

Part of the turbulence associated with the support for some of the more obviously outrageous attacks by populists like Trump is that the high-status individuals (commonly referred to by populists as 'liberal elites') such as in academia, non-governmental organisations, Democratic politics, and journalism, are increasingly indulging in the "anti-white ideology" of the cultural left. Previously known as 'political correctness', this mutation into 'wokeness' or 'social justice ideology' is increasingly on the ascent within high-status institutions. One key component of this ideological framing of Western society is a sacralisation of different identity categories with white, straight males epitomised as the principal cause of social oppression. Kaufmann argues that a few decades ago, making generalising (and clearly derogatory) comments about groups of white people could be shrugged off. Now, however, with declining share of population and beset by the insecurity of collective disintegration, more and more white individuals refuse to abide by these kinds of racialised attacks.

The consequence is that a discussion of the effects of mass-immigration and national identity is made deviant and off-limits in the name of anti-racism. This forces the issue underground, opening a space for populist right entrepreneurs like Trump or Farage to fill. In part, their success resides in the ability to articulate anxieties about lack of control over cultural and ethnic change in ways which bypass the heavy cultural taboos around this area. It is clearly not by chance that the Vote Leave campaign for Brexit won with the slogan 'Take Back Control'. They are also to redirect these sentiments into vehicles which have no demonstrable connection to the identity politics status games of urban elites. Massive cultural instability like Brexit or Trump is among the consequences. More recent evidence for this claim can be found in the fact that in the period since Brexit, anxieties about immigration have dropped considerably (YouGov 2019).

Whiteshift's (2018) approach to the ethno-racial dimension to Brexit is highly generative. It is true that the book can be criticised for assuming that assimilation only happens one way, caricaturing the influence of the 'woke' cultural left, and sidestepping the legitimate anxiety of non-whites toward a reassertion of white cultural dominance (Ford 2019). But overall, the strength of the work rests in that although many scholars have decried an apocalyptic and Manichean situation of unprecedented racism throughout the 2016 referendum, Kaufmann provides a more grounded account of the seismic ethnocultural shifts in Western societies. By seeking to understand the populist-right on their own terms – rather than simply dismissing Brexit as racism pure and simple – this approach opens the possibility for a nuanced reading of the cultural context since 2016. Not economic grievance, but culture and identity, ethnicity, and race.

Overall, a perspective foregrounding ethnoracial tension as a powerful sentiment within the vote for Brexit seems undeniable, even if there is considerably more debate to the problem than just this one factor. Yet, there are also reasons to be sceptical of this position. One criticism of much of this literature rests on the fact that most of the 'racism' of Brexit descends largely from anecdotal references and, often, inferences from media representation. Certain scholarship is clearly comfortable with making claims about the Brexit vote with little by way of solid evidence. However, narrative-based arguments, without ethnographic or statistical data, count little for making sense of the situation on the ground. If racism truly was the cause of the vote, it is expected that scholars proposing this line of argument be able to empirically demonstrate so. The reality is that racism as a concept is as difficult to define as it is to accurately measure. Attempts to psychologise this problem by conceptualising it in terms of the inclination towards prejudice or group narcissism (Zala et al. 2017) do little to help in making sense of a complex question.

Beyond the paucity of evidence in favour of racial hatred as a mobilising component of voting for Brexit, the question of whether Brexit was an essentially 'white' (and thus inevitably racialised) phenomenon is also contentious. Norris and Inglehart (2019), in perhaps one of the most data-heavy texts on Brexit, demonstrate that being in the category of 'White British' does *not* predict whether someone voted to Remain or Leave. There is an expectation that being ethnoracially 'white' would have had a far more mobilising power than this if Brexit was really about race. But these explanations remain altogether unconvincing in that they may simply reify the categories of race and racism as the *sine qua non* for understanding polarised social cleavages.

Finally, but no less importantly, the question of the legitimacy of concerns about immigration are central. Much of the scholarship on the issue of xenophobia, racism, and Brexit works with several assumptions about the legitimacy of these questions. Post-1997, during the years of Tony Blair's governance, Britain saw the biggest rise in immigration in its recorded history. Between 2001 and 2014, for instance, several millions of people arrived from outside the UK, largely as the consequence of a dynamic combination between government laxity and the freedom of movement accompanying integration with the EU. Yet, there was always much less public support for such immigration than either the government or the minority of 'Somewheres' supposed (Goodhart 2017). Many British citizens felt that they were never asked about the sweeping ethnic and cultural changes that were occurring across the country, especially in urban centres (Coleman 2016).

The question of whether they were justified in feeling anxious about immigration transcends the limit of this chapter. This would require both an analysis of demographic issues and the far more epistemologically complex questions about where the limits of social identity and solidarity in relation to ethnic or racial groups are legitimately allowed to rest. We cannot avoid bumping into the eternal human dynamics of in-groups and out-groups, many of which overlay much more easily onto ethnic 'others' (Laurence et al. 2019). The complexity of how these anxieties map out and translate into voting should be taken seriously as sociological facts in their own right – one which hints at the complexity of interaction between human diversity, assimilation, and belonging. Many people clearly felt that they were unable to change government policy about something they felt demonstrably uncomfortable about and voting for Brexit was a consequence of this frustration. The fact that immigration has dropped off the list of major concerns since Brexit, this framework – rightly or wrongly – appears to have been vindicated.

Cultural Backlash

The next paradigm, 'cultural backlash', treats Brexit as the consequence of long-term structural change in the value composition of Western populations. Two central texts, *Cultural Backlash* (2019) and *Brexitland* (2020), associate the referendum result around turbulence associated with the shifting culture and identity of generationally divided population groups. Indeed, one of the major strengths of this framework is that it is one of the few which provide a meaningful and coherent explanation why divides in age are one of the most replicable findings for populist support across the developed world.

Both texts draw from the paradigm shifting work of Inglehart, whose 1977 book *The Silent Revolution* marked a turning point in cultural sociology. The core claim of the text is that norms and values which prioritise security and collective identity gradually erode in periods of affluence. In the post-war context, this unprecedented material and existential abundance for Western democracies produced a great shift in value-orientation for the young. Increasingly representing the values of individual fulfilment and free expression, this recent period saw movements for the environment, sexuality, human rights, and ethnic diversity all became culturally hegemonic. The glacial shift from previously 'materialist' values of collective security, strong leadership and closed social groups gives way, over the course of several generations, to a society dominated by individualistic 'post-materialist' ones. Freed from anxieties over threat to collective life, whether economic or military, younger generations onwards tended with increasing frequency to have values orientated to more liberal, cosmopolitan, and openly aspirational goals.

Of all the main structural drivers of these value changes, education features as the most prominent. Access to university, an institution reserved just a generation ago for a small intellectual elite, has increased exponentially. University education is important in this context not only for economic reasons connected to technological skill and capital accumulation but because it is linked to cultural worldview, the central site of transformation across the past half-century. As the Western world moves from a majority school-leaver population to a majority graduate one, this causes profound shifts in attitude towards a wide variety of cultural markers, including sympathy for the role of international institutions and comfortability with population centres marked by diversity, mobility, and rapid change. In part, this is increasingly a description of global trends in urban areas. A great many 'global' cities are marked both by the same 'hyper-diversity' of people and many of the same chronic resource issues.

The increase in urbanisation, ethnic diversity and gender equality all contribute to a generational divide in which less and less is shared or even recognised as a meaningful political concern across ages. And although education itself tends to make people more comfortable with social diversity (Ford and Jennings 2020), the younger generations who grew up surrounded by more of it than their parents and grandparents increasingly reject exclusionary social attitudes towards ethnic or racial outsiders which were practically universal within living memory. Additionally, the proliferation of technological literacy and the digital divide has accelerated these attitudinal divergences, especially when it comes to having constant, open contact with people who are outside of one's local geographical community. The cumulative result of is this is that the social segments attached to either broadly 'liberal' or 'conservative-authoritarian' norms and values are starkly divided by age. This fact is also something which the authors are keen to point out is not caused by life the periodic shifts in lifecycle. In short, attitudinal changes are not the product of youthful idealism or naivety, but rather represent long-term value trends which will not be reversed soon.

The link between long-term structural changes and the 2016 vote emerge in ways that can be replicated across the Western world. In the eyes of the authors and a considerable array of other scholars, there is a clear relationship between Brexit and other right-wing populist elections such as that won by Trump. Norris and Inglehart (2019) explain that what these populist moments represent are the 'tipping point' at which older, whiter, and non-college educated generations – psychologically much more associated with 'materialist' values of the past – react to their decline in social position and the values associated with it. Although from a demographic point of view these individuals are far less hegemonic than they were even ten or twenty years ago, they are still narrowly the majority. How they vote can still cause tremendous changes across both the national and international political system.

Sobolewska and Ford (2020) in *Brexitland* examine the British social landscape in more depth using the same tools of cultural sociology. Although they build on the same framework, the authors generate a new tripartite division of social categories to make sense of the identity polarisation exposed by the Brexit vote. They argue that there are three main 'types', roughly approximating a Weberian 'ideal-type' framework (Weber 2019). The first, *conviction liberals*, consist of university educated graduates, comfortable with diversity, socially cosmopolitan, and politically liberal. The second, *necessity liberals*, are usually ethnic minorities who align with the former for pragmatic rather than ideological reasons. Thirdly, *identity conservatives* are the mostly white school-leavers who have seen a rapid descent from hegemony in the past couple of decades. This last group is strongly attached to the ethnic in-group and displays a characteristic hostility to national or ethnic out-groups (usually immigrants).

Brexit can be understood in large part as the tipping point when *identity conservatives* react to their declining share of the population in relation to the coalition between both types of *liberals*. In this sense, the argument aligns with Norris and Inglehart's argument about the decline in materialist values compared to post-materialist ones. *Brexitland*'s strength is both in the development of this paradigm and in invoking *necessity liberals* as a coalitional element to voting to Remain within the EU without necessarily adopting all the same liberal values – many of which may be distant to first-generation ethnic minority immigrants were socialised in materialist conditions of scarcity, poverty, or conflict. Finally, the authors also provide a cogent explanation for the polarisation in contemporary Britain which is high (and growing) in large part because no one group is broadly hegemonic, as it was in the past few decades. As none are large enough to set the terms of debate, the boundaries of permissible speech or values is constantly in play, rendering politics itself extremely polarised, adversarial, and dynamic.

Moreover, the authors expand upon Norris and Inglehart's (2019) emphasis on the role of tertiary education as the highest predictor of identification with the *conviction liberal* category rather than the *identity conservative* in contemporary Britain. They concur that while university used to be the reserve only of a privileged minority, its unprecedented expansion (mirrored in nearly all affluent Western democracies) has brought a "slow but relentless transformation of the electorate" (ibid, p. 22). The result is a situation in which there is a radical difference in political outlook, cultural worldview, comfort with ethnic diversity, and residence in urban or rural area. Regarding this latter point, the authors would appear likely to concur with Kaufmann's (2018) point that the urban/rural split in voting for populist candidates does not represent anything connected to geography itself but rather the reality that university education almost everywhere leads to employment in urban areas in which the service sector predominates.

This cultural backlash theory remains one of the strongest theoretical paradigms for understanding Brexit and similar populist movements across the world. Of its many strengths, are accounting for the generational split in the vote, as well as explaining the clear role of immigration and diversity without resorting either to circular reasoning or an oversimplification of the issue. However, scholars like Schäfer (2021) argue quite convincingly that the broad empirics of texts like *Cultural Backlash* are simply incorrect. He argues that the data extracted simply does not correlate with the broad narrative conclusions that Norris and Inglehart present. Although reviewing this critique would also require a considerable knowledge of statistical methods, there seems to be reasonable ground for scepticism when it comes to adopting the conclusions that are claimed to follow from the empirical data presented in this book.

The British Empire

The British Empire has had something of a strange resurrection in the British cultural space, especially since the global protests surrounding the killing of George Floyd in 2020 catalysed global reflection on the legacy of slavery. A flurry of texts, both popular and academic, have emerged in the past few years which mediate on the issue (Dorling and Tomlinson 2019; El-Enany 2020; Gildea 2019; Gilroy 2020; Mitchell 2021; Sanghera 2021; Ward and Rasch 2019) with many positing a direct triage between racism, Brexit, and the British Empire. These have become popular ways in which people have begun to make sense of what historical antecedents may explain the vote to leave the EU. Overall, many of these approaches can be summarised in the claim that Brexit represented a kind of 'postcolonial melancholy': one which continues to resonate throughout contemporary electoral politics (Gilroy 2020).

This perspective, popular both among scholars and the public, is that of Brexit as indelibly connected to the history of imperialism, both ghostly present and yet simultaneously unpresentable or unspeakable (Cummings 2020). This view is taken by Colley (2016), who sees in the aftermath of the referendum a group of "nostalgics in search of a lost empire". As the building blocks of British national identity, such as majority Protestantism and a culture of constitutional liberties have faded away, Colley claims that the British are left feeling bereft and without a project for national revival. This energy was transferred, predominantly by English MPs, into a new an opportunity "for a new start, however illusory".

The historical context is an indelible part of this puzzle. The British people's anxious and conflicted relationship to the EU was pre-empted by the Dean Acheson's quip that by the 1960s Britain had "lost an empire but not yet found a role" (Brinkley 1990, p. 599). From WWII onwards a considerable majority of British statesman came to believe that projecting power through the EU would give Britain the capacity to project its power on the world stage, such as it was able to during the imperial era (Saunders 2020). Europe would be a vehicle through which British prestige and influence could carry into a global arena increasing dominated by countries like India, China, and Russia. A great percentage of 'Remainers' adopt a discursive position roughly analogous to this. Their position is that Britain's place in the world, especially as it relates to maximising influence while minimising trade-offs (like shared sovereignty), can be located as principal members of the EU (Adonis and Hutton 2018). From this more sympathetic perspective, Brexit could be understood as the result of collective anxiety and identity crisis in the face of national decline, not sublimated longings for imperialist revanchism.

Yet, this softer approach is not shared by all scholars. Explanations that link Brexit to ethnocultural antagonism have been mirrored in discussions of Britain's relationship to empire. Cummings (2020) argues that both Brexit and the Windrush scandal (in which Caribbean immigrants who had lived in Britain for decades were deported) are both examples of "border anxieties" that structure contemporary Britain. Drawing on the observation that Enoch Powell left Heath's Conservative Party over its attempts to join the EEC, the suggestion is that "Black Atlantic Diasporic histories and British-European border politics have long been interlinked" (ibid). Drawing a connection between period of great post-war immigration from former colonies of the British Empire, this framing sees Brexit as a kind of afterlife of empire – one fuelled by memories of British imperial supremacy that disregard the suffering of former colonial subjects.

Another approach sustains the criticism that Brexit rests on an inflated, post-imperial grandeur. Danny Dorling and Sally Tomlinson (2019, p. 13) argue that part of the reason why Brexit happened was because "a small number of people in Britain have a dangerous, imperialist misconception of our standing in the world". The result of the EU referendum as one of the last parts of Britain finally coming to terms with the last vestiges of its declining empire. This text attacks what it perceives as the jingoism, stupidity, and nostalgia for what is otherwise morally irredeemable project of Britain's colonial past. Moreover, they insist that voting in Brexit was at least in part built on a fantasy of creating an Empire 2.0 – one which will usher in "some great new era of superiority where an inborn British ability and predisposition to trade, to earn, to invent, and to invest will cause the country to be great again" (ibid, p. 96).

The authors further suggest that there is a profound connection between the British ruling elite and this imperial mentality. Drawing connections between the wealth brought by empire, including for many of the wealthiest donors to the Conservative party and leaders of Eurosceptic parties like the United Kingdom Independence Party (UKIP), they argue that an overconfidence, swagger, and delusion about superiority is the hallmark of British political elites. It is something which is cultivated in the top private schools and finalised in universities like Oxford and Cambridge. The fact that much of the Brexit side was driven by these elites is taken as evidence of a profound connection between British elitism, the spoils of empire, and the promotion of Brexit.

However, there is a danger in proclaiming direct causal relations between these phenomena. One persistent issue among the scholarship is a tendency to conflate nostalgia and amnesia (Saunders 2020). The word 'nostalgia' is also a kind of pathologising discourse, one which precludes meaningful debate and replaces with a treatable psychological disorder. A similar critique of this psychologising discourse is posited by both Müller (2017) sees it as a vehicle for delegitimising political opinions. This is not to altogether deny the existence of a pining for a better past as an integral to the cultural imaginary of many Brexit voters. Rather, it is that we must be wary that this kind of emotionally pathologising of the vote simply does not help us understand the result in any clear way.

Moreover, while the Remain side may be harsh to criticise what they perceive to be a fixation on global supremacy, it is not clear whether they themselves are not also enrapt with leadership of Europe and of exerting global power through its institutions. As I touched on, much post-war diplomatic policy was driven by using the EU as the new vehicle for Britain's imperial mission after the empire had dissolved. Even Roy Jenkins thought that one could have, through leadership of Europe, an attachment to imperial commitments "worthy of Chamberlain, Kitchener, or Curzon" (Saunders 2020, p. 1146). The desire to *lead* Europe, then, was always at least as strong as to leave it, and the concern that a Britain outside the EU would be cold, lonely, and irrelevant suggests that 'postcolonial melancholia' has "haunted the supporters of membership as much as their opponents" (Saunders 2020, p. 1148). In addition, there remains an argument that EU is itself an 'liberal imperialist' entity, and it is not altogether clear whether Brexit can really be represented as the pro-imperial position (Streeck 2019).

The delineation between ostensibly imperialist Brexiteers and open, liberal Remainers is at the heart of much academic discourse on the connection between Brexit and the British Empire. Empire has often been made to be such a totalising and all-pervasive aspect of national history that near all racial inequalities or border discipline (El-Enany 2020) can be attributed to it. Yet, as Saunders (2020) notes, the ghosts of empire must surely haunt supporters of EU membership too. While this does not negate the sense of bereftness that might have influenced the vote, it destabilises any straightforward connection between the referendum voting and Britain's imperial past (Saunders 2020).

Overall, finding a connection between the British Empire and Brexit is probably the most contentious explanation of all those presented in this review. At its core, the argument rests on something like an articulation of cultural mood (Borneman and Ghassem-Fachandi 2017). This is broadly the proposition that there is a sense of restless decline and pessimism in British cultural life that is difficult to express verbally and comes out in instances of collective transference. This neurosis is ostensibly more common among older and wealthier generations, many of whom will still have personal recollections of an era when British global dominance was only very recently challenged.

However, the strength of an argument which seeks to capture the trans-discursive sense of mood may also be its weakness. As it cannot be spoken but merely 'felt' as a shared affect, mood is an almost impossibly difficult object of analysis (Borneman and Ghassem-Fachandi 2017). No metric can adequately measure the unique moment of a pervasive melancholic sense of decline, nor any empirical evidence provided to prove it was a factor. It remains, perhaps like the best ethnographic descriptions, entirely non-quantifiable, non-falsifiable and beyond the best attempts of any scholar to provide convincing evidence of it other than a vague sense that it emerged when people spoke about it. At most, it can be subjectively inferred from scatterings of often unrelated cultural artefacts and narratives. This means that the ostensible 'imperial' moods and motivations which may have influenced the Brexit vote can never have the same quality of empirical evidence as other forms of data. Being so hard to prove, centring post-imperial affect cannot but remains a contentious claim in the wider debate.

Finally, arguments concerning the relationship between social elitism or educational privilege and Brexit (Dorling and Tomlinson 2019) are open criticism. Studying Politics, Philosophy, and Economics (PPE) at Oxford or Cambridge has been a social marker associated with most influential individuals in British political life. A more recent small-scale study by Zhu and Carl (2018) suggests that of all Members of Parliament that have a PPE degree, 95 per cent of them voted to Remain inside the EU. Although this does not necessitate any causal link, it complicates any argument that posits the British elite class as the cause behind the Brexit vote.

Neo-Nationalism

A considerable sub-literature details the role of nationalism in the vote to leave the EU. The importance of the nation as an 'imagined community' (Anderson 2016) was a key feature of the debate on leaving the EU, especially when it concerns the problem of sovereignty in a federal system. However, it is unclear the extent to which this issue was a motivating factor for the vote. Nevertheless, anxieties about national decline, belonging and identity were all features to a varying extent in the debate since 2016. Many of them were framed in explicitly national or nationalistic language that concerned both physical and social boundaries as well as the health of the nation.

The foundational argument in this regard sees Brexit as the culmination of decades-long growth of nationalist politics, exemplified by fringe political parties like UKIP (Ford and Goodwin 2014). Although the British have often thought of themselves as 'reluctant nationalists' – this may be attributable to escaping foreign domination and instead managing the responsibility of imperial domination over others (Kumar 2006). The more recent growth in nationalist politics across the UK is evident and perhaps in large part attributable to the process of regional devolution of Scotland, Wales, and Northern Ireland since the 1990s. Given the rise in nationalist parties like the

SNP and Plaid Cymru, it is reasonable to assume that England also saw a slow rise in nationalist sentiment. Owing to the constitutional uniqueness of the UK however, these forces may – given the absence of *English* devolution – have expressed themselves through a vehicle like Brexit (Denham and Devine 2018).

A more cynical approach sees the Brexit programme focused on the "ostensible problems of immigration, multiculturalism, and ethnic diversity" only as a justification (Valluvan and Kalra 2019, p. 2394). This approach clearly dovetails with literature highlighting the role of ethnic anxiety in the vote to leave but frames the problem in more instrumental terms: a demographic explanation would be considered merely an apologetics for revanchist chauvinism. Rather, the new nationalist paradigm of Brexit which "present[s] itself as the voice of the dispossessed, the working class, the welfare state and other cognate left-of-centre twentieth century emphases" is a cynical fig leaf for what is a much more ambitious, if delusional, turn towards an "anxious, defensive and resentful" nationalist temperament or mentality (ibid, p. 2393). This neo-nationalism is predicated on a political discourse with an "outsized place for the problems putatively posed by those who do not belong", ultimately as a tragic iteration of the same processes of scapegoating and exclusion that mark Europe's earlier history (ibid, p. 2395). Scholars with this position thus argue that nationalism has returned to the centre of the European stage.

One alternative reading sees the EU itself as part of the cause for the growth in nationalist politics. For Wellings (2020), Brexit should make us more cognisant of how nationalist politics remains an independent variable occurring within the assembly of creating European institutions. In other words, Britain's integration into Europe has produced a "heightened salience of nationalist politics rather than its containment" (ibid, p. 326). As a result, re-invigorated nationalism surfaces not despite but *because* of federalist attempts at uniting the continent. The historical irony here is that even if divisive nationalism across Europe was the forebear to the EU, today's institutions may have inadvertently served to revive its salience. Such a framework complicates an already tendentious founding myth that European integration is the solution to nationalism (Lähdesmäki 2018) by instead suggesting that it could be its consequence.

A last alternative intervention downplays the nationalist fervour of Brexit while retaining a balanced understanding that national identity played a large role in the vote. Reynolds (2019), for example, argues that Britons living today feel challenged about their sense of national identity in the complex and shifting world of globalisation. Rejecting the ostensible provincialism of what he sees in the national-focused campaign to leave the EU, he suggests that the historically contingent period in which Britain had the role of global supremacy is something of an illusion. Like problems with the British empire, 'nationalist' agitation may be closer to a sense of impeding identity crisis than it does with any overtly sinister agitation towards the exclusionary and ultimately murderous nationalist regimes of the 20th century.

Although Reynolds (2019) is careful to avoid an overly psychologising approach, others bring in Lacanian understanding of Self and social identity to understand how a fragmentation of national decline could have led to the referendum result. For Mandelbaum (2020, p. 451), a Lacanian-psychoanalytic framework make sense of populism because it "appeal emotively and thus interpellates, at least partially, their subjects by offering unity and a 'fulness to come', the promise of filling the void, the promise of full jouissance". In other words, the Brexit campaign fulfilled the fantasy of a lost Golden era of greatness and made the Other, in this case the EU, the cause of emptiness. Brexit was thus a "failure-based utopia" which played on the desire for a wholeness which can never truly be satisfied (ibid, p. 453). Browning (2019) posits a similar perspective: Brexit promised a return to a kind of 'lost home', a nostalgia which was nourished by grievance and discontent. Both of these scholars see an empirical interplay between internal, psychoanalytic dynamics of identity and the nationalism which inspired the vote to leave the EU.

Anti-Politics

Finally, another profoundly influential paradigm with which one can understand the rise of populism is through the framework of 'anti-politics'. Although a generative paradigm, it too has a something of a protean form. Vines and Marsh (2018, p. 434) note that any simple definition of anti-politics "would be too bland or heavily contested". After all, much of what scholars put as conceptually outside traditional politics could be perceived to be 'anti-politics'. Influential works in anthropology on resistance (Ortner 1995; Scott 1985) could easily fit such a definition. Although the extent to which resistance literature can work with Brexit is highly contestable, we should keep an open mind about how individuals relate to institutional – and especially neoliberal – politics where the distinction between apathy, revolt and grievance are hopelessly mixed and confused.

Broadly conceived, however, anti-politics refers to range of attitudes and practices that reject mainstream politics *in toto*. It is heavily rooted in popular mistrust of a political elite and a rejection of the wisdom of established powers. As such, it is likely to be either connected to or synonymous with populism: the definition of which distinguishes between treacherous elites and true people (Mudde 2004). From a historical perspective, one can observe this general feeling in Britain going back decades, although flashpoints like the 2003 Iraq war or the advent of mass-immigration during the period of Blair's premiership are examples of where a sense of despondency towards national leadership peaked. Popular discontent with mass immigration has increased year on year since his election in 1997 and is surely likely to have impacted public conviction that the government does not care enough to prevent the unprecedented ethnocultural change (Flinders 2018). Anti-politics, from this perspective, is the logical outcome of a system which is unresponsive to the wishes and desires of the national electorate.

There appears to be strong empirical evidence that anti-politics in this sense is part of any coherent explanation for Brexit. The idea that voting to leave was about 'sending the government a message' is evidenced in ethnographic explorations of the aftermath of the vote in 2016 (Koch 2017). The historical irony, in the long run, is that although anti-politics led to Brexit, it seems likely that it will simply increase it. Brexit offered a very simplistic solution to the very complex problem of globalisation, regulatory alignment and shifting geopolitics. Leaving the EU does not seem to result in the capacity to respond to these problems in any meaningful way. As much as the EU is a cause of the discontents of globalisation, it was also an attempt to be a solution to it.

There are two basic explanations of anti-politics: a supply-side one and a demand side one (Vines and Marsh 2017). For the former, anti-politics is created this same political culture in which citizens have lost faith in government and generally feel disempowered in their political lives. Politics is defined not by hatred but by apathy. The demand-side, for its part, sees anti-politics as part of poor performance by the government, even if this itself is caused by the very apathy that supply-side talks discusses. Altogether, is unclear the extent to which these two can really be disentangled. Most likely the reality is that both are acting in concert. And although explanations of what causes anti-politics may differ, all would probably agree that the climate of the decline in voter participation, party membership, lack of excellent party leaders and general contempt for (and lack of trust in) politicians speaks to the climate of anti-politics in the UK that contributed to the vote for Brexit.

Perhaps the most powerful single approach to understanding anti-politics is developed by Mair (2013). Broadly, he argues that the most salient post-war development in European politics is that individual citizens are essentially becoming 'non-sovereign'. Part of the reason for this is that political parties themselves – the very sustenance of mass democracy as we understand it today – have been dissolving rapidly in the age of social atomisation. Traditional parties of the kind analysed by Weber (2010) find it increasingly difficult to engage ordinary citizens, who are voting less and with less partisan consistency. They are also unable to provide the base for the activities and status of their own leaders who are more likely to focus on careers in other external institutions. If, following Weber, we can think of parties as essentially machines for producing leaders; then the incapacity for traditional parties to hold and train these leaders is an ominous sign of their impeding dissolution.

Mair's (2013, p. 16) central idea is that there is thus a "process of mutual withdrawal or abandonment", in which both citizens withdraw into private life *and* the party leadership moves further into other, non-formally political institutions. A more concrete example of this would be the tendency for politicians to circulate between directorships or boardroom roles at financial, consultancy or arts institutions, with their role as a Member of Parliament being simply one career stop among many. (Current examples include Chuka Umunna, who went from corporate solicitor to Labour politician to PR consultant to investment banker in the space of less than a decade; or George Osborne, who switched from Chancellor of the Exchequer to editor of London's *Evening Standard* to investment banker). Parties serve as springboards for elites to access other lucrative or high-prestige careers in which their status, connections and wealth can allow them to accrue even more advantages for themselves.

One of Mair's (2013) key insights is that the experience of mass affiliation and involvement in political parties that characterised the earlier half of the 20th century is simply disappearing. This is because party organisation is no longer really rooted within wider society. The churches, clubs and neighbourhood organisations which gave the foundation to mass politics have simply dissolved in a general context of industrial anomie. The idea of the British Labour Party as the mass membership vehicle for the working class of the 19th century seems virtually unthinkable today.[2] Not only does this diminish the role of party affiliation and identification, but it also arrests the transition from what we can think of as a class 'in itself' into a class 'for itself' (Andrew 1983).

Another important factor is that, as many scholars note, governments are no longer truly capable of formally managing the economy because of globalisation. Moreover, the problem-solving and decision-making practices that characterise public policy have become substantially more complex. Difficult (and often irresolvable) trade-offs must be made in a fast moving, globally competitive environment – especially operating under infrastructure of a neoliberal regime. One consequence of this is that popular understanding and control simply cannot catch up. The political context becomes substantially impoverished as a cluster of un-related (and usually superficial) issues dominate the news cycle. In addition to this, there becomes a general acceptance that depoliticised and technocratic modes of decision making through international institutions is the only legitimate (or even possible) option. The 'void' created, according to Mair (2013), results in a cleavage between populists on the one hand and distant technocrats on the other.

Though *Ruling the* Void was written in 2013 – three years before the referendum – there is perhaps no other text which quite captures the dynamic which led to the Brexit referendum as much. Mair's argument that national elites have become increasingly preoccupied with the opinions of 'horizontal' (i.e., their peers in international institutions or countries) rather than 'vertical' (i.e., the voters) is extremely important. From one angle, this is perhaps an inevitable fact of globalisation – as people encounter new people, one of the many possible responses is kinship affiliation. The high-intermarriage rates of traditional elites (like European monarchs) are one historical example of this (Fleming 1973). But it also speaks to the fact that it is precisely *elites* who are acting in this way. Their preferences for the opinions of other global elites are part of a story in which they become decoupled from the local context of their national publics: something which inevitably stimulates a 'pushback' by disaffected individuals who feel that they can no longer influence the world around them.

In short, understanding the vote to leave the EU as a kind of 'anti-politics' is pivotal. It helps us make sense of both the generalised social decay of communal institutions and the weakness of traditional political parties. The idea that the vote was less about Europe and more about 'sending a message' to the political elite should resonate strongly with anyone involved in these political developments over the years (e.g., Koch 2017). This broader 'politics of depoliticisation' has characterised the neoliberal era of the Blair years onwards and contributes just as much as any economic or cultural explanation. Notwithstanding the influence of parties like UKIP, we cannot forget that Brexit was caused by an arbitrary referendum result and was categorically *not* the consequence of collective, long-term social pressure (except perhaps UKIP's nipping at the heels of the Conservative Party). My own ethnographic research in addition to much that I have presented here suggests that 'anti-politics' was a highly important aspect to understanding Brexit.

Conclusion

All these frameworks provide generative and insightful perspectives on what drove the vote to leave the EU in 2016. Each of them chooses to emphasise distinct drivers, attributes, characteristics, dispositions, or social forces. However, little that has been explored here is necessarily mutually exclusive. A focus on aggregate authoritarian personalities, for instance, does not necessarily collide with a sense of bereftness that may accompany a decline in economic position. Neither could this be entirely extrapolated from the entrance of foreign groups ethnic or cultural groups with distinct attitudes towards production and exchange. It is likely, in sum, that many or all these various perspectives meet somewhere in the middle. Populism has no simple and identifiable cause but is rather the consequence of both contingent political decisions and wider structural changes in Western democracies.

There is still considerable direction forward on this issue, and this book looks to tackle some of the questions that emerge from the literature. Despite the vast proliferation of populist scholarship since 2016, there is plenty of opportunity for a greater exploration of the issues raised in this book. One of the more fertile avenues for future discussion would be qualitative or ethnographic explorations of profound structural changes that drive educational polarisation. Although scholars have plainly demonstrated the salience of higher education as a key marker for 'post-materialist' or anti-populist values, it remains broadly unclear why that is. Inroads have been attempted to capture how education relates to both worldview and exposure to cultural difference, but this literature would be greatly enhanced by richer ethnographic explorations of how young adults experience sense of generation (Mannheim 1952) which blossoms in these moments of great sociocultural turbulence.

Moreover, key questions remain on what the drivers of discursive interest in historical moments like the British Empire represent. The *Black Lives Matter* galvanised great swathes of the Western world was the single biggest factor that ignited public conversation on the legacy of the Atlantic slave trade and the role of state memorialisation for complex historical figures. However, Britain's great populist moment predated these events by half a decade and deserves deeper examination. If it is true that Brexit was in some sense influenced by either the mood or memory of a lingering 'postcolonial melancholy' (Gilroy 2020), this situation merits deeper ethnographic investigation on why these types of discourses resonates with some individuals and not with others. Questions surrounding the transformation in the discourse of race will necessarily delve into the concept of "wokeness" – something which was almost entirely absent from the pre-2016 world but is now a reliable feature of trans-Atlantic political discourse. Understanding what people think this word means, and how they experience it in their daily lives, will be another central component of this book.

Brexit was almost certainly the most important geopolitical event in the UK's post-war history, except perhaps for the Suez crisis in 1956. While the long-term consequences of leaving the EU are likely to remain undetermined for a considerable amount of time, the causes still present fascinating questions about the social cleavages in modern Euro-American societies. Despite the vast array of possible explanations, there are laudable reasons both to try and understand events like Brexit and pre-empt the damaging effects of long-term polarisation in Western democracies. When Prime Minister Theresa May was asked what Brexit meant, she replied: "Brexit *means* Brexit". The following chapters will make some modest headway in approaching this bizarre tautology from an anthropological perspective.

Notes

1 Although I take pains to refer to 'Brexiters' using this term, my interlocutors themselves (and much of the wider world) still uses the term 'Brexiteer' – insinuating a kind of buccaneering spirit to those who wanted to leave the EU. While I believe that such terminology is ethnographically interesting, I have refrained from reproducing these folk terminologies in line with the more analytically suitable alterative.

2 With the obvious exception of Jeremy Corbyn's leadership of the Labour Party, which after his election in 2015 grew to over 500,000 people (Seymour 2015). However, as this number was considerably inflated by virtual members, who paid £3 for the privilege, it is limited whether we can see this as genuine political membership or not.

1

BRITAIN'S SACRED? SACRIFICE, RENEWAL, AND THE 2019 DECEMBER GENERAL ELECTION

> "It is only thanks to the Brexit Party that we hear about the truth, the horrors, the abuse, and the excess of what goes on in Brussels"
>
> *Richard Tice, Chairman of the Brexit Party, speaking at a rally in Southport, England*

2.1 Introduction

Democratic elections appear mostly as disenchanted, routine, and bureaucratic exercise in national governance. Yet under the scrutiny of the ethnographic lens, there are times in which we glimpse not merely a striving for a change in management but rather a drive towards the transcendental; something wholly other, what Rudolf Otto (1923) might have thought of as the *numinous*. Through an investigation based on both personal conversations and the electoral rhetoric of populist Brexit Party supporters, this chapter will argue that the 2019 British general election represented one such 'ritual of renewal'; an event which attempted to transform the moral order, create the sacred, and revitalise the political alienation which increasingly defines West European democracies.

By January 2020, after several years of unprecedented political turbulence, the pro-Brexit Conservatives had won an enormous majority in the preceding 2019 election. This gave them enough political dominance in the House of Commons to end the parliamentary gridlock and approve the revised Withdrawal Agreement, cementing the United Kingdom's exit from the European Union (EU). Much like the 2016 referendum which preceded and in some sense determined them, the events of the time were extraordinarily

DOI: 10.4324/9781003458517-2

contentious. Minor changes in historical pathway could have seen a hung parliament and a more trepidatious coalition, one which may have produced a second referendum or even reversed the Brexit process altogether. In those short months after Prime Minister Boris Johnson called a snap election announced on 31 October 2019, there remained all to play for on both sides of the ideological divide.

In setting out my research objectives for the election, what I found most worthwhile to study were neither the ambivalent voters in the periphery nor the senior leadership in the centre. There has already been considerable scholarship on the demographic makeup of national voting for Brexit, as well as the charismatic mandate of individuals like Nigel Farage (Ford and Goodwin 2014; Goodwin and Milazzo 2015; Kelsey 2015). Instead, what I wanted to focus on were those that were somewhere in the middle: the more regular ideologues and activists. Who were these political candidates standing for the Brexit Party in seats across the UK, many of whom would risk professional scorn and public ridicule for doing so? Clearly, they were authentic believers in Brexit, unlike the many millions who may have voted Leave out of either a fuzzy anti-political sentiment or the assumption that it wouldn't actually happen.[1] But neither were they people like Farage – individuals who had gained fame (and fortune) from being the symbolic figurehead of an anti-establishment movement. Instead, these individuals represented interlocutors for whom I could have a serious intellectual and emotional relationship without the condescension inherent in studying people who were framed as "left-behinds", forgotten by mainstream society.

What then can we learn about Brexit from understanding Brexit Party activists? What modest literature on this populist movement which already exists tends to focus on its role within formal electoral politics: standing MPs, MEPs, contesting seats, or winning vote shares (Dennison 2020; Ford et al. 2021). Little emphasis has been placed on what was said and felt by activists, campaigners, and leaders during that volatile era in which so much of Britain's future hung in the balance. Although a great deal of scholarship has focused on Farage and UKIP, almost nothing has been written on the 283 Brexit Party candidates that were drawn to this ideology and mission. This is curious given the wide-ranging literature on both populism and Brexit (Eatwell and Goodwin 2018; Kaufmann 2018; Norris and Inglehart 2019; Sobolewska and Ford 2020), especially as it concerns the voting behaviour of ordinary individuals (Evans 2020; Koch 2017; Ringel 2020). Instead, I ask: what of the 'organic intellectuals' (Gramsci 2011) who shaped the Brexit narrative, devoted themselves to the cause, risked intense public scrutiny and indeed broke personal relationships over their political stance?

This chapter will examine some of these questions by providing a snapshot of the 2019 general election and the months leading up to it. Unlike a broad survey analysis, ethnography cannot easily capture what was happening during several months of fervour at the national level. Each individual's experience of both Brexit and the 2019 election had a singular, unrepeatably emic quality. This 'native point of view' (Geertz 1974) may testify to the uniqueness of anthropology of a discipline, but it makes generalising particularly difficult. I can only provide limited descriptions about what I consider relevant to the things a small selection of people were discussing and try to describe the mood in which they discussed them. Overall, my approach to researching elections is sympathetic to Clifford's (1988, p. 19) ideal of the ethnographic attitude: one which conceptualises "culture and its norms – beauty, truth, reality – as artificial arrangements susceptible to detached analysis and comparison with other possible dispositions". I have endeavoured to frame what I discovered with an anthropological approach that prioritises salient theoretically concepts like ritual and the sacred. Ultimately, however, this analysis is only my reading of it – the data can speak for itself.

In endeavouring to understand these pivotal individuals, my research started by focusing just on the electoral process itself: strategy, campaigning, rhetoric, canvassing, and party aesthetics. Much of this could fall under a Latourian framework for analysing the electoral techniques which produce truth and knowledge within democratic elections (Coles 2004; Latour and Woolgar 1987). However, rather than trying to squeeze the intimate diachronic personal relationships that I had with my interlocutors into this chapter, I have kept them for the rest of the book. Here, I will attend mostly to what I found compelling during the singular events that made up election season.

Once again, it is worth making clear that this chapter is concerned primarily with the public character of electoral ritual, such that intimate conversations have been de-emphasised in favour of public-facing elite rhetoric. Both the descriptive and the analytical focus will be on the discourse and performance of the speeches presented to crowds of supporters over the many rallies that the Brexit Party held during those months. Although they did have other policy platforms, as far as I could tell, the only reason why anyone stood as a candidate or voted for them was because they were authentic believers in the necessity of leaving the EU. The language they used to articulate their political worldview and the tactics they used to mobilise their supporters are the core interest for my ethnographic work in this area.

The overall argument is that what the 2019 election represented for many Brexit supporters was a fundamental transformation of the social: the destruction of a deteriorating old order and the birth of a wholesome new one. This framework pivots on Borneman's (2002) theory that sees democratic elections as a ritual practice in which the ruler (here 'ruling party') gives up their life and power such that the social body can rejuvenate through an infusion with the transcendental. What I found startling about the election was that in every single Brexit Party rally I encountered there was at least one instance in which speakers invoked the war dead as an example of those who gave up their lives for democracy. And as Borneman makes clear; if sacrifice functions by creating the sacred through an act of loss, then the ritualistic invocations of these dead seemed to midwife a transformation of the referendum result from a "socio-material apparatus for producing particular political facts" (Green et al. 2016, p. 480) into a sacred vehicle for collective moral transformation.

By thus leaving the EU, my interlocutors seem to feel that the faith, trust, and sanctity in democracy could be replenished, the sacrificial dead could be honoured, and the social could once again become whole. The question of whether they feel vindicated for this decision will be explored in the following chapters. But the essence of this process is that Brexit supporters put the European project quite literally on a sacrificial alter in order that the pain of economic loss would result in the gain of holistic social rejuvenation. Understanding the arbitrariness of the EU as a symbol here is important: it is a target which merely approximates the general sense that things have been morally and culturally deteriorating over the past several decades. National decline, economic inequality, and rapid demographic change are eminently pivotal causes of this general sentiment, as outlined by considerable number of scholars throughout this book (Dorling and Tomlinson 2019; Gusterson 2017; Kaufmann 2018; Norris and Inglehart 2019; Sobolewska and Ford 2020).

However, abstract cultural change cannot so easily function as a 'master symbol' (Wolf 1958), 'empty signifier' (Laclau 2005) or 'transformational object' (Bollas 2017) in the same way that a technocratic and largely distant organisation like the EU can. This is at least partly connected to strong taboos around immigration issues, as Sobolewska and Ford (2020) demonstrate, which I believe prime political discourse for instances of collective transference.[2] It also explains the intense drive – almost always completely vacant of intellectual argumentation about the trade-offs and economic consequences of leaving the EU – that characterised these Brexit supporters.

Our context is a society marked by ever-declining trust in moral authorities – especially towards political elites – and moments like the election are a ritual which provide that essential 'collective effervesce' (Durkheim 2008) that can transform the social, reverse its course or cleanse it of impurities. This collective binding does not necessarily rest on positive affect: negative emotions like paranoia, anger, and hatred share in the potential to unite groups against others, as historical examples of the scapegoat clearly demonstrate (Borneman 2002; Freud 1990; Girard 2013). And as Bloch (1992) has shown, in a ritual context such a transformation necessarily involves aggression and destruction. This is because they are signifiers of the political vitalism inherent in violently subordinating and overcoming the old social order. I believe that this explains the rejection of all compromise on Britain's membership of the EU – exemplified by the so-called 'Norway Option' – despite at least half the population being strongly against leaving at all. The quasi-millenerial insistence on a 'Hard' or 'Clean Break Brexit' without any concessions whatsoever was not mere political rhetoric: it was the discursive manifestation of an aggressive vitalism which is indispensable for transforming the social hierarchy through ritual.

Understanding the sanctity of 'honouring the referendum' is thus key. It was not simply about Brexiters getting their way from the result; neither whether the referendum was simply advisory.[3] Nor can we think of it as the unsatisfactory answer to an academic question about representative versus direct democracy. What was in play was ultimately of transcendental rather than quantifiable value; and repeated invocation of the war dead who defended democracy is yet another example of a sacrificial victim who acts as the spiritual conductor between the sacred and the profane (Bloch 1992). It is the key illustration of Borneman's (2002) major insight that sacrifice may be displaced but never truly eliminated from society lest it disintegrate. It is no coincidence that the language of 'honouring' the referendum throughout the election campaign so powerfully evoked the aura of sanctity and holiness.

I thus also hope to show that much of what can appear bizarre and incoherent rhetoric emerging from Brexit supporters does indeed contain more than a kernel of logic and meaning. While the aim here is not to write an apologetics, there is certainly an opportunity to elucidate something that I believe has poisoned much of our public discourse since 2016. The reason why arguments about the economic drawbacks of leaving the EU may have made such little impact on Brexiters is not because they are innumerate, stupid, or indecisive.[4] Instead, I propose that this confusion arises out of a broader and perhaps more interesting misrecognition. Many Brexiters are in pursuit of that which is *not* bound by trade-offs, compromises, and concessions: or indeed anything contained in the profane world of day-to-day exchange. They are looking for that which *transcends* all of these contingencies, the only thing that can transform moral fragmentation and the disintegration of the social (and 'fix broken Britain'). However my interlocutors themselves understood this process; an etic perspective would frame that thing in pursuit as the sacred, and it must therefore be reached (even if only discursively) through the notion of sacrifice (Borneman 2002). In short, for social renewal to be achieved, the European project itself must be ritually placed on the alter and slain.

To sum up, then: I argue that Brexit Party activists coalesced as a group because they were drawn to the message that Britain as a moral community has profoundly deteriorated in recent decades. There are many ways of thinking about this disintegration, but perhaps the most germane is in terms of a rupture of trust in political authority. This is something which has both a reasonable exposure to empirical analysis and a genuine ethnographic presence in conversations and discourse of these voters. This sentiment only intensified between 2016 and 2019 when it became clear that the political class as a whole had little intention of following through on the referendum result (Copus 2018). The 2019 election represented the apex of mobilisation for almost any kind of arrangement (including 'No Deal') which would sever Britain's relationship to the EU; something that my interlocutors believed was the root cause of this general anomie, especially at the level of leadership. This was not necessarily an unreasonable perspective, as scholars more critical of the EU's weak democratic foundations, technocratic centralising tendencies, and supranational elite unaccountability have cogently suggested (Mair 2013; Shore 2000, 2006; Streeck 2019).

The key here is that the sacred value of democracy was embodied in Brexit – something which symbolised both the honouring of a democratic referendum and final severance from an undemocratic EU – and represented the transcendental value which could revitalise the social solidarity of the national group as a moral community (Durkheim 2008). But achieving any contact with this transcendental requires a sacrificial element: this explains the invocation of a discourse on soldiers who died to defend democracy. Their deaths are the lightning rod which brings together the profane world of voting choices and the sacred world of nation, freedom, continuity. When Brexit candidates implore people to vote against the EU, it represented the latest link in the chain of sacrificial practices that might culminate in revitalisation and renewal. In line with Borneman's (2002) adaption of Frazer's (1998) work, we can interpret the severance from the EU via democratic elections as a culmination of this process. Once again, that which seems the most mundane example of governmental practice leaves us pondering whether if indeed it is still not true that, for many democratic voters today, "the world remains a great enchanted garden" (Weber 1971, p. 270).

2.2 A Winter of Discontent

The 2019 election was simultaneously the first, the most significant, and the ethnographically richest period of the fieldwork which led to the creation of this book. The contrast between those initial months of energy and the years of boredom that would shortly ensue owing to the effects of coronavirus was enormous. Before an even more totalising experience of this phenomenon during the pandemic, I do not recall at any point in my life the news cycle being utterly dominated by just one issue: Brexit. The election marked the last period in which almost nothing could appear on mainstream British news without some reference to leaving the EU.

During the period 2016–2020, but especially between the 2017 election (won by Theresa May) and the 2019 poll (won by Johnson), parliamentary businesses seemed to have little else on the agenda. In March 2017 May had triggered 'Article 50' of the Lisbon Treaty – the process by which any country could willingly leave the EU – and thus started a two-year countdown clock in which Britain would have to completely sever sovereign ties with the EU. Even under the most auspicious circumstances – involving a high degree of collective will and social solidarity – this process would have been immensely challenging.

As it was, nothing like this characterised the period. The country was deeply divided: not only polarised along the Remain/Leave axis but also within them. Some – such as the *People's Vote* campaign group – argued for a fresh referendum on an issue which they felt had been illegitimately won. Others believed that Britain had no choice lest it cease to become a democracy; and the ideal was to stay as close to the EU as possible, such that re-entry would be easier in the future. People remained bitterly divided about whether Brexit meant total severance in all political and economic arrangements or having a 'Norway' or 'Switzerland' option in which there was still a great deal of co-operation without full membership. Regardless of which position was taken, the debates across the country were fractious and all-consuming. It is no coincidence that Johnsons 'Get Brexit Done' mantra was so popular in the 2019 election: years of often tedious discussion had taken its toll on the attention of the British public.

Unable to muster either the charisma or the political *nous* to deliver Brexit (as she had promised in the election of that year), May was removed from office and replaced in a leadership contest by Johnson. A leader of the Leave campaign in 2016 and canny political operator with the mayoralty of London behind him, Johnson was perhaps one of the few politicians who would have been able to finalise a British exit from the EU. Partly this was because of an uncharacteristic ruthlessness of personality, examples of which include expelling 21 Conservative MPs (including Winston Churchill's grandson) from the party for opposing Brexit, in addition to proroguing Parliament in 2019. A great deal of these issues was of his own making: like the rest of the leadership behind the Leave campaign, there was nothing close to a blueprint for what would happen should the nation actually vote to leave the EU. At the time, few believed that they would win, and the consequences of not having a plan for victory reverberated throughout these years as one of the significant obstacles to achieving what was promised during the referendum.

It is not the focus of this chapter to provide a minute play-by-play account of those years in terms of what political actors were doing, nor indeed will I focus even on this for the general election of 2019. Considerable efforts have already been made to provide high calibre scholarship on the period, much of which provides a highly generative reading (Ford et al. 2021). But to give a summary: the era was one pervaded by a great sense of insecurity and political turbulence. This was defined by oscillation and instability around Parliamentary votes and deals, specifically the Withdrawal Agreement, the

Northern Ireland backstop, and the applicability of a 'No-Deal Brexit' (whatever that would mean). It was also marked by the eruption of Jeremy Corbyn's populist insurgency in the Labour Party, one dogged by accusations of widespread antisemitism (Heppell 2021). By the time of the 2019 election, frustrations had ripened. Few people were not eager – regardless of their view on Brexit – to simply forget about the whole thing such that the news cycle would finally move on.

It was during this period that I began research on those who will be a focus of this chapter and indeed the rest of my book: members of the Brexit Party. Formed in 2018 as a response to a 'betrayal' of the Chequers deal, which Farage claims represented sell-out of British interests, the party was set up as the successor to his former outfit, The United Kingdom Independence Party (UKIP). Now condemned as being fundamentally Islamophobic and obsessed with immigration, Farage gave up leadership of UKIP to find a new vehicle which would promote his vision of leaving the EU. This was something which he had spent the past thirty years of his life promoting; and having come so close to achieving it, he clearly felt a sense that the Leave movement was about to snatch a defeat from the jaws of victory. This was in large part because he was faced with a growing backlash of both pro-Remain groups (who were mobilising for a new referendum) and a Parliament which was overwhelmingly against leaving the EU at all. His response was to register a new party with an otherwise esoteric politician called Catherine Blaiklock: a figure who then quickly resigned after it came out that she had shared anti-Islamic media posts on Twitter. In the event of European Parliament elections – Britain was at this time still a voting member of the EU – Farage and others would use this new party to push through their vision of a Britain completely unshackled (in their eyes) from membership with any supra-national body.

From the outset, the Brexit Party was dogged by financial scandal. This was primarily because it was not a conventional political party at all: it had no members nor any kind of administrative infrastructure. Almost everything was ordered by decree from Farage and the brief addition of Richard Tice, a businessman who had headed the *Leave Means Leave* group after the referendum. Instead, enthusiastic individuals were offered the option not of being party members but 'registered supporters'. By the time of the European Parliament elections in 2019, there were 100,000 such persons, each of whom had to pay £25 for the affiliation. Contravening British balloting regulations, the party was quickly investigated by the Electoral Commission, possibly under the direct influence of the Prime Minister. The Commission found that despite 'very serious concerns', there was no substantial fear that they had broken the law (Ford et al. 2021). What was also unique about this episode was that like many other populist ensembles throughout Europe, the Brexit Party merged business and politics in such a way that complicates traditional demarcations between social spheres, although in ways which align with neoliberal impetus towards dissolving social relationships into exchange ones. In this case, a common scandal of a political party corrupted by business interests came closer to a business corrupted by party interests.

In 2018, one year before the general election which constitutes the ethnographic component of this chapter, European elections were called. The Brexit Party put up several dozen candidates, many of whom became some of my most trusted interlocutors. There was no manifesto and no mission other than Brexit. Taking up the mantra 'Change Politics for Good' shortly before the election, the party stood as the authentic vehicle for those who wanted nothing less than a total divorce from the EU. Winning an unforeseen 30 per cent of the vote, the Brexit party rapidly transformed the characteristics of British representation in the EU Parliament. (Perhaps counterintuitively for those who saw Brexit as irredeemably racist, it was also most ethnically diverse party in the chamber's history). The reason for its victory was predominantly because it had become the principal vehicle for airing grievances of those who felt that Brexit was being 'betrayed' by an untrustworthy and even treasonous 'establishment'. Although it was to some extent a protest vote – much like its antecedent in the 2016 referendum – it was also ultimately coupled with dissatisfaction with the Conservative Party and the leadership of May.

Just a few months later, when Johnson called a general election in 2019, the Brexit Party would go on to win 600,000 votes. Although this did not place them with even a single Member of Parliament, it produced a series of other consequences. The first and most important one was splitting the vote: Ford et al. (2021) suggest that they cost the Conservatives up to 25 seats over Labour. When Farage chose to stand down candidates in Conservative constituencies so as to ensure a pro-Brexit coalitional majority across the country, it was another example of him being a skilful political operator. This manoeuvring would ultimately ensure that there was a 'Clean Break Brexit' in line with the wishes of many Brexit hardliners. If not for these electoral innovations, it is highly possible that a resurgent and well-organised Remain/Rejoin coalition could have fought back to prevent a Brexit landslide, keep Britain more or less inside in the EU, and set the conditions for a gradual re-entry. What ultimately transpired was the opposite: during the time of writing, Britain is firmly and formally outside of the EU with little view to coming back anytime soon. The Brexit Party can be rightfully seen as one of the most influential populist parties in European history.

At the 2019 election, the Brexit Party – despite considerable speculation about impropriety of its financial management – promoted a diverse array of candidates for office across the UK. Very little substantial changes occurred by virtue of the party's mobilisation: they did not win even a single parliamentary seat. In my own constituency in London, the local candidate of the

Brexit Party achieved only 1.8 per cent of the vote. Yet although the party itself was unable to win even one constituency, it played a pivotal role in shaping both the re-election of Johnson and the Conservative Party, as well as the final fulfilment of a 'Hard Brexit' for the UK. This is because on 11 November Farage announced that he would stand down all his candidates in the Conservative held seats. The remaining contenders would try their luck at election against progressive candidates who opposed Brexit, many of whom I also interviewed for this book. The trick seemed to have paid off: the Conservatives won a majority with 365 MPs, defeating any chance of a 'progressive alliance' that could block Britain's exit. The UK then formally left the EU on 31st January 2020. This ethnographic section follows those that fought the election which was so pivotal for Britain's relationship with its European neighbours.

During those fast-paced months when I began my fieldwork, the Brexit Party adopted an electoral strategy of both traditional canvassing and a digital broadcasting. Understanding that social media advertisement had a key role in winning the Leave vote during the referendum, the Brexit Party wasted little time in organising many kinds of political advertisements, interviews, and general online content. These were aimed directly at their sole demographic of voters who felt that the referendum was not being honoured but were ambivalent about the Conservative Party's ability to deliver an 'authentic' Brexit. Many of these videos are still available on Farage's YouTube channel: a source I found invaluable for keeping up with various political events which I was unable to attend in-person. However, I have chosen to mostly keep the social media material for later sections and focus just on electoral rhetoric: an amount of content which is still overwhelming even when abridged enough for a book chapter.

One of the particularly curious features of their campaign strategy – one perhaps in line with overall suspicions about their administrative operation – was in holding usually quite secretive rallies across the country. It's true that there were some grassroots campaigning tactics, such as handing out leaflets and meeting people in the street. But these were significantly less voluminous than one would have expected for a party contesting the national election. In fact, I found it a challenge to even locate where these candidates would be meeting and campaigning. Much I managed to trace only through small Facebook groups and word-of-mouth. This may have simply been due to their small size, but the entire operation felt suspicious. Despite hosting candidates across the country, their presence was so limited that it was near impossible to get hold of them. For a political party looking for national recognition – even if it was modest by the standards of the Labour or Conservative parties – their opacity and aloofness was unusual. They were in fact true representatives of the new wave of 'digital populism' that bypasses traditional media gatekeepers and is constituted by an ethereal and spectral presence, lacking the physical enlistment of mass political parties that so defined the 20th century (Mair 2013; Schroeder 2018).

Around the time that the election was called, the leadership mostly avoided many of the typical metropolitan areas and instead focused on less well-known constituencies which had strong support for Brexit. All led by then chairman Tice, the central campaigning happened Doncaster, Sedgefield, Southport, Telford, Newport, Exeter, Maidstone, and eventually London. Except for the capital, the demography of many these urban centres resembles contain many of the populist voters who feel shut out from the fruits of globalisation: older, less educated, and less diverse (Eatwell and Goodwin 2018). The only real examples of those from a more diverse ethnic background were the individuals who appeared on stage, late, for photo opportunities at the end of the rally.

Condensing all of what was said will necessarily be difficult in such a short space, so let us begin by sketching an overview of each rally was like, before delving deeper into the themes which repeatedly permeated them. Hundreds of people attended each one. The audiences were almost always the same; draped in the blue and white Brexit Party flags, the speakers would walk on stage one-by-one to the sound of rock-guitar stringing. Each stage was covered with giant blow-up signs with 'We Are Ready' written behind the podium. Although each rally had a unique set of local speakers and candidates, a few key figures from the party were a constant presence on stage: Richard Tice, Ann Widdecombe, Annunziata Rees-Mogg (who later defected back to the Conservatives) and, of course, Nigel Farage.

Almost all the speeches and discussions contained a similar set of grievances and tropes about who the enemies were and what problems they had created. One of these themes was a direct complaint about the Northern Irish backstop process: essentially a legal wrangling over whether there would be a hard border between the Ireland and Northern Ireland if the former but not the latter would have full membership of the EU. These objections reflected a profound suspicion over the direction of Brexit, much of it along the lines that excuses were being conjured up to find problems with leaving at all. Much of them contained wrathful rhetoric about "betrayal" and "liberal elites", the insistence that "we must stand up for our democracy" being the overriding and quintessential aspect of all of them. There was unique rage directed at what Tice named "pretty perfect policy wonks" in Westminster, a label one would interpret as a slight against an archetypal technocrat with a condescending metropolitan attitude about Leave voters.

Another key theme throughout the campaigning, leafletting and digital media was the complete sense of humiliation. A quintessential example of this is from Widdecombe, who claimed at a number of rallies that Britain "has become an international laughingstock" with "the worst Parliament since the Civil War". (A bizarre irony, given Parliamentarian opposition to the most unelected of all liberal elites: a divinely appointed Stuart monarch). A number of videos that circulated on social media echoed the same sentiments: in one, a series of individuals line up and say: "our country has been humiliated / by politicians we trusted with our vote / we deserve so much better than this". At a rally in Exeter, candidate Christina Jordan's speech included the complaint that "we sit in that chamber and listen to speakers belittle, insult and humiliate the UK because we have the cheek to say we are leaving". At a rally in London, Farage protested that "I think we've really had enough of being talked down to and humiliated by the bureaucrats of Brussels and many other European leaders". These are just a few examples of the similar sentiments that circulated throughout the election.

The significance of these affects for understanding the appeal of populist parties cannot be underestimated. Based on my own embeddedness in these conversations, I imagine that the majority of the British population at the time viewed delays to Brexit as the obvious consequence of indecision and resistance operating at the domestic level. Between 2016 and 2020 the gridlock, polarisation, and arguments about Brexit were visceral and all-consuming. Little concerned the political authorities in Brussels: it was almost entirely a national conversation which divided the country into two bitterly opposing camps. I found few people during that era who believed that obstructions and delays were caused by a cynical attempt to humiliate a patriotic nation.[5]

Yet this discourse eminently has great moral authority: insights from thinkers like Nietzsche (2013) demonstrate that victimhood has a transformational power. And while I am extremely cautious to make any comparison to fascism, when I heard these relentless discourses of national humiliation and victimhood – which I saw as largely operating on the level of total fantasy – one is reminded of Nazi adoption of the same rhetoric in periods of economic crisis (Borneman 2002; Eghigian 2002; Scheff and Retzinger 2003). These speeches demonstrated that for a considerable number of populist supporters, the domestic opposition of half the country could only be conceived through a prism of elite malfeasance. This one point of connection that helps us make sense of the cross-fertilisation of conspiracy theories and right-wing populism – both of which are built on alienated and low-trust political relationships – that I will explore in later chapters (Goertzel 1994; Miller et al. 2016).

Beyond these sentiments, another key concern was that a great many of speeches testified to the cliche that 'all politics is local'. To a surprising degree, the reasons people gave on stage for supporting the Brexit Party operated at a tremendous distance to anything even vaguely related to the EU. Some candidates, like Dr David Bull, complained that the problem was about GP triaging systems. Others spoke about the concerns of parents who had kids bullied at school. One voter during the campaign said that they supported Brexit because nobody was coming to clean up the neighbour's dog waste. Another wanted Brexit so we would respect our elders. One archetypal version of this theme comes from Tegan Lucas, candidate for Lewisham Deptford. In the capital's biggest pro-Brexit Party rally, she claimed also drew an otherwise unintelligible connection between medical provision and the EU by saying that:

> "I do now work as a mechanic, but before that after [sic] facing mental health difficulties on my very own. I worked at a training initiative, one that supports those with mental health needs, to re-join the working world. And it's because of this I cannot help but feel like the crows [sic] in Westminster still refusing to enact what we voted for three years ago, means serious injustice is in our country are being ignored. I am determined to ensure democracy is delivered and crisis in our countries such as poor mental health provisions to be rectified".

Many speakers echoed similar sentiments, often comfortable with the folksy aesthetic that defines much populist rhetoric (Hall et al. 2016; Moffitt 2016). At the rally in Doncaster, one speech from a young woman named from Lucy Harris is worth quoting in full:

> "Now, my degree as Richard has touched on was in music. Now music is a lot of fun, but it doesn't pay the bills at the end of the day. And what I found that was the biggest experience in my life, was taking a job as a fishmonger for five years in my local Waitrose[6] as I did that degree. I learned so much more from talking to the general public, understanding what they're about understanding what they wanted. Was it a sea bass? Was it a slap? It doesn't matter.. understanding what they wanted. And it really got into the idea of what it meant to be to be part of a community. And I'm trying to say to people my age, and people who are younger, that you don't have to follow the same road. You don't have to be part of the mould. I hope that you have the confidence to go out there and build yourselves as individuals, as ordinary people who can crack the mould and be something different than to what a government or a state system will tell you. You can be you, can be someone else and you can be different! I reject the paternalism of the EU; I reject the idea of a nanny state. I reject being told what to do, and I hope young adults my age will understand the importance and the freedom that lies behind rejecting so much control over every aspect of our lives. We do not need the approval of anyone to be successful in our own lives, be rebellious. Question those in power, not yourself. Question the status quo. Not yourself. Question the mainstream not yourself. Be rebellious. Vote for the Brexit Party".

Others bordered on a distinctive (but largely old fashioned) distrust of Britain's European neighbours. Although they often attacked the EU's democratic deficit, they mostly represented what I discovered to be typically pro-Brexit suspicion that Europe was less a domain for enacting shared sovereignty than it was a cynical confidence trick. At a rally in Telford, Rupert Lowe epitomised this low-trust attitude when he said:

> "We just had another very active week in Strasburg as Richard says, with all 29 MEPs continuing to challenge the bureaucratic behemoth, which is a sorry excuse for a Parliament. Truly a democratic fig leaf. It is a sham designed to uphold the veneer of democracy in a place where there is none. It is paid for by us and the Germans, but ultimately run by our historical foe, the French".

A fair few stressed their grievances about the direction of surplus government aid. Much of this is based on a common objection, recognisable to anyone who has read the British tabloid newspapers, that the UK is profligate and financially ill-disciplined about international charity. Although this is usually directed at incompetent liberal technocrats, it also emerged throughout in the Brexit Party's campaigning. At the same rally in Shropshire, Elaine Adams said:

> "When we spend more than 1 billion pounds every month on foreign aid – which has included financing a girl band in Ethiopia to the tune of 5 million pounds – and sending 98 million pounds to India. A lovely country, lovely people, but a country which has its own space programme and nuclear weapons. Why is that? Here in Telford, our own Telford and Wrekin council has cut 123 million pounds over the past decade, and they've got an extra 25 billion pounds to cut over the next two years. Indirectly, therefore, Telford and Wrekin Council has helped fund India's nuclear weapons programme".

In addition to much softer rhetoric of "global trade" and "reconnecting outside of the borders of the EU", there was much more pin-pointed criticism of individual political leaders. Jokes and fixations on Anna Soubry, the former Conservative (and vociferously pro-Remain) MP, implied an abundance of either animosity or infatuation. Speakers adopted a characteristically populist rhetoric ridiculing by elaborating the vision of a distant and wealthy liberal elite against a pure, honest 'people' (Mudde 2004). One common refrain from Farage was that politicians like her:

> "[Are] about Islington not Islwyn, about Hampstead not Huddersfield, Dalston not Doncaster, about comfortable elites and no longer standing up for the working classes".

At other points during the campaign, speakers took a far more aggressive and confrontational tone. Farage combined quasi-apocalyptic rhetoric with a folksy and Trumpian manner when he claimed in a London rally that:

> "If you rob people of their identity, if you rob them of their democracy, then all they have left with is nationalism and violence. People fought and died so that we could be an independent, self-governing democratic nation that was able to hire and fire its leaders".

After he spoke, Widdecombe took to the stage to add:

> "These sensitive souls in Parliament don't really like words like betrayal and surrender. They don't like words like surrender. And betrayal. Then let them stop betraying and surrendering! MPs voting to take 'No Deal' off the table by quite deliberately weakening Britain's position at the negotiating table are guilty of betrayal. What else do you call it to give a foreign power an advantage when Britain is trying to negotiate a deal? What treachery! You're right that is what that is. What else do you call it? If you are prepared in perpetuity to let the law of a foreign power override your own law except surrender. That is what happens when a country loses a war".

In another particularly baffling example of this rhetoric – one which flips what many scholars have seen as the relationship between Brexit and the British Empire on its head to make Britain a *victim* of imperialism – Widdecombe's previous speech to the European Parliament went viral among Brexit Party supporters before the election, when she said:

> "One of the many reasons why Britain is right to leaving this place, [...] and is right to do so, is because there is a pattern consistent throughout history of oppressed people turning on their oppressors, slaves against their owners, the peasantry against the feudal barons, colonies – Mr. Verhofstadt – against their empires... and that is why Britain is leaving and it doesn't matter which language you use we are going, and we are glad to be going".

Farage echoed this rhetoric when he claimed at another rally that:

> "This is now a much bigger question. This is about whether we are a democratic nation or not. It's that fundamental it's about who we are. As a country. It's about how the rest of the world sees us. It's about what we want to hand down to our children and grandchildren. Are we to be a great, proud nation, or are we to be a colony of a new United

States of Europe? But I tell you what, if we're not prepared to stand up and fight, it'll be the latter. So I'm prepared to stand up and fight. These people are prepared to stand up and fight. Are you prepared to stand up and fight?"

Dovetailing with the more aggressive tone I have outlined here, perhaps one of the most important themes that emerged was an insistence on what was variously called a 'No-Deal Brexit', a 'Hard Brexit' or a 'Clean Break Brexit'. These unique phrasings were ubiquitous throughout the rallies, especially by Farage. They mostly implied that this form of absolute separation was the only option not only to save Britain but to arrest its decline and propel it back to the global influence. One quintessential example of this type of discourse comes from a rally in Maidstone in Kent. John Longsworth took to the stage and argued that:

"If we give away our sovereignty to the European Union, if we stay in rather than having a 'Clean Break Brexit', we will find that certainly in my children's lifetime, Britain no longer exists. So don't be afraid of a 'Clean Break Brexit'. On the contrary, a 'Clean Break Brexit' will make us more wealthy, and it will actually make the regions like Yorkshire and North Lincolnshire boom again".

Writing this nearly two years after Brexit, it goes without saying that none of this actually happened. If anything, much as anti-Brexit commentators predicted, the economic consequences of leaving have been just as calamitous as predicted (Sampson 2017). Nowhere in the North of England has industry had a "boom". Regardless of this financial reality, Longsworth's discourse created a sense that total divorce and separation from the old status quo was necessary to begin the process of social renewal (Bloch 1992; Turner 1970). Whether this had any substantial connection to reality impinged little on the power of this rhetoric.

This last point links with what I found curious about much Brexit oratory: that even the most radically pro-Leave candidate would not admit that at least half of the British population wanted to Remain, often vehemently so. For a group of people concerned with democracy, unity, and collective purpose, this was perhaps an undesirable reality. So why was there nothing by way of compromise? Why did Farage and others insist on a complete and total severance from the previous order – one which consciously invoked a language of destruction, partition, cutting-off? Could there not have been a compromise such that countries like Switzerland and Norway had? I do not believe that this fact simply reflects an arbitrary campaigning tactic nor the personal proclivity of Farage. Rather, as I elaborated on in the introduction, this requires us to think about the politics of moral revitalisation through creating the transcendental by means of a violent destruction and overcoming of the old social order (Bloch 1992).

2.3 Those Who Died For Us

What stood out most from these rallies was the fact that in hardly a single one did the theme of sacrifice not at one point come up. What I initially imagined as simply an example of Second World War nostalgia (Williams 2021) transformed into something far more significant as the election ran on. At one of the first rallies in Newton Abbot, a small town in rural South Devon, Farage took the stage after several other speakers had proclaimed their vision of transforming the British political system. He went on to say:

> "I didn't spend 25 years of my life, I thought to myself, to allow the greatest democratic exercise in the history of our nation to be overturned. And that, ladies and gentlemen, is why I formed the Brexit Party, to fundamentally reset, realign and change British Politics. It is rotten, it is dishonest, it is broken, it doesn't work; and we can do so much better, because we believe in our country, we believe in the legacy that was handed down to us – from generations that made massive sacrifices – so that we could be free people".

At another Brexit Party rally in Cornwall a short time later, Farage invoked evoked a comparable sentiment:

> "I grew up and I'm sure many of you grew up understanding something that you may not agree with somebody else's opinion but in a democracy, you respected the right of other people to have different opinions. This is this is what those generations who sacrificed so much for in two world wars for us to live in a free independent nation in a democratic system".

This nascent imagery of sacrificial fallen only intensified throughout the rest of the campaign and was remarkably similar throughout the diverse regions of England. At Doncaster racecourse in the North of England, another enormous rally took place closer to the time of the election. To another crowd of supporters, Farage ended his rally speech:

> "I admit I made a mistake: I did not believe that a vicar's daughter [Theresa May] could be so wilfully duplicitous with the British nation. If we win these elections and we win them big, then perhaps something starts to matter again. We actually made huge sacrifices twice in the 20th century to defend the very notion of democracy. It is democracy itself that has been betrayed – we must fight for it!"

The crowd shortly burst into cheers. They sung "Nigel, Nigel, Nigel!" in unison as the energy of the room alighted in ritualistic solidarity with Farage's speech. More speakers lined up to talk about the revolutionary effects of Brexit: lower taxes, stopping the "fat cats" from lining their own pockets, investing in industry, and creating a fairer economy. All these linguistic articulations seemed to add up to the general sense that Britain simply was not quite right: there was not enough of what Durkheim (2008) would call "social solidarity" between individuals. People could not be relied upon, honesty was in short supply, not everyone was pulling their weight, our leaders were duplicitous and did not serve the community as they should. There was a much greater sense of both personal and cultural alienation than people felt comfortable with. Something had to be the solution that could renew this moral decay.

At this same rally, a woman called Barbara had asked a question to Tice, who read out the script for the audience. "How", she had ostensibly asked, "how can it be justified to just forget about democracy and forget about us Leave voters that won the referendum?". After a short interlude by another disaffected Brexit candidate, Farage once again leaped onto the stage to give another small speech:

> "I was in Lincoln this morning, and I went to visit the new Bomber Command museum that's been put up there in the last couple of years. And it's a pretty humbling place: humbling in terms of the massive sacrifice that was made, scary in terms of the realisation what total war meant for ordinary people in this country and Germany, and around much of the world. But I did think to myself, as I walked through that garden looking at all the names of people that Bomber Command had lost including, including women, of course who worked on bases that have been bombed, all of those things. When you talk, sir [sic], in your question about democracy – what right do we have to throw away the massive sacrifice that those before us made to live in democracy? What right does anybody have to do that?"

The crowd roared with delight. One smaller question followed, and a discussion about split voting and the treasonous character of the "liberal elite" came up once again. Little else followed from the rally: the crowd slowly dispersed after a wave of Brexit Party placards shimmered across the hall. As the cameras went down, the hundreds of people then winded their way outside of the auditorium and made their way home.

Two weeks later, a similar rally was held in Newport, Wales. Once again, the audience consisted of primarily older, whiter British citizens who had come from the local area in a mostly Leave voting region. The content of the rally was almost the same as that from Doncaster: there was a set pattern of speech given by Tice, and then various political candidates would talk for about twenty minutes on a subject related to their own personal relationship with Brexit. The same topics continue to emerge: foreign aid budgets, inept "bungling bureaucrats in Brussels", the Irish backstop, the stupidity of "pretty perfect policy wonks" in Whitehall and, of course, May's Brexit deal ("a stinker and a polished turd" originally attributed to Johnson but ridiculed throughout the rallies). All the discursive contents of these speeches could be categorised under the same sentiments as before: the nation has gotten worse, leaders are corrupt and untrustworthy, our conventional values have declined.

Near the end of the rally, the Brexit Party candidate for Caerphilly, Nathan Gill, gave a long speech on the epoch-defining significance of Brexit. As with the other candidates, the speaker textured what he told the crowd with evocations of cultural transformation and renewal. Towards the climax of his speech, he said:

> "A couple of weeks ago, I met with one of the leaders of a Eurosceptic party in Brussels. And she was very downcast and negative, and she was basically saying: if you guys can't leave, none of us can. It's all over. There's no hope, there's no chance for a result. And I said to her, just imagine that you was [sic] living in Germany in 1945. And you looked around and saw every single city, desolated [sic] by the bombings, and you saw that all of your men have been taken away to Russia or America or wherever to pay reparations. And said you would have had no hope at all, you'd have literally just wanted to get out of your country and leave. Twenty years later, Germany was the third biggest economy in the world. It's never ever too late and we should never ever lose hope in ourselves, in our country and in our abilities to succeed".

Evidently, the theme of hope, redemption and national renewal had a powerful effect on the crowd, who seemed enrapt by these stories. Nathan continued and described how Westminster politicians (as he saw them) had no belief in the nation, nor did they think that there was any possibility that anything could improve. He ended his speech with another analogy and an exhortation to collective effort:

> "Many, many years ago, I was brought up in an old people's home, and when I came home from school, my mother would make us go and speak to the oldies. We had to go and listen to them for about 30 minutes before we were allowed to watch TV. So we go down, and of course we would hear the same stories, day after day, and there was quite a few there but we would move around, and they'd tell us all of these stories. Initially, there were people who had been in World War One, and then

> there were people that had been in World War Two, and these people instilled in me that knowledge and that belief that our country was simply worth fighting for: it was something that was worth sacrificing for. [Massive applause and cheering]. And I just thank the Lord that I am not being asked to storm the beaches of Normandy or parachute into Arnhem. My sons hopefully will never have to do that either. But this is our battle: remember that when you put on your favourite walking boots and your coat, and you go out there to campaign for the Brexit Party. Remember that this is your battle: and you must win!"

A few less charismatic speakers followed Nathan's speech, before the Brexit Party candidate for Newport East, Julie Price, also took to the stage. She began with a winding monologue about how terrible the Labour Party were, before launching into another story about why leaving the EU remained a sanctified task:

> "I told you a little bit about my upbringing, and I mentioned my mother's side of the family but today I'd like to talk about my dad's side. They are much loved and much missed. My grandparents met during World War Two. Their names for Fred and Kate Batten. We know them still as Grim and Grump. He was from Cardiff, and she was from the northeast. He returned to Cardiff from the war alive but not unscathed. In fact, the family made headlines like many others at the time of the Cardiff Blitz, while his father had remained in Cardiff as a serving police officer, grandpa was away serving in the Air Force when their house was hit. His dad was injured and hospitalised. Buehler, his mum died instantly aged 40. His little sister Patricia died a couple of days later, aged 18. At 19, he'd had to come home to deal with all of this. And he never really talked about it ever".

After detailing her family's history, she continued:

> "Every single person in this room will have stories like this to tell. Families scarred by battles for freedom and democracy, long past and more recent. Those memories must never, ever fade. I don't know how they would have voted in 2016. But what I do know is that they would expect the decision made then to be enacted. As do we: still!"

The tragedy of war seemed to evoke great sympathy in the crowd. She continued her narrative:

> "In May [2019], I told you that I thought politics is broken. What an understatement that was! I really didn't think it could get any worse.

> And I suspect we have not yet reached rock bottom or peak hysteria. The behaviour of the majority of our elected representatives makes me sick quite frankly. They are not fit to lick my grandparent's boots. I remain in no doubt at all that we need to leave the European Union properly and cleanly and respect that 2016 vote. If we don't, I don't know what sort of country this is. If we don't, I don't know what we fought for in the many conflicts that saw the sacrifice of literally millions of lives. And I really don't know what will become of us as we lose complete faith in our democracy that has been subsumed into the coming chaos of ever closer EU integration. There's a couple of things I do know. I do know we desperately need a general election to finally rid this country and the charlatans who are presiding over this rotting corpse of a democracy".

As for many other Brexit Party candidates, the emotion in her words was palpable. In the rhetoric of disgust, we see evidence of affectual demarcation of in-group and out-group boundaries, something noted by both psychologists and anthropologists (Buckels and Trapnell 2013). Clearly the sentiment of treachery and treason was close to mind. This dovetails with arguments about the illegitimacy of the 2016 referendum: it is not at all clear how an advisory referendum should have played out, and ascribing moral failing to logistical challenges is a problematic position. Ascribing duplicitousness to the general confusion of those years demands some sort of explanation, and this is especially salient regarding the palpable unreality of many statements ("chaos" of integration or "rotting corpse of democracy") that repeatedly emerged from speeches like Julie's.

An alternative reading of these sentiments, once again links back to the notion of the sacred. Berger's (1990) approach to religion argues that it is the consequence of shared categories which are revitalised through ritual practice, an idea that has much in common with both Bloch's (1992) and Durkheim's (2008) general framework. The key here is that the sacred – that which is an externalisation of our collectively shared social values – must always be counterposed to the idea of chaos. Berger argues that the latter, explicitly featured in a great number of cosmogonic myths, represents the disintegration of the categories which structure a sense of reality. It must therefore be avoided at all costs. If we see the transcendental value of democracy here as symbolised in Brexit, as I have suggested throughout this chapter, it makes sense why candidates like Price or Widdecombe ("the Conservatives offer us division and chaos, Labour offer us division and chaos"), and Tice could make claims that remaining within the EU in any form represents a destructive pathway towards complete social disorder. This binary opposition fits the definition of the sacred, something which adds further justification that this is the applicable etic category for making sense of these electoral discourses.

Finally, in one of the final (and perhaps best covered) Brexit Party rallies during that season, in London, another series of candidates gave long, impassioned speeches about how Britain would survive and rejuvenate through Brexit. In the middle of one particularly long piece of rhetoric, Farage once again invoked the sacrifices of the noble dead. He stood proudly and said:

> "This is now actually about more than just delivering Brexit. This is in fact about democracy itself. This is about our nation. This is about those who for hundreds of years, built this nation, defended this nation, sacrificed so much so that we could be a nation. This is about who we are as a people and as a country".

Once again, the invocation of the sacrificial dead was juxtaposed to the transcendental value of democracy, in effect sacralising what would in other contexts be considered as a merely academic question on the relative merits of representational versus direct democracy.

Farage continued:

> "But it is also about our place in the world. And our standing in the world. And I have to say I've met so many people who said to me: what an earth is happening to your country? We used to have great respect for the UK. We thought you were a great nation. We have been reduced by all politicians on the world stage to being a laughingstock and I want us not just to deliver Brexit, but I want us to re-establish where we should be in the world. Being represented, being represented in the higher councils across the globe by somebody from the European Commission is – I would suggest – not worthy of who we are as a people".

Most of Farage's speeches at all these rallies circled back to those same topics which I have outlined within this chapter. But it is worth highlighting this fragment of Farage's many speeches for another couple of reasons. The first is as an empirical example of the outsized collective narcissism and inflated sense of greatness that may have accompanied the vote to Leave. It is manifest here through imagining that Britain is so uniquely special and powerful that it is beneath us to be represented as equal member of a broader European sovereignty, a position analysed by a range of thinkers (Barnett 2017; Covington 2018; Dorling and Tomlinson 2019; Mandelbaum 2020; Reynolds 2019). Those from a psychoanalytic background, for instance, have noted that there is a sense of "narcissistic injury" present for many Brexit supporters, who see a puncture in the overly inflated sense of self (Covington 2018). Joining the EU implies that Britain is simply one European country among many, even if it is more financially, technologically, and militarily powerful than most of the others. (As one interlocutor told me, "it would be nuts to talk about Global Poland or Global Sweden. So why does it make sense for the UK?"). To paraphrase Dean Acheson, Europe was not a suitable role for space left vacant by the dissolution and loss of the British empire. It is evident from speeches like these that this sentiment is widely shared by the leadership of the pro-Brexit factions like Farage and Tice.

2.4 Britain's Sacred?

I have thus shown that sacrificial discourse permeated the electoral season of the Brexit Party. To make sense of this unfamiliar context, let us outline the key features of the debates around sacrifice in anthropology. At the earliest stages of its study, scholars like Frazer (1998) and Tylor (2016) took a broadly historical approach to sacrifice which traced its evolutionary development through evolutionary stages of human mentation. This was followed by Hubert and Mauss (1964), who took a more sociological or analytic approach which looked at it in terms of cross-cultural functions. Both approaches have their relative merits and demerits, and they were followed by scholars were much more critical of attempts to create vast generalisations about sacrifice (De Heusch 1985; Detienne 1989). One significant component of this debate concerns whether or not all sacrifice follows a simple logic of exchange in which one thing is lost in anticipation of the creation or reception of something new (Bataille 1991; Keenan 2005; Mayblin 2014). All these complex issues lend credence to the sentiment that we should not generalise too much about topics as vast and heterogenous as sacrifice.

Yet this trepidation has pernicious consequences when it forecloses moving forward with what we can positively associate with the practice. Let us summarise with what I believe are the two most irreplaceable features of the phenomenon. The first is that, as Borneman (2002, p. 3) claims, sacrifice can broadly be understood "as the constitution of a loss necessary for the creation of the sacred". Fixing an immutable bond between sacrifice and the sacred is, I believe, at the fundamental core of the often wildly divergent examples of how ritual sacrifice plays out cross-culturally in practice. Regardless of whether it always operates under a logic of exchange, there is no feature of sacrifice which can be found not to involve the creation of, contact with, or aversion towards, some feature of the transcendental. Whether this takes the form of the nation, the *Volk*, spirits, tutelary deities, mystical ideologies, secret societies, or any such other type is superfluous. The key is that all sacrifice involves something greater than the individual; and as Eliade (1959) notes, mankind cannot live without the sacred.

The second important feature which I wish to bring to attention in my ethnography is the schema outlined by later anthropologists. For Turner (1970), sacrifice is the archetypal ritual practice linked with social renewal. Its fundamental aim is the alteration of the moral quality of the social order. In times of extreme crisis, for instance, sacrificial practices can help individuals manage the shifting requirements that they face in their physical and cultural environment. Most importantly, these rituals can transform the moral essence of those who are enacting them. For Bloch (1992), the fundamental purpose of ritual is to mediate the unresolvable tension between the transience of human biological life and the necessity for durable social institutions. To manage this problem, groups seek to deny this very transience by creating a transcendent entity to which they can identify. This then becomes established as the legitimate social order. These explanations thus falls more along the lines of sociological than historical, and we would expect to find that such rituals are as necessary today as they would be in other periods in history, even if de-traditionalising tendencies (Giddens 1991) of late modernity have transformed the social nearly beyond recognition.

If sacrifice remains an unalterable feature of all human social life, then, where can we begin to find it today? It is of course true that in many contexts, the sacred is produced through sacrificial rituals in a manner familiar to traditional scholars of sacrifice. Goat-sacrifice continues in temples in Southern India, the Paschal lamb is slaughtered by Samaritans during Passover, and Afro-Cuban Santería worshippers have constitutional protection to continue the ritual killing of animals. Moreover, the religion in which sacrifice has a key (if now mostly figurative) role – Christianity – is still the most dominant belief system on the planet. Although both the human and animal sacrifices which conform most closely to the work of anthropologists have significantly diminished in volume since the advent of modernity, it is a mistake to imagine that it has been wholly eradicated even along its most traditionally morphological dimensions.

Notwithstanding many other cases in which sacrifice may continue to play a considerable social role, there is one sphere in which scholars converge to name as a site of the continued existence of sacrifice: democratic elections (Banerjee 2007; Borneman 2002).[7] To frame this question, it is worth briefly discussing how to define democracy. It can be identified by a great many constituent parts, including civil rights, a free press, high living standards, the rule of law and an open selection of political candidates (Paley 2002). However, we should remain cognisant of the vast heterogeneity in interpretations of democracy across ethnographic contexts (Schaffer 1997). For the sake of this case, following Borneman (2002), I shall concur with Schumpeter's (2010) definition that democracies are symbolic political systems in which the ruled chose who rule them using a selection mechanism known as elections.[8] My only intervention in this particular framing is that high levels of social trust are necessary for a healthy functioning democracy (Warren 2018; Zmerli and Newton 2008). I will return to this point at the later stage of this chapter.

Following these perspectives, Banerjee (2007) argues there are two principle means by which scholars have teased out the relationship between the practice of elections and the democratic system as a whole. The first is one manifestation of rational choice theory; a set of assumptions which is tremendously popular with economists and political scientists, but far less so with anthropologists, psychoanalysts, and many sociologists (Chibnik 2011; Foy et al. 2018). Indeed, the latter two tend to be considerably more suspicious about any claims to rational decision making, either in lieu of the influence of the unconscious (Freud 1961) or the constraints of a substantive economy over a formalist one (Polanyi 2002). Many of these thinkers would argue that rational choice theory is an embedded component of neoliberal cosmology rather than a reflection of any universal proclivity of human mentation, even if it does speak to a truth that humans certainly do engage in a degree of maximising behaviour.

In the framework of rational choice, people use their vote in a democratic election to maximise leverage, self-interest, and the fundamental conditions of their lives. There are certainly instances where this can be empirically observed: Chandra's (2004) ethnography of patronage networks in the Indian Punjab demonstrates that people make strategic decisions to vote in ways which increase the flow material services towards them. Elections in this framing are little more than transactional relationships between agents of differencing social and economic capital vying to gain the best deal out of a system they were born into and have little chance of fundamentally changing. There is clearly substantive degree of truth in the idea that humans rationally choose to maximise personal advantage through electoral means.

However, this approach to democratic elections, or indeed any framework which derives from its assumptions and principles, can be critiqued from several directions. The first is that in many instances voting simply has no point because the incumbent is hardly ever likely to lose. In West Bengal for instance, the Left Front have been in power for over thirty years, and a point Banerjee (2007) makes about her observations of a consistently high voter turnout cannot be made sense of in terms of maximising gain given the inevitable outcome. This is also true in contexts less involving hegemonic parties than archaic voting systems (such as Britain's) in which a first-past-the-post system largely precludes substantial social change through electoral means (Ford et al. 2021). A second critique, expertly illustrated by Lennon's (2018) ethnography of Trump voters, demonstrates that voting or party affiliation itself is hardly ever rational. Instead, it is largely an incoherent bundle of fractured and fragmentary subjectivities with little by way of relationship to any empirical political reality. It is difficult to attribute much degree of rationality however defined to nearly all voting behaviour in any global context.

As an alternative to the rational choice approach, the second major way in which scholars have thought about elections and democracy is in ritual terms. From this perspective, we can think of elections as having a symbolic or mythical role in helping to discursively constituting the people, maintaining structural equilibrium, and encouraging a cohesive society. It can be compared to a safety valve in which pent up frustration can be securely vented before it ferments mass unrest. However, in flipping the social world before putting it back again, this approach sees elections as ultimately reifying the status quo and precluding real social change (Bakhtin 1984; Dunn 1980; Lukes 1975). Scholars who adopt this framework must thus reckon with the epistemological barriers to assuming that the population colludes in gigantic misrecognition "of the emptiness of its procedures and of the lack of any significant changes which this ritual brings about" (Banerjee 2007, p. 1556). Indeed, such a framing has been vigorously critiqued by scholars like Spencer (2012), who see elections as closer to moral dramas than systematic mystifications. Such approaches would deeply resonate with Geertz's (1980) interpretation of politics in Bali, in which he saw the poetics of the theatre-state as the source rather than the dressing over royal power. Moreover, conceiving of elections as fundamentally conservative cannot explain how genuine change can indeed come about in democratic systems, even if that change is mostly minimal compared to revolutionary upheavals.

Such an approach means that we can open up the study of democratic elections in a way that converges with the knowledge produced by anthropologists who were looking at ritual in traditional societies. Although they may emerge in a "denuded" form which lacks either "intentionality or instrumentality" of other examples, seeing elections in this way helps us understand why they take the form of collectively performed, socially meaningful events in which pageantry and mass participation are usually the norm (Banerjee 2007, p. 1559). As Coles (2004, p. 553) notes, by virtue of their "formalism, traditionalism, disciplined invariance and repetition, rule governance, sacral symbolism, and performance", elections fit well into a framework that categories them as a form of ritual. Indeed, a similar observation is made by Herzfeld (1992), who sees modern bureaucratic rationality as another example of how ritualised behaviour can create the transcendental form or identity.

Thinking of democratic elections as a form of ritual can begin to help us connect the process towards the genesis of the transcendental. In Banerjee's (2007) ethnography of West Bengal, she describes how vivid pageantry and extremely high voter turnout problematise a rational choice theory of elections, much as they also do to critique the idea that elections are nothing short of gigantic social illusions. Rather, democratic elections represent a kind of sacred duty, one of "only a handful of institutions (the army, railways, cricket, and movies) that are genuinely pan-Indian and can serve to bind the vast and varied country together" (ibid, p. 1560). Elections thus generate "patriotic faith in the idea of India itself" and signify that no matter how socially insignificant any individual is in terms of the greater whole, they have a sacred duty to create the transcendental moral community of the nation (ibid, p. 1560). It serves to validate each person – no matter their station in life – as a citizen and member of their country. In short, the significance of democratic elections as ritual is that they represent "an end in themselves" and "a means to better society" by nearly a billion people across India (ibid, p. 1560).

I have suggested that this ritual approach to democracy is a tremendously generative approach to understanding their function in contemporary social systems. Yet, there is something lacking here in terms of intellectual cohesion. Little of this scholarship offers a sustained and serious elucidation of the actual mechanics of electoral ritual. James (2003) has argued that we should instead swap the term for 'ceremony', given that 'ritual' is too reminiscent of religious practices to have valence in the context of understanding contemporary social norms. This is a useful intervention, but I do not believe that it solves the problem either. Instead, I will suggest that thinking through ritual in terms of *sacrifice* will take us further to understanding the complex ways in which this unique cultural practice remains a cornerstone of sociality in the modern world. It will also tie up these theoretical sections of the chapter with the descriptive richness of my ethnographic material.

Borneman (2002) notes that before 1945, traditional forms of sacrifice were used to create the transcendental through ritual violence in Europe as historically elsewhere. Examples of this in Germany include a heroic death in the First World War and latterly in the unprecedented genocidal persecution of the Jewish scapegoat during the Holocaust. Both instances involved the practice of sacrificial ritual violence to create the foundational social act and means of spiritual sustenance which midwife the social into being. He notes that since the war, these conventional forms of sacrifice have become impotent to the central task of uniting disparate individuals under one single collective. In the past, the transcendental was produced by sacrifice either of the sons (in the First World War) or the scapegoat (in the Second World War). Today, these forms of sacrifice are "not entirely convincing to most of the people living in the European states", especially Germans (Borneman 2002, p. 16). Yet this empirical reality must be squared with the knowledge that although the "social and institutional form can be displaced", it can "never be truly eliminated without risk of dissolving the social" (Borneman 2002, p. 5).

If sacrifice is so necessary to society's functioning, where then can we find it today? This riddle is solved when we recall that the first stop in the historical model proposed by Frazer (1998) is that of the self-sacrifice of the ruler. In the past, this ritual took the form of a king being burned or bludgeoned to death. Today we can see the core of this performed in the guise of democratic elections. This is because we have in these moments a process of ritualised turn-taking and, most importantly, self-sacrifice of the ruling party through electoral loss. This dissolution mirrors the ancient act of royal suicide, one in which the monarch who symbolised sovereignty could die such that the group would rejuvenate. This idea of divine monarchical legitimacy is clearly no longer the case in the context of popular sovereignty. Yet that universal human ritual, sacrifice, is still required to create the transcendental collective known as 'the people' out of inchoate and heterogenous monads that make up the general population (Luhmann 1990). We can thus understand the function of democratic elections as the periodic sacrifice of the ruler (i.e., the ruling party) which renews and rejuvenates the social body.[9]

2.5 Fixing 'Broken Britain'

Having described the recurrent existence of sacrificial discourse throughout the election, one's attention is naturally turns on the question of why this was invoked at all. As I have shown, it is immediately clear is that very few of these grievances have any material relationship to the institutions of the EU. This was something one can get a sense of from political science literature on negative voter misperceptions of the EU (Stoeckel et al. 2020), but even so, I personally found it startling. With the few exceptions about the Irish backstop, there was close to zero engagement with anything even vaguely connected to Britain's geo-strategic relationship with an external and autonomous political entity known as the EU. The lack of anything close to what Freud (1991) termed the 'reality principle' on this issue is of supreme ethnographic relevance. In this case, speakers seemed disproportionally focused on emotional sensations rather than rational arguments. Problems in the external world of geopolitical relations did not in any meaningful sense impinge upon the 'collective effervescence' (Durkheim 2008) of these rallies. The 'pleasure principle' (Freud 1991) – propelling voters towards an idealised future of absolute transcendence and gratification with zero trade-offs, compromises, or downsides – seemed hegemonic. The psychological dynamics of this situation merit serious investigation.

An associated problem emerges from another observation: that what reasons are indeed offered for voting for Brexit seem to reflect little more than projected local grievances constituted by unique but fundamentally irrelevant obstacles in these candidates' own lives. Mental health provision, community feeling, respecting our elders, South Asian foreign aid budgets, and poor local waste management are just a few examples of the issues invoked to justify leaving the EU. But none of them had any discernible connection with Europe or any part of Britain's relationship to it. All these issues could have been tackled from within the EU as much as from outside. The responsibility and capacity for fixing them has always been squarely in the hands of British Parliament, which retained sovereignty over all of them throughout the decades of the country's previous membership.

The last but perhaps most disconcerting observation is that many candidates (including Farage) chose to employ provocative and inappropriately disproportional rhetoric (such as about slavery, colonialism, and violence) to make a point about freely leaving a system of pooled sovereignty. This behaviour in some sense clearly mirrored his friend and fellow populist Donald Trump, whose abrasive oratory was also marked by a disturbing proclivity towards aggression and confrontation. In this context, questions around whether anxieties about being colonised are indicative of unconscious projections of an imperialist mindset would be necessarily speculative. But they are likely to contain a great deal of merit. Many scholars have posited a link between Brexit and the British Empire (Colley 2016; Dorling and Tomlinson 2019; El-Enany 2020; Gildea 2019; Gilroy 2020; Mitchell 2021; Sanghera 2021; Ward and Rasch 2019) and I believe it reasonable to imagine a psychological relationship which explains why this otherwise bizarre and inflammatory rhetoric has such resonance over many British voters.[10]

I appreciate that many pro-Remain voters will take this ethnography as evidence that motivations to vote leave the EU were based on little more than ignorance, stupidity, deceit, myopia, or xenophobia. But I do not wish to make this claim; not only because I believe in the ethics of generosity which defines anthropology, nor to simply avoid making a negative value-judgement on my interlocutors. When early anthropologists went to study cannibalism, headhunting and infanticide, they sought to explain these cultural behaviours in their rightful context. At no point did they feel the need to attribute vice and idiocy to their informants. Like them, I believe that these otherwise incongruous statements do add up to *something*, even if they are verbally articulated in such a way that make little apparent or obvious sense. This of course becomes doubly frustrating to the vast majority of scholars who were furious about the decision to leave, many of whom were quite consciously searching for a way to delegitimise the vote. But if is the nature of the anthropologist to make the "familiar strange and the strange familiar", such a task is clearly at stake here in interpreting cultural behaviour which seems otherwise totally illogical and nonsensical.

Of all the potential hermeneutics for making sense of this incoherence, I believe the strongest interpretation rests on the idea that this material speaks to is an inarticulable sense of lack of trust in the political class of contemporary Britain. The bonds that ensure social co-operation, what Durkheim (2013) calls 'social solidarity', are an essential element of human life. But they are not eternal; they decay and expire like all natural phenomena, and they need to be periodically rejuvenated through the rituals that create a shared sense of belonging, meaning and purpose. Collaboration among strangers cannot be taken for granted, even if the contemporary world Anglo-American world has had relatively few recent instances of internecine conflict. This is especially true at a level of 'imagined community' (Anderson

2016) which operates at an incredibly high degree of abstraction compared to our day-to-day experience.

What is the state of this social solidarity in Britain as a whole today? While I am conscious that trust as a relational concept cannot easily be metamorphosed into a statistical concept, it is worth remarking on attempts to capture it through polling (Marková et al. 2007). A recent report from the *British Social Attitudes* Survey shows that trust has declined rapidly in Britain since the Second World War; year on year, there is even less of a belief that politicians serve the public in good faith. Around the time of the 2019 election, only 15 per cent of those questioned believed that the government was trustworthy most of the time (Curtice et al. 2020). In addition to this, a wide and vast literature on populism – of which Brexit is clearly a manifestation – firmly places low-levels of trust at the heart of causes for why people vote for populist parties, movements, and candidates (Galston 2018; Keefer et al. 2021; Norris and Inglehart 2019; Sobolewska and Ford 2020).

Thus, grievances about poor local services and a distant elite, betrayal, humiliation, lack of control – such discourses that have defined this snapshot of the election – may well all be verbal articulations of this phenomenon. This is because social trust is fundamentally an emotional sense of the honesty and integrity in relationships with others: it is more like a precondition of human life and does not easily translate onto linguistic verbalisation (Erikson 1968; Marková et al. 2007). As a pre-discursive (or even non-discursive) phenomenon, it cannot align easily with intellectualisation and language. Trust in political authority and a form of social solidarity between centre and periphery are difficult to measure and often just as hard to observe ethnographically. However, I believe that the sentiments, affects and discourses I encountered during the election – like brokenness, rottenness, dishonesty, incompetency, and chaos – all index the process in which cultural anomie has become cemented among individuals and political communities.

Moreover, my argument that these otherwise incoherent discourses are attempts to verbally articulate frustrations over declining sense of trust and social solidarity are not based simply on my own interpretation of the ethnographic material. There are other examples in which candidates were able to express these feelings more explicitly than many of the others. One speaker, Matthew Pattern (candidate for Folkestone and Hythe), explains:

> "I'm standing for the Brexit party because I believe in unlocking Britain's potential. For early fifteen years I've worked for some of Britain's leading charities, helping children and young people and families in some of our most challenging communities. We all believe that British politics is broken. We all share a burning desire to put trust back into our political system. The thing that we all really share is a deep sense that trust in

British politics has been broken. I really identify with that feeling that we need to make this better if we can believe in ourselves".

At a rally in Exeter, Alex Waugh – who as a note of historical curiosity is the grandson of the eminent writer Evelyn Waugh – took the stage to deliver a speech as Brexit Party candidate for Bridgwater and West Somerset. He finished his colourful speech and announced:

"I hope that there will come a time when our grandchildren and our great grandchildren will reach for the dictionary look up Brexit VERB: to bring honour, integrity, and trust to democratic politics by application of courage!"

I suggest that these are further empirical demonstrations of the scholarship that frames declining social trust – manifest through fraying social bonds and frustrations over political control – as one of the more pivotal factors in understanding the lead up to Brexit and the general trend towards populism (Geurkink et al. 2020; Keefer et al. 2021). They were not, as I had initially suspected, little more than rhetorical flourishes (although they may have been that too). Rather, they took the form of real admonishments towards challenging the status quo, fixing a damaged or broken social body, and instigating authentic social change. There was a genuine yearning a sense of wholeness, co-operation, and renewal: it was a vision of wholesale collective transformation. The mood or *Stimmung* (Borneman and Ghassem-Fachandi 2017) of the campaigns were not conservative: it was revolutionary. The Brexit Party was promising that the general election would transform Britain and replenish the fractures and divisions that had characterised it for decades. We should not write them off as simply reactive: leaving the EU was an agentive decision *towards* something new as much as it was *away* from something old.

Why has trust so much declined both between and among voters and their leaders in Britain? There are of course many explanations that have been explored in great depth. One is simply that neoliberalism acts to depoliticise the economy and dissolve more collective and harmonious relationships into ones of alienation and antagonism (Brown 2017). Another perspective correlates a breakdown of social trust with an increase in ethnic diversity (Dinesen et al. 2020). Alternatively, Mair's classic text *Ruling the Void* (2013) argued that it derived from the collapse in membership of mass political parties, itself the result of alienation and dissolving social institutions that arise in late modernity. This process causes the political disengagement of both voters elites: the former become populist, the latter technocratic. I believe that this is the most convincing of the many theories, especially as Mair's work seems to pre-empt the vote for Brexit by several years.

Regardless of which explanatory framework is made, there can be little doubt that trust and solidarity for a great many (if not all) voters in the UK has changed considerably for many decades, and this is much more likely to be true for demographic of voters who support populist parties (Eatwell and Goodwin 2018). What I have brought in this chapter is a demonstration of how political communities attempt to arrest this decline through collective ritual. The moral authority of the rulers naturally declines with time: this is why in archaic societies there needs to be periodic ritual destruction and replenishment (Frazer 1998). My ethnographic material leads me to believe that the same process is occurring here in the context of political alienation from the British political elite.

2.6 Conclusion

For Brexit Party candidates, the mood (Borneman and Ghassem-Fachandi 2017) of those late autumn months was one of decline and disillusion: the social body was in a pitiable state, leaders could not be trusted, old values had collapsed, Britain had lost its strength, and people did not believe that they could give Britain the future it deserved. This chapter has shown how little the discourse that emerged through the election had anything concretely to do with the EU, and I have tried to explain this problem in terms which try to make sense of, rather than delegitimise, these ostensibly 'irrational' voting choices. Moreover, I have tried to provide both sides of the argument, but part of the frustrations with writing about Brexit is understanding why people were so motivated by something so abstract and disconnected from their day-to-day lives.

But what I hope this chapter suggests is that there is much more to Brexit than has been captured in much of the literature so far. As I detailed in the introduction, cross-disciplinary approaches have taken a wide variety of perspectives which analyse authoritarianism, ethnicity, race, anti-politics, economic grievance, social media, and a whole host of other factors. They all played a role: but there is a missing element here too. What little ethnographies of Brexiters do exist tended to portray them in negative terms: poverty-stricken, innumerate, volatile. While I have shown clearly that much of these pro-Brexit discourses were indeed irrelevant, incoherent, and illogical, I have also tried to demonstrate that there is some meaning behind all of them. One of the foundations to the discipline of anthropology is the eternal oscillation between sacred and profane: it is the foundation of social cognition and there is no such thing as a culture without them (Durkheim 2008). I believe I have provided a demonstration of where we find this reality today in my ethnography of sacrificial discourses within the 2019 general election. In my reading, Brexit was more than a decision about trade rules or economic valuations: it was a moment for transformation, a point of renewal that offered the potential for growing social solidarity in the face of structural decline.

It also links back to my first discussion about the nature of sacrifice. The recurrent invocations of the sacrificial dead throughout the election could be understood as a kind of discursive substitute for the practices of traditional behaviour in which ritual sacrifice connected the profane world of individuals to the sacred one of transcendence (Bloch 1992; Borneman 2002; Keenan 2005; Mayblin 2014). Those that had died to defend democracy were invoked throughout these rallies not as mere rhetoric: they had acted as the spiritual conductor between the profane world of a broken Britain and the transcendental 'Clean Break Brexit' that could transform it. It perfectly mirrors the situation of process of ritual destruction of the ruler in archaic societies (Frazer 1998). The moral community, then as now, is sustained always on the periodic cycle of sacrifice and renewal.

Finally, how does this connect to the 'paradox of sacrifice' (Keenan 2005), the insight that the practice must simultaneously give selflessly yet do so in the expectation of a return? I can only end this chapter with a note of ambivalence. There does after all appear to be an undeniably *quid pro quo* aspect to sacrifice in this ethnographic context. Farage clearly implied that those who died did so *in order* that democracy might live, thus creating a sense of obligation towards the living that they continue to honour them and the values they perished for. Could it thus have been that these men and women died within the context of a reciprocal trade expectation – such that a free and democratic Britain might live – or did they give themselves selflessly as the ultimate sacrifice? No matter how much these individuals may have been invoked as a 'spiritual conductor' to the sacred, it is difficult to disentangle the reciprocal basis for their deaths. Ultimately, it seems that just as it is true that there is no such thing as the free gift (Mauss 2001), there is no such thing as the unrequited sacrifice (Mayblin 2014).

Notes

1 I have little survey data on this point, but quite a considerable number of people I have spoken to over the previous years testify to one of these two options. It makes Brexit even more difficult for those who sincerely wished to remain: the reality is that if people had not voted in such a reactive way then Britain would still easily have stayed a member. It speaks to the campaigning skill of the Vote Leave faction that they were able to manipulate these sentiments so powerfully.

2 This tends to take the form of transference onto charismatic leaders, as Freud (1990) demonstrated. But it can also take more abstracted forms, as I believe happens here with the EU.

3 These were both claims made by pro-Remain activists before the 2019 election that saw Britain finally leave the EU. Neither of them was particularly convincing on their own terms: politicians repeatedly insisted that 'the referendum will be honoured' throughout the summer of 2016. But they provided a small (and

ultimately futile) window of opportunity through which Remainers could provide a counterattack and try to reverse course.

4 Dorothy Bishop (2019) summed up the feelings of an entire demographic when she wrote: "as a Remainer, I am baffled as to what Brexiteers want".

5 Although I am not claiming that Brussels did not take an influential role: the EU clearly had its own negotiating interests, especially towards Britain's exit, when it came to a number of policies involving borders, resources, and legal questions.

6 A high-quality supermarket in Britain, roughly comparable to Whole Foods in the United States.

7 Several scholars the question of what an 'anthropology of elections' might involve, including taking an ethnographic perspective from the United States (Damon 2003), Bosnia-Herzegovina (Coles 2004), Lebanon (Obeid 2011), and Kenya (Matter 2010). However, for the purposes of this chapter, I will focus on two key theories each deriving from unique ethnographic contexts: contemporary Germany (Borneman 2002) and contemporary India (Banerjee 2007). Then I will apply these insights to my research on the 2019 British general election.

8 As Graeber (2014) pointed out, it is widely forgotten that elections were historically associated far more with aristocratic forms of governance than democratic ones, having only later become associated with popular emancipation.

9 Borneman (2002) outlines four key means by which rites of sacrifice are performed during the period of democratic elections. The first involves the periodic sacrifice of the ruler or ruling party, such as when the elected group loses power. The second involves the dissolution (and then reconstitution) of the 'people', who are at one moment broken up into disaggregated monads to be discursively reconstituted after the election. Next, the sacrifice of time, wherein individuals give up their way for the non-monetary component of 'having their say' and effecting the political process. Lastly, the ritual excess which, in line with Bataille's (1991) theory of sacrifice, involves the massive over-expenditure of money, time, effort and mobilisation to effect specified outcomes.

10 However, I believe it is important to present a steel-manned case for the other side. Certain scholars have indeed suggested that Europe is a kind of 'liberal empire' (Streeck 2019), and the extent to which countries become peripheral units of an 'ever-closer' federal union is still unclear. While I do not personally believe that the EU makes colonies out of its members – the very fact that Britain did freely leave the EU is an empirical demonstration of this reality – the exact mechanisms of centre/periphery governance are not completely clear for the EU as a 'political unit of a novel order' (Borneman and Fowler 1997).

2

BRITAIN ALONE: READINGS ON MYTH, FANTASY, AND REALITY

> "To grasp the native's point of view, his relation to life, to realize his vision of his world… we must study what concerns him most, ultimately, that is, the hold which life has on him"
>
> *Bronislaw Malinowski,* Argonauts of the Western Pacific *(1922)*

3.1 Introduction

Panoff (1988) has echoed Lévi-Strauss's insight that politics in contemporary society looks very much like mythology in traditional ones. Anyone who has spent even cursory time involved in conversation with British Eurosceptics will confirm this recognition wholeheartedly. Common fantasy narratives include: a singular Britain can and should 'stand-alone' once again, the European Union (EU) is a dangerous re-run of European totalitarianism, we once ruled the world and thus do not need to be 'bossed around' by a menacing continental government, our military is in danger of dissolving into a European army, a globalist pro-EU agenda desires open and uncontrolled migration, we didn't fight Hitler in order to lose our freedom to Brussels, etc. In addition, there is a prevalent sentiment – especially among the older generation – that anxiously frames our victory in Second World War as preclusion of us from merging our national identity with Europe.[1] Some scholars have attributed these feelings to a cluster of psychological states, including narcissism, melancholy, nostalgia, and longing (Campanella and Dassù 2019; Covington 2018; Kenny 2017; Kulz 2020; Mandelbaum 2020; Manners 2018). But these explanations only go so far in explaining the psychological power of these stories to captivate people's sense of what has exactly happened between Britain and Europe over the past half-century.

DOI: 10.4324/9781003458517-3

This chapter explores this problem in the following ways. Firstly, I present my ethnographic observations of one man, Terry. A late middle-aged businessman and Brexit Party activist, Terry's archetypal views on Europe was soaked in the narratives of resisting servitude to EU totalitarianism. His engagement with these kinds of stories testifies, I believe, to the irreducible power of myth in political life (Cassirer 2009). This observation I develop anthropologically in two ways: firstly, I utilise a structuralist reading of the Britain/Europe relationship to illustrate Lévi-Strauss's (2021) argument that the human mind generates meaning out of binary conceptual oppositions. I then invoke a Malinowskian (1948) reading of myth to show that its function remains indispensable as a charter or map of social reality. Fantasies about fighting Nazis or communist technocrats provide more than just a *conceptual* orientation to modern geopolitics: they prefigure a practical course of action in the face of an almost overwhelmingly complex problem. In other words, perhaps myth is meaningful because it helps us order and make sense of the world in rational terms.

Yet this too only goes so far. If we talk about myth purely as narrative storytelling, we remain incapable of explaining the relentlessness of its influence and the obduracy of its moral authority. We may be able to trace 'mythic contents' through time – such as the idea of an English exceptionalism from the Reformation down to the British Empire – but this does not quite explain why they re-emerged with such virility during the referendum. There are many things in history which can be appropriated as fuel for the engine of political myth: why these? What is it about the mythic images of an isolated Britain, a looming continental threat, or a sense of inner erosion and imminent takeover, which so animates a considerable demographic segment of the population? It may be true that much of our "island story" (Reynolds 2019) is myth, but what are the psycho-cultural mechanics by which these fantasies support and sustain themselves?

I argue that the concept of 'ontological insecurity' (Laing 2010) may help us in making sense of this problem. This approach emphasises the link between threat to the autonomy of the self ('engulfment') and behaviour which seeks stability and safety through self-contraction and acute withdrawal. Symptoms become considerably worse when identity becomes more porous and uncontrolled, such as we observe in the context of globalisation (Giddens 1990; Van Marle and Maruna 2009). For Brexiters like Terry, these annihilation anxieties intensify when they can no longer take their self-identity for granted or feel that it is dissolving in the face of rapid ethnocultural change. The impending sense of catastrophe, dread, disintegration, and being overrun are thus all responses to the liquid, disembedded nature of late modernity which relentlessly impinges on and destabilises our collective attempt to create a stable psycho-cultural base of shared values and norms (Bauman 2000; Giddens 1990). Terry's anxieties about loss of boundaries and engulfment reflect a terror at the dissolution of the self – whether personal, cultural, or national – in the 'Other' of Europeanisation or Islamification. These are then expressed *mythically* through shared narratives about a time when it was 'Britain Alone': isolated from continental federalism, hostile immigration, neo-fascism, or dictatorial Russian meddling.

Terry may represent an extreme case in his obsessive fear of annihilation, but the overarching point still stands. Mythic narratives represent culture as an elaborate collective fantasy to protect against individual anxieties of destruction (Paul 1989). And what we observe on the level of individual psychology can hold true for entire demographic segments. It was overwhelmingly older people that voted for Brexit, and this may reflect both the anxieties of a generational post-war experience *and* personal memories of a Britain where national identity was significantly more stable and homogenous than it is today. Rather than seeing these myths about 'standing alone' against the Germans as a form of nostalgia, then, we should investigate how human culture operates in tandem with the psyche to rationalise political action and stabilise against the threat of dissolution. In short, my intervention suggests that Brexit may be an unconscious move to shore-up intolerable anxieties about cultural dislocation through national withdrawal and stabilisation of boundaries between 'Self' and 'Other'. Perhaps myth is meaningful not because it helps us order the world in rational terms but precisely because it helps us *rationalise* the world in ordered terms.

3.2 The Child of War

"I am a child of the Second World War". This was how Terry, a roughly 70-year-old businessman and Brexit Party activist introduced himself to me when we first spoke on the phone some few months after the 2019 election. It was our first real conversation: I had been unable to contact him until after the energy of those crucial moments had passed. Terry was one of the more interesting candidates that I had met during my ethnographic research on Brexit, not least because his character, lifestyle and background could not be more distinct from other ethnographic portrayals of Brexit voters. Although it was impossible to really get a handle on his financial situation, it was clear that Terry was far from the kind of economically marginalised individual that is usually portrayed as the driving coalition force behind the vote to leave (Evans 2020; Koch 2017; Ringel 2020). If he had been in anyway affected by neoliberalism, his social location as white, middle-class and the owner of multiple businesses made him much more of a proponent than a detractor. Indeed, I noticed that one of his political preoccupations was the enormous danger of reversal from the many social and economic advances that Thatcher had pushed through in the 1980s. Smart, articulate, and fiscally solvent: Terry's life and career spoke to the reality that populist voters are often just as much some of the financial 'winners' of our globalised society rather than they are precarious members of the so-called 'left-behinds'. Economic marginalisation and social alienation provided a very limited explanation for the discontent and dissatisfaction expressed by Leave voters like him.

Like many of the candidates I interviewed throughout this book, he was difficult to get hold of, sceptical, concerned about what I represent, and generally somewhat busy. He made the time for me, however, on several occasions during my fieldwork. This included both telephone calls and in-person interviews. Many of his anecdotes and expressions came up repeatedly: a point I found stimulating when thinking about the careful stage management of politicians. For instance, he announced that he "was a child of the Second World War" twice; first on a telephone call, and second the first time we met in person. He also repeated the same anecdote that his wife had told him that his various public musings in favour of Brexit were an "apology to [his] deceased parents". This seemed to refer their own views on the matter: he repeatedly noted that after the war they saw the EU as a vehicle for peace, solidarity and goodwill between formerly blood-stained neighbours. Indeed, he claimed that even his younger self was so pro-European that he demonstrated his support by standing outside the House Commons on the day that Britain was taken into the European Economic Community. Whether this was an admission of guilt I could not say, not in the least because he promoted Brexit for at least half a decade. He evidently forgot that he had mentioned this story and was reasonably attached to it. How much this may have been a show (or simply a rationalisation) remained a mystery to me.

Despite the theatricality of these statements, Terry had clearly cathected to the Brexit process. I had befriended him in person, followed him on social media during lockdown, read his online blog, and generally got a relatively good picture of the man. Although I never quite understood his personal life as satisfactorily as one could have – a common occurrence among politically sensitive interlocutors – much of his online activity kept me alert to his internal emotional landscape. Mostly, the content of his observations throughout my fieldwork experiences both in person and online took the form of various lists of unsatisfactory social problems. Almost everything that came up was an aversion to the state of contemporary British society: incompetent governments, inept civil servants, useless journalists, malicious EU commissioners, corrupt corporations, the failures of the police, the failures of COVID-19 policy, the dishonesty of banks, and the all-pervading coercive power of political correctness. As with my ethnography in the previous chapter, his perception of Britain was textured by a profound sense of cultural disintegration and unease.

He also held particular scorn for politicians who didn't appreciate the risk of near apocalyptic threats. When the initial coronavirus outbreak happened, for instance, he recalled insisting (much to his wife's frustration) on buying several new freezers in which to store enormous amounts of food for the imminent disaster. He also predicted that the exodus from in person office work would lead to the mass bankruptcy of pension funds, in turn causing the global economy to collapse (it did not). I noted that this degree of catastrophising was much more common among the Brexiters I spoke to than the Remainers. For instance, the latter mostly perceived lockdown to be in their overall interest, while many of the former became convinced that the victory of the totalitarians ("lockdown fanatics") now all but assured. Partly this may reflect the degree to which each side was able to work from home or not, but the key insight here is simply to note the parallels in shared experience between two ideological groupings. This may suggest some underlying psycho-cultural dynamic behind any ostensibly 'rational' foundation to the referendum vote. This includes shared perceptions of catastrophe, threat, and most of all, a dread of confinement and loss of control. I will return to the salience of this observation later on in this chapter.

Perhaps Terry's most significant and reoccurring emotional preoccupation was the anxiety over the existential military threats which continue to hover over the nation. There were many examples of how these phantoms came up in-person. At one London event in 2021, the *Battle of Ideas* – a conference run almost entirely by the network of ex-Brexit Party candidates – I ran into him once again.[2] Although our conversation was briefer than usual owing to the excitement of the event – much to my own disappointment – the conversation with Terry was once again terse, dramatic, penetrating. "We are in another 1939 moment" he exclaimed as he paused halfway up a small flight of stairs.[3] It seemed to me that his worrying about an impending disaster was not an infrequent concern. Conceptualising global events came more easily to Terry through a narrative of military catastrophe isomorphic with the Second World War. There was a recurring pattern in which this sense of external and imminent threat impinged upon his consciousness as a mental representation, and encouraged him to adopt narratives which matched his experience of political change in such unsettling terms.

As we stood and caught up on the other candidates, he began outlining his anxieties over the build-up of dangerous capitalist states. "There has never been a more perilous situation than the one we are in now", he exclaimed, before mourning that the tragedy is that the West has "lost its way". If there is hope, he exasperatedly told me at the end of our conversation, it is "in the wisdom of the crowd you see before you today". Terry saw in this conference of anti-progressive, COVID-sceptic, and largely pro-Brexit attendees a last holdout of patriotic and level-headed citizens in a world that was heading towards total disaster. This unique network of populist activists represented the resistance which he saw as pivotal to preventing the further cultural decay of Western civilisation. Most importantly, they are the only people who cared about saving democracy in Britain: whether it is against foreign enemies, the EU, or authoritarian coronavirus policies. He didn't stay much longer, and instead returned to his home in a prosperous suburb outside of London where he resides with his wife and family.

This ethnographic vignette is a suitable demonstration of the internal contents that seemed to animate Terry's lifeworld, at least to the extent that I was personally privy to. His sensitivity to foreign aggression was on constant display: he had commented earlier on in the year that we were "three to four years away from World War Three". (A hyperbolic statement – although this chapter was written during the early stages of the Russian invasion of the Ukraine). More salient is his insistence that we are witnessing the same expression of dictatorial capitalism in China and Russia as we saw in 1930s Germany. Conversations like these would recurringly emerge to weave such topical strands into a tapestry I could make sense of only much later in my fieldwork. China, Russia, the EU: they were all in some sense homogenised as external, malign forces which impinged upon (and even existentially threatened) more than something as profane as economic regulations or negotiations around tariffs. Something much greater and more dramatic was at stake in what increasingly seemed to be interpreted as a cosmic war happening on multiple global fronts. I felt like we were closer to the world of *The Ramayana* than we were debating articles from *The Economist*.

One way of understanding these kinds of views would be to interpret them as the result of an overactive sense of threat perception. This has been routinely demonstrated to be integral to more authoritarian types of personality structure that correlate with populist voting trends (Feldman and Stenner 1997; Norris and Inglehart 2019; Sobolewska and Ford 2020). Terry is clearly not wrong in being concerned about the human rights practices of Vladimir Putin's Russia or Xi Jinping's China. But what I found interesting was the way it always circled back to Britain and Europe, as if all of these things were subplots in a much larger narrative. The key point here is that he saw in Brexit the latest manifestation of this same fight to defend the collective from continental aspirations of pan-European dominance. This was one whose aims were to subordinate England just as both Hitler and Napoleon had intended to do in previous centuries. Paranoia wove the first into the second, confusing functionally distinct historical changes and misrecognising (at least in my opinion) the ultimate objective of the European project.[4]

For Terry, the EU was never more than a hair's breadth from creating a new European slaughterhouse. He often talked about his friends in Ireland, Poland, Lithuania, France, and Germany, and I once asked him once if any of them were not perhaps surprised at his support for Brexit. "They were totally appalled", he replied, somewhat taken aback (I thought) by his own response to the question. I asked him whether or not that had in any way changed his mind, or at least given him second thoughts, about his political activism. "No", he replied, adding:

> "They were totally appalled, because we were one of the military bedrocks, one of the three pillars [along with France and Germany] that supported the EU. No, they were horrified by my decision. For us not to be there was nothing less than a massive betrayal. But I said to them, look, if we don't leave now, then there will be civil war. It will be just like the United States [in the 1860s], with the South trying to break free from the North. The EU military is building, and we had to get out now, before it was too late to stop them".

This idiosyncratic reading of political reality only led to more confusion and misunderstanding between us. When I listened to Terry's (and others) justifications for claiming that the EU was akin to a totalitarian continental regime – one which does not value democracy or personal freedom and was trying to conquer Britain militarily – I felt bewildered. Yet comments like this were hardly unusual: around the 2019 general election, for instance, Terry wrote that the fight against what he termed the "EU oligarchs" was exactly the same as being "in a fight for our democracy as in 1939". Staying within Europe, he repeatedly claimed, was akin to "years of servitude", and the collective transformation from a "citizen" to a "subject". Justifications for such accusations rarely had much empirical grounding; however, he occasionally supplemented his allegations with the reference to what the EU had done by "enslaving" the Greek people with a policy of financial austerity. This was attributable to the malice of Germany, he thought, a viewpoint which does appear to have at least some vague degree of basis in reality (Varoufakis 2017, 2018). Curiously, it has also been found to be a common explanation or folk theory among other pro-Brexit interlocutors (Shore 2021).

This kind of rationalisation is also typical of the experience of mutual incomprehension between Remainers and Brexiters. Part of the difficulty in making sense of these opinions was that they seemed to disconnect so much with the reality that Remainers experienced around the EU. For almost every single individual within my wider personal and professional network, for instance, the EU represented openness, tolerance, travel, and freedom. To some degree, it also signified a transcendence over the historical forms of oppression, xenophobia and racism that characterised much of the previous century. This idea did not come about my accident: scholars have noted that EU policymakers cultivated a sense of pan-continental identity in contrast to an 'Other' which is not different in traditionally ethnic, cultural, or geographical terms but instead Europe's own past (Diez 2004). Indeed, public relations for the EU have consistently taken advantage of this when framing the project as a unifying system based on 'civic' values of democracy, freedom and pluralism over 'ethnic' values of nation and locale (Shore 1993, 2000). One observation here is that this concerns generation: Terry was forty years older than me. Fascism and war in Europe shaped his childhood environment in ways that neither I nor millions of others can relate to. Yet even so, the notion that Brussels and London would end with mass blood-letting seemed delusionally out of proportion to the problems presented by either remaining in or leaving the EU. Why this conspiratorial framing – one so completely severed from Freud's (1991) notion of the 'reality principle' – seemed to personally preoccupy Terry so much, continued to elude me.

My initial (and rather two-dimensional) explanation for attitudes like this was the same as that proposed by many other scholars. This approach sees Brexit supporters like Terry as having been fooled, misdirected, and taken in by sophisticated right-wing propaganda (Rawlinson 2020). In this reading, Eurosceptic attitudes professed (mostly) by the working-class are a form of scapegoating which emerge out of a misdirected recognition of the injustice and poverty of neoliberal globalisation. It also of course feeds on the fear of ethnic outsiders, a common enough object of blame for economic problems. This interpretation views such a process cultivated assiduously by right-wing newspapers like *The Daily Mail* and *The Sun*. It has increasingly taken the form of a 'moral panic' (Cohen 2011) which helps people (usually Remainers) to make sense of a shocking sense of loss over Brexit.

While Terry rejected the United Kingdom Independence Party (UKIP) as "objectively racist", he informally agreed with many of the prevailing narratives about the EU which I had heard in those circles over the years of fieldwork. One was the constant comparison to communism: the EU's ostensible "tyranny" represented something like the historical re-emergence of this totalitarianism. I had heard this discourse a number of times before; many UKIP supporters had even gone as far as claim that it was the *Soviet EUnion*, a description I found uncomfortable and lacking even a modest semblance of contact to reality. Yet this framing of the EU has had popular support at the highest levels of anti-European mobilisation for decades. One example is a speech to the European Parliament in Strasbourg in 2013, where then MEP Nigel Farage gave a long diatribe over the fiscal crisis in Cyprus that had followed the then not stabilised issue of the fallout of the 2007–08 financial implosion and viability of the Euro currency. He claimed:

> "Mrs Thatcher recognised the truth behind the European project, she saw that it was about taking away democracy from nation states and handing that power to largely unaccountable people... Not even me and my most pessimistic speeches would have imaged that you and others in the *Troika* would resort to the level of common criminals and steal money... how ironic to see the Russian Prime Minister, Dmitry Medvedev, compare your actions to some of the decisions taken by the Soviet authorities... This European Union is the new communism. It is power without limits. It is creating a tide of human misery and the sooner it is swept away, the better!"

The problem with framing Terry's views with the idea of psychological manipulation is that debates in the literature still question the extent to which media reflects people's baseline sentiments and attitudes about the world rather than crafting them (Entman 1989). It could thus be an error to attribute these views to right-wing newspapers: these broadsheets sell to those people who are already more or less convinced by these kinds of stories. While it is true that there is value in a tracing discourses through the actors who articulate them (Marcus 1995), causal alignment is much more difficult and, I suggest, challenging to penetrate with ethnography. I do not believe understanding why people like Terry feel that Europe is a malign entity can be explained in such terms. Rather, we need to understand the affectual basis which is then open to a process of *post-hoc* rationalisation, not least in the form of salacious newspaper stories or social media posts.

Beyond these problems, one last interesting feature of Terry's mental life came from his personal fidelity to memory and sanctity of the nation. This is particularly relevant in the case of remembering the dead who sacrificed their lives to protect democracy: a subject I treated at length in Chapter 1. After retiring from several decades in business, including a small stint in the United States, South Africa, and Moldova (where he investigated the feasibility of privatising the post-communist wine industry), Terry had devoted himself to writing war novels. This four-part series chronicles the rise and fall of his own extended family: a massive literary project involving "an excel spreadsheet with over 55 columns and 169 rows" of his own kinship network that stretches back over a century to Second World War. The novels themselves tell the story of all these people as they encounter the difficulties of war, loss, betrayal, and scandal across the European mainland during the early 20th century.

If we can think of myth, dream, and fiction as different fruits from the same unconscious (Freud 2001, 2008; Jung 1991), we are perhaps close to understanding that the emotional pre-occupations that emerge from Terry's writings. Both his fiction and his political stance were emanations of a deeply embedded symbolic landscape, one which is imbibed by a sense of catastrophe and loss of the previous century. The fact that individuals like Terry clearly *live* these narratives in some way suggested to me that there was more to this invocation of the 20th century than a kind of political opportunism. As for many other Brexiters I spoke to, particularly the older ones, mythopoetic imagery of war in Europe impinged on his consciousness constantly. It proved to be a powerful vehicle for orientating himself towards the consequences of leaving the EU. A sense of threat and impeding dissolution seemed to be inexplicably linked in both his inner world and the cultural form (myth, fiction, narrative, dream) in which he focused his emotional attention.

Indeed, much of his personal emotional output seemed to be dedicated to keeping the past alive through these literary projects and his own political activism. The dead were never far away: whether they took the form of pictures or in the novels which absorbed so much of his personal time. And while it is patently not true that *every* Brexiter was influenced by the conflict, I have found that this unique period has tended to play an oversized role in the various narratives that came up for people making the pro-Brexit argument. But the salience of the war was rarely (if ever) in indexing any demonstrable empirical relationship to the actual EU (like the 2007 Lisbon Treaty or the 1992 Maastricht Treaty). Rather, it repeatedly came up in analogous form. For Terry and others, things seemed *like* this or that, rather than *were* like this or that. He was haunted by ghosts, not writing an academic monograph. The narratives clearly gave texture and form to the political events of the past few decades, midwifing the process of sense-making and justifying why it was worth fighting for at all.

Terry had acted as an executor for the estates of many of his father's friends and told me on a number of occasions that the entire generation was exceptionally pro-Europe, because they felt that it could keep the peace. I once asked Terry if he thought his parents would have changed their minds about the EU, like him, if they had still been alive. He looked at me solemnly and paused for the longest time in any of our conversations. Adopting a tone that mingled sadness and reflection, he said:

> "I couldn't answer that. No, I couldn't answer that. You know, I've been very privileged in my life, not having to be burying the man on the left and the right of me in battle. That judgement... that judgement can only be made by those who made that sacrifice. No, no, it would be too presumptuous to answer that question".

*

Finally, Terry's sense of impeding threat from the EU, Russia and China were supplemented by another great anxiety: Islam. This was not something which was immediately apparent from our first meeting. Much of what I gleaned from his thoughts emerged much later, either from deeper intimacy or keeping an eye on his public writings and social media. These overall perceptions of Muslims in the United Kingdom fell into a few distinct conceptual categories. The first was anxiety about Muslim men sexually assaulting British women. One particular manifestation of this was a fixation on the 'grooming gangs scandal', an interest he shared with many others on the political right (Cockbain 2013). This broadly refers to the tragic case of many poor, young white British girls being sexually abused by men of Pakistani heritage in the north of England. In the eyes of Terry, this story has been purposefully buried and ignored by mainstream media, either for fear of being seen as 'Islamophobic' or because the leader of the Labour Party, Keir

Starmer, is somehow involved in the lack of prosecution. Those guilty members were seen as the same corrupt bureaucrats, civil service workers, politicians, and other members of the 'globalised elite' who were responsible for mass-immigration and attempts to derail Brexit from the very outset.

The actual facts of the case are outside the remit of this book: the point is merely to show that this particular phenomenon pressed heavily on Terry's consciousness. So much so, in fact, that it seemed to spill over and would appear in otherwise barely credible ways. For example, he told me received a phone call from one of the workers at a business he owned who said that they couldn't come to work "because now fifty migrants have come and they're too scared to go out". (I reasoned that this was almost certainly the case of a young person taking advantage of Terry's paranoia to bunk off work). He followed up with a second point which was connected to the first: "that there have been some rapes in the local area that the media are not reporting". Although he refused to plainly tell me the connection, it was not hard to discern the obvious mental associations in his mind between these (ostensible) rapes and the Muslim grooming gang scandal in the north of England. He connected them quite explicitly to Islam, tweeting once that: "the rape of a schoolgirl by a gang of Muslim men MUST be on the agenda too. This Islamic nonsense has to be stopped for a cult, based on the 1,400-year-old sayings of an illiterate peadophile [sic], has no place in UK society".

Another is a general fear and threat of violence. He said: "Islamophobia is not an irrational fear... to be frightened of Islam is fully justified and those who claims this term is an expression of racism doesn't know our language... the term is being misused and abused for religious advantage... multiculturalism must stop". He connected this to various fears about female genital mutilation, claiming that "if I veherementy [sic] disapprove of FGM (which I do) then apparently I am to be condemned as an Islamophobe. Well, if standing against this vile, barbaric behaviour, then I'm proudly guilty as charged". He was very concerned about the general violence associated with the religion, using the same derogatory language about Mohammed in saying that: "don't anyone dare tell me Islam is a religion of peace... Islamophobia (a fear of Islam) is not irrational... there is much to fear about this 1,400-year-old 'religion' lead by an illiterate peadophile [sic] from the dessert [sic]". His general outlook was that the police and politicians turn a blind eye to assaults among certain ethnic communities in order to evade looking at a difficult subject. Although perhaps not entirely untrue, his overall rhetoric clearly indexes an agenda which is profoundly suspicious of British Muslims and the threat that he thinks they have brought with them into the UK.

A last reflection of these anxieties were his sense of being overrun or dissolved by the sheer number of Muslims in England. What particularly resonated for me on this was that this fear of being taken over mirrored his perception of the EU's relationship with Britain. One characteristic outburst came shortly after the stabbing of Salman Rushdie in 2022. Terry announced publically that:

> "We've had an Islamic invasion taking place here for the last 30 years with the UK Muslim population now exceeding 3.3m people. Many take leading roles throughout our society and institutions are free to practice their 'religion' although they want the infidel (me) dead".

He supplemented this with the claim once again that "one should be proud to be called Islamaphobic [sic] for it is perfectly rationale [sic] to have a fear of Islam". Snippets like this represent more or less archetypal examples of general sentiments that he had remarked to me personally, if perhaps in less blunt a form. (Why he was more brash in public rather than private remains a mystery, especially given the risks of reputational damage to his career and business). He was clearly trying to justify the extreme anxiety he was feeling around Muslims by repeatedly announcing that his anxiety was "perfectly rationale [sic]". I suspect that this is a case of rationalisation in the psychoanalytic sense, in which the statement must be announced precisely to justify non-verbal feelings that have arisen from the unconscious (e.g., Fenichel 1996).

One way of approaching these examples could be to look at the example of mood. Borneman and Ghassem-Fachandi (2017) note a similar process at work during a New Year's Eve party 2015 in Cologne, in which a number of German women were sexually assaulted by migrants. This led to "activated latent fears and mobilized a xenophobic mood – primarily fear of Muslim male's sexualized aggression" (ibid, p. 110). The majority of these men were North African and the sexual assaults themselves were largely co-ordinated – police were unable to effectively intervene. The consequences were a general shift in the dominant mood from xenophilia to xenophobia. Much in Terry's idea, attacks on German women were "sometimes framed as experiences of German defencelessness in the face of a mainly Muslim onslaught" (ibid, p. 124). Part of this cultivates a dangerous sense that foreigners were taking advantage of Germany, much like Terry's overall anxiety that Britain was being overrun and abused by hordes of migrants.

However, Borneman and Ghassem-Fachandi's (2017) approach pays attention to the ways in which events like this shift the public mood. Despite following Terry's general trajectory over the years, I was never able to exactly connect it to this broader sense of *Stimmung*. The reality is that these issues have far less of a national reverberation than this ethnographic example in Germany. Although it may have influenced many voters, it was mainly individuals who were already quite involved in right-wing populist politics who felt emotionally and intellectually preoccupied with this framing of Islam. A considerable literature exists which details the often-toxic relationship between this right-wing populism and fear or hatred of Muslims (Betz and Meret 2009; Hafez 2014; Mudde and Kaltwasser 2013; Oztig et al. 2021; Williams 2010). But this chapter is not exactly concerned with augmenting it; rather, it is corned with how Islam is named and ordered alongside other existential terrors, which for Terry includes Russia, China, and even the EU. By putting these together, we can see that for him (and many others), the symbol itself seems to be arbitrary. What connects all of them is the sheer terror of annihilation, dissolution, disintegration, or take over by an external threat which impinges upon the sense of self. This is what merits the exploration I will make in this chapter.

3.3 Democracy Dies in Darkness

The apocalyptic anxieties that I have demonstrated here are worthy of deeper investigation. But my primary objective is to portray the man and his relationship to Brexit in the most holistic and honest way possible. This means avoiding a caricatured representation epitomised by Wodak (2015, p. 2) in her claim that populism endorses an "appeals to common-sense and anti-intellectualism [which] mark a return to pre-modernist or pre-Enlightenment thinking". It is worthwhile exploring how Terry's views did have at least some modest anchor in the reality of EU institutions and policymaking. It would be both personally unfair and professionally bad faith to talk as if the comments I mentioned defined his entire relationship to Europe. In fact, what is remarkably more curious and interesting is that he took a quite unusually serious and mature approach the EU, even if his overall emotions towards it seemed so bizarre and unrealistic. This tension itself is a topic of investigation.

We can observe this fact in his perception of democratic accountability. During the 2016 referendum, much of the electoral discourse tended to focus on sentiments like 'sovereignty' and 'freedom'. By 2019 these tensions had altogether faded under the weight of feeling that the establishment was somehow going against 'democracy' itself by not following Brexit towards legal completion. The arguments about the democratic legitimacy of either the EU or the referendum itself are topics that have been treated at length by other scholars (Follesdal and Hix 2006; Meunier-Aitsahalia and Ross 1993; Moravcsik 2003). In this example, the salient fact is the emotional resonance for many Brexit candidates that the referendum was not being 'honoured' was too much to bear. Indeed, almost all of them claim to have been instinctively drawn towards Farage's new venture directly because they felt that this unique expression of real 'democracy' was about to be lost.

If this was the general context of mobilisation for the 2019 election, Terry's personal experience was unique. The dichotomy between a genuine British democracy and an EU *un*democracy or oligarchy was not simply the result of imbibing sensational news articles about the nature of the EU. For many I had spoken to over the years, the idea of fighting for democracy seemed little more than a rhetorical device or rationalisation for things that they already believed. In contrast, Terry had a concrete experience of what this means. One tangible example of this comes from a particular discussion we had not too long after the election. The discussion turned to Terry's palpable disgust about the various tax arrangements that were occurring on the European mainland. Having discovered that the EU charges a VAT on educational materials (like books), he narrated to me that he felt a compulsion to personally change the law. This is something that he claims he has done on three separate occasions in the Houses of Parliament.

When he decided to change the law such that it would align with a morally reputable position, he discovered an obstacle in the legal realities of the Brussels. Sitting back in his chair outside a tearoom, he described his experience in the following way:

> "The first thing that people don't realize is that there were these 'comitons', familiar with the 'comiton'? These are committees that sit there, and their job is to effectively, they are the advice of the great and the good, so what you get is you get a situation whereby you have large institutions like the W.W.F., sitting on a comiton, sitting on a comiton advising Europeans, being paid by the European Union, so we'll come back and advise them. So, I decide I'm gonna change the law, so you start with spending 200 quid to go down there [to Brussels], you then find people to hire a load of consultants, find that you're then going into a committee with a guy that's has no idea about what you're talking about. If you think our SPADs [Special Advisors] are bad. Yeah. And suddenly you realize that this is the most... When you look at these comitons, you realize that you've got the most undemocratic process in the world. And it is an institution for itself. And so, I thought shit. This was a really, you know, this was a real eye opener to me because I thought some common sense would apply".

Having only a modest personal acquaintance with the intricacies of either European or British legislatures – despite writing a book about the EU – I was intrigued that Terry had genuinely attempted to alter legal rules around an issue that he cared about. Not only did he seem to authentically experience the participatory democracy of the UK – and the lack of it on the mainland – his narration of trying to change the law in Brussels also adds substance to his claim that the battle over Brexit was indeed one that had a real connection to functional democracy. Moreover, it was a situation which I understood to be broadly in line with both the opaque reality of the EU legislature and the inherent tension between the British Common Law system and European Civil Law.

But the important point we can draw from this vignette is that, for Terry at least, the tension between British democracy and the EU was indeed something like an empirical reality. In at least one small sense, then, scholars must not be afraid to come to terms with the fact that there is indeed a legitimate criticism of the democratic deficit in the EU (Moravcsik 2003; Follesdal and Hix 2006), and that a not inconsiderable amount of people were genuinely motivated to rectify this problem. It is of course *also* true that Britain has deep problems with its democracy, including the FPTP voting system and the very existence of the House of Lords (Colley 2016). But to many varying degrees, Brexiters do care about this 'democratic deficit' in the European Commission – it is not *simply* cynical political opportunism.

Anthropologists and others have so far mostly evaded this question, attributing the vote to leave to sociologically measurable factors like attitudes towards race, trust, or party alignment. But there has been considerably more intellectual reckoning with the EU than is commonly assumed for Leave voters. My own fear is that, in attempt to overturn the referendum, Remainers (including many academics) have been reticent to address structural issues within the EU for fear that it might damage the case for either staying or re-joining. It is a pattern in human psychology that we are more likely to excuse the faults of our in-group than those of our out-group (e.g., Tajfel 1974), and, with the notable exception of Cris Shore (1993, 2000), I suspect that such a dynamic is one of the factors at play in cautiously side-stepping this issue.

However, I am conscious of the limits to this contribution. For even if Terry had had genuine experience with this problem – something I do not doubt – it did not explain the mobilising power of leaving the EU to most voters (or indeed him). After all, a great many instances of the absence of genuine democracy exist across the Western world, but few (if any) have the rallying influence that Brexit had. As Colley (2016) notes, few of those Brexit voters seemed equally motivated about the undemocratic House of Lords.[5] In this case, I found it difficult to believe that Terry would stand for public office to pull Britain out of Europe simply because he felt that there was an extra 15 per cent tax on high-school textbooks. The entire justification seemed so much like a verbal rationalisation of processes which were operating on a much more unconscious level – such as those we find in dream, myth, and emotional attachment which both precede and shape conscious mental contents. Too little is elucidated simply by taking verbal rationalisations at face value, especially when the contents of our discussions on the same issue could be so radically distinct.

3.4 Myth and Meaning

Let us then consider how to make sense of the popular worldview that Brexit represents a fight *against* European fascism, one epitomised in this reading by interlocutors like Terry. As I previously noted, some of these thornier criticisms of the EU can be attributed in good faith – although still contested – to issues around a real 'democratic deficit'. However, the unique instances of encounters with this political reality pale in comparison to the myths surrounding European 'totalitarianism' which colour so much hostility towards Britain's membership of Europe. These voices take the anti-democratic foundations of the EU as evidence both of moral degeneracy and a potential military threat. How can we account anthropologically for the mismatch between perception and reality? Is it necessary to invoke 'propaganda' or 'brainwashing' by news media as cogent explanations for this fact? Or is there something operating at a deeper cultural or psychological level that can midwife a more holistic explanation?

By noting that there is a problem between empirical reality and something more like 'narrative fictions' around the EU – especially as it recalls great battles, stories of defiance and the sacrality of territorial boundaries – it becomes apparent that we have entered into the world of myth. This section of the chapter is therefore an invitation to make sense of Brexiter ideological hostility to the European continent by drawing on how anthropologists have examined myth since the 19th century. However, it is important to note the wide variety of what the term 'myth' actually means. In its most colloquial and common usage, it refers to something which is objectively not true. In such a case, the 'myth' of the "Soviet EUnion" indexes a patent untruth: whatever its faults, any comparison between Stalinist Russia and the EU is little short of delusional. Many commentators have insinuated that this meaning of 'myth' as basically falsehood is the most applicable to these Brexiter framings of Europe, especially in relationship to the economy (Tilford 2016). Nevertheless, I do not refer to this meaning of the word 'myth' when I refer to the worldview of people like Terry, although I do not deny a degree of validity to the charge.

If we put aside this colloquial definition, we are left with a wide variety of approaches to myth; including that which sees it as an explanation, a symbolic statement, a function, a legitimation, a rationalisation of ritual, or a projection from the unconscious (Cassirer 2009; Cohen 1969; Durkheim 2008; Frazer 1998; Freud 2008; Jung 1991; Tylor 1958). What tends to distinguish 'myth' from other narratives like folk-tales or conspiracy theories are its sacred quality, usually pertaining to some dramatic transformation or origin (Cohen 1969). There is certainly a porous boundary here – both analytically and descriptively – between what anthropologists would call 'myth' in contrast to a 'cosmology', which is much more like a general set of ideas. I leave this distinction purposefully ambivalent in this chapter; not only because I personally find it hard to nail down whether the object of my analysis is myth or cosmology, but also because the object itself seems to fit both. It is a problem both of observer and observed.[6]

I believe that an anthropological analysis of my ethnographic material would most usefully fall into two basic categories: the structuralist account and the functionalist one. I shall thus begin with the former.[7] In the structuralist account, then, our preliminary way of understanding this ethnographic complexity rests on the argument that the human mind makes sense of social reality through the generation of dichotomous and oppositional framings. Myth does not exist to provide a metaphysical explanation or account for the physical world, but rather as the "science of abstract relations" (2021). This means that its principal function is to meditate 'contradictions' or 'oppositions' between categories that are experienced in reality. This framing, one influenced by early 20th-century linguists like Roman Jakobson, sees cultural forms as emergent from the basic 'structural' characteristics of the human mind. All cognition, in Lévi-Strauss' view, operates through these binary framings: everything is divided into X and not-X, the interplay of which are constantly in a state of mental process and flux. This perpetual mental activity Lévi-Strauss calls the "science of the concrete" (ibid.).

This transformation defines mythic patterns of thought because while the contents are subject to the contingencies of *bricolage*, the hard structural core remains broadly the same. If such a model could apply in this context, then, we would expect to find a situation in which the cultural contents seem to vary while the underlining 'structural' element of binary oppositions remains. I argue that we do indeed witness such an example. Explaining why Terry and others are fixed on the idea of democracy/undemocracy as Britain/Europe seems to be a perfect example of cultural oppositions requiring meditation. This seems to part way explain the otherwise unreasonable assertion that the EU is the newest iteration of both Nazi Germany *and* the Soviet Union. These two polities contained fundamentally distinct forms of governance, ideology, and territoriality. The comparison between them – let alone the idea that either resemble the EU – never stops infuriating the pro-European side.

For many Brexiters, however, it was often taken for granted that this binary division of politics across the channel could be perceived in such a way. Despite an unbridgeable ideological gulf between them, what Nazism, Communism and (I suspect) the ghosts of Bonapartism have in common is that they are all not fundamentally democratic systems. That they are also both found on the European continent to the east of the British channel may strengthen their narrative grip, but it does not fundamentally explain it. Instead, they function as symbolic placeholders within a structuralist dichotomy of opposites that allow people like Terry to generate meaning and orientation from the world around them. The contingencies of the mythic contents here are less important than the fact that a hard structural core of binary oppositions between them remains. The initially inexplicable confluence of various distinct ideologies can be ascribed not to ignorance but to *bricolage* (Lévi-Strauss 2021).[8]

Most importantly, these examples support my previous chapter's argument that democracy has become the sacred, transcendental value which holds an otherwise fracturing national group together. For England to be sacred, Europe is profane; if the sacred is democratic, the 'Other' is a living archetype of an anti-democratic establishment on the mainland. If the British nation-state can be defined as 'democratic', then, the opposing signifier of non-democratic is more important than the content which fills it. The particularities of whether it is Nazi Germany, the USSR, or the EU is of much less concern than the more universal aspect that it is a 'non-democratic' mytheme (Lévi-Strauss 1974) filling this space. It also makes much more sense why people like Terry are concerned with other threats – China or Putin's Russia – which follow the same pathway. They too are both fundamentally *non-democracies* that can also fit the semiotic tension that all structuralist binaries require, although on a much more global scale.[9] In short, meaning is made, as Lévi-Strauss (1955, 1974, 2021) claimed, not standing on its own but through the movement of these binaries in relationship with one another.

Finally, another interesting conclusion that can be drawn from the structuralist account is Lévi-Strauss' explanation for why myth is so important in pre-modern cultures. Unlike in the alienated flux of modernity, traditional societies depend heavily on references to the past. This is because social practices are generally legitimated in reference to previous ways of doing things; relations about property, marriage, territory and kinship all rely heavily on lines of historical descent. The symbolic contents of myths are in some sense archives or records of that which occurred before. Are we then unsurprised that justifications for remaining outside the EU are anchored in mythical conceptions of a historical past in which Europe was the enemy? One approach would thus frame Terry's worldview not as a *misperception* of an empirical reality but a kind of rationalisation for the traditional boundaries and moral authorities of the national community as anchored in a kind of mythical past. Brexiters like Terry wish to keep traditional boundaries of the moral community static and stable, especially concerning the issue of immigration. It is therefore incumbent on him to invoke a mythic conception of the past which would justify the maintenance of these boundaries. The myth comes after, not before, the political reality.

*

The structuralist account is a generative means for understanding many of these issues, but it is not the only one. If we draw from the rich tradition of British social anthropology, particularly the work of Bronislaw Malinowski, we are resourced with another means of understanding myth. This is despite the reality that British anthropology has been rather reluctant to deal with myth on its own, preferring instead to incorporate it within a broader framework of belief and custom (Rapport and Overing 2000). At its most basic level, Malinowski (2014, p. 317) saw myths as "founts of ethnographic information" which tell us a great deal about the beliefs and wishes of a culture. But what distinguishes his theoretical paradigm from someone like Lévi-Strauss is the fact that he is the originator of the idea of *functionalism*. This is an approach to the society which sees categories like myth, custom, and ritual all as having a useful purpose (or 'function'). Their existence is justified on the grounds that it *does* something, however modest, for the community in which it is embedded. It is therefore not simply an epiphenomenon of cognitive processes. If we accept with him, then, that myth only exists because it has some kind of function for each culture, we are faced primarily with the need to conceptually isolate it.

For Malinowski, a workable definition of myth was to label it as something special or out of the ordinary. It cannot be reduced, content-wise, to any particular focus on heroes, deities, ghosts, or any some such supernatural occurrence. What is or is not a 'myth' is neither objective nor clearly signposted: a great deal of ethnographic interpretation must go into discerning whether that which anthropologists can fruitfully identify and study as a 'myth' actually is one. The reason for this confusion is because the term 'myth' is indigenous to Western categories of thought: it has no precise translation in other contexts. For example, Malinowski (2014) claims the Trobriand term *lili'u* should be equated with the term "myth" because it is a uniquely important class of stories for the native Trobrianders. It is a not simply a set of stories but a *venerated* set of stories that plays a significant role in the Melanesian culture. But it is unclear whether the natives themselves would necessarily agree with such a schematic ordering.

Moreover, for Malinowski, the myth itself has no intrinsic meaning outside of the context in which it is embedded. This is to say that they are not primarily texts, as someone like Geertz (1973) would go on to suggest some many decades later. They are, Strenski (2006) notes, "texts *merged* with contexts" [emphasis mine], and this has profound implications for how an anthropologist might make sense of them. We cannot isolate them as a piece of literature, although Biblical or Homeric stories testify to the sublime aesthetic value of myth which far succeed their author's lives. Social context remains central to their purpose. As Malinowski (1979, p. 138) claims: "to understand myth, you must have a good knowledge of their sociology, religion, customs, and outlook… then, and only then, can you appreciate what this story means to the natives and how it can live in their life". Such an approach supports the importance of experiential fieldwork as equal, if not superior, to text-focused approaches to culture. This argument is supported by scholars like Borneman and Hammoudi (2009), who also remain sceptical of anthropological work which relegates physical encounters to the sidelines.

Overall, then, we can think of Malinowski's functionalism as placing a holistic form of attention on the way in which an entire culture holds together through time. These sacred stories – these myths – are deeply embedded within all the internal relations of a culture and function to maintain a sense of coherence and co-operation across the social whole. The core purpose of myth, Malinowski (1948, p. 85) claims, is as "a warrant, a charter, and even a practical guide to the activities with which it is connected". It is thus not quite a theoretical explanation for the world as it appears before us, but something more like a legitimising mechanism for the social institutions as they currently exist. The legitimacy of our collective arrangement is solidified through the existence of myths; hence the correlation between myths about female untrustworthiness and pollution and highly patriarchal social structures (Godelier 1986).[10] In short, then, the necessity of myth is based on the fact that it "expresses, enhances and codifies belief; it safeguards and enforces morality; it ... contains practical rules for the guidance of men ... a pragmatic charter of primitive faith and moral wisdom" (Malinowski 1948, p. 101). Like sacrifice (Borneman 2002), no society – traditional or modern – can really function without it.

What Malinowski (1948, 1979, 2014) further notes, however, is that the indispensability of myth in human culture is not simply a socio-cultural function but a biological one, too. Heavily influenced by the early ideas of the Freudian (1991) psychoanalytic movement in Europe, his overall theory of myth considers that the reality that social institutions overlay a deeper and more foundational reality: biological necessity. Our most salient characteristic is our fallible nature as animals, and myths can serve as a profound palliative to the anxieties that accompany our human mortality. In our fears of death and total annihilation, we unconsciously craft narratives which speak to this basic fact of our organism. Mythic thinking is "born from the innermost and emotional reaction to the most formidable and haunting idea", that is, the inevitability of death (Malinowski 1979, p. 110). It is for this reason that Talcott Parsons (2002) sees Malinowski and re-establishing the connection "between man as a biological organism and man as a creator of culture" (Kempny 1992, p. 56). Symbolisation is important, but cannot adequately be explained in purely mental, cultural, or intellectual terms.

Yet, for all the criticisms of the functionalist view,[11] there remains something elucidating about Malinowski's framework. Let us once more sum up his approach to myth. We note that it acts as a symbolic guide to practical action, one which justifies particular contingent and often arbitrary social arrangements. Myths resolve the unavoidable "inconsistences and irreconcilable demands" of claims in the present-moment by recounting events "of an invented or partly-invented past", creating a story which transcends the mundane and often highly doubtful nature of "real history, real patterns of migration and settlement [and] real claims to property and power" (Cohen

1969, p. 344). Despite the disenchanted character of modernity (Weber 1971), these dynamics are clearly visible to us.[12] In short, Malinowski posits a 'charter' theory of myth: one which functions to resolve these ambivalent issues through sacralised narrative storytelling. It by no means demands a necessary connection to empirical reality as social scientists understand it, although it is highly likely to involve at least modest contact with the 'reality principle' (Freud 1991).

How can we connect this to the ethnographic material? Terry's reading of Brexit, in addition to much of his personal life, was bathed in the myth of the Second World War. His fantasy life reflects this fact, as we can see from the material artefacts of his personal life, the business he keeps, the videos he promotes, the novels he writes and most saliently of all in his justifications for Brexit over the past several years. Invoking the Second World War was not *just* a rationalisation of leaving Europe: it truly animated the way he thought about Britain. But unlike his parents, for whom the war as a real experience shaped their attitude towards European peace, Terry only experienced the war as fantasy. As he himself claimed, he "was a child of the second World War" – not exactly a participant, but instead someone who was generated from the matrix of that conflict. He was a spectator of this great drama – not an actual player. Terry lived on the stories and narratives about war that were passed down to him and wrote copiously about the period in his spare time. He decorates his life with the memories of great battles and heroic deeds of his ancestors, although he himself played no role in them – and partook of no risk.

The 'charter' aspect of mythmaking is apposite here. Terry invoked the myth of the Second World War – of Britain 'standing alone' against European dictatorship – throughout our many discussions of why he supported Brexit. The implicit relevance of this myth is that it created a "web of meaning" (Geertz 1973) around what he already desired: strong borders on Europe, buttressed by a healthy suspicion of the continent, and the desire for national renewal stimulated by the feeling that Britain has somehow "lost its way" compared to its previous ability to "commit to total war" to defend itself. The idea of Britain as uniquely destined to defend the free world from continental threat is clearly a myth which provides guidance and orientation for individuals trying to make sense of complex topics like membership of the EU. It takes in every sense the form of a narrative 'charter' much like the *lili'u* stories of the Trobriand Islanders in the Pacific, even if it is not exactly condensed into individually replicable stories.

At this point, one approach might ask: where do these mythic contents actually come from? Genealogically, we might endeavour to trace a sentiment of isolation and supremacy down to at least the Reformation and era of Elizabeth I (Mason 1994). This could be supplemented by the subsequent Cromwellian and Miltonian notions of England as an elected nation – a 'new

Israel' – and later 18th-century notions of Britain as a uniquely free, literate, and Protestant island (Chernaik 2016). Such myths seamlessly developed through the anti-Napoleonic era into the broader imperial notions about bringing Christian civilisation to the world, some of which grew in embryo from internal colonial domineering of a Celtic fringe located principally in Ireland (Armitage 2000). We might invoke Lévi-Strauss's (2021) notion of *bricolage* here and note that Brexiters who feel this way are re-assembling free-floating mythic contents in order to structure and order thought in the synchronic moment of the referendum.

But there is a significant problem here. Notwithstanding the richness of the mythic contents which British people have to work with, understanding the historical origins of these ideational features cannot support any blanket assertion that past here *explains* anti-European sentiment. One cannot look at the myth and see the 'reason' for why Britain left, although it clearly contains a general guide or orientation towards the continental policy. Myth might be a charter, but it does not have any kind of causal agency by itself – despite Lévi-Strauss's (2021) somewhat peculiar suggestion that myths can talk to one another inside the skulls of human beings (Godelier 2018). Rather, in Malinowskian fashion, we must see the myth as speech-acts which aid the sense-making that draws on both internal and external objects – threats, sensations, anxieties, thoughts, dreams, and so on. Most importantly, the content of his mythic storytelling pointed to something deep in Terry's inner life that sensed a 'nameless dread' (Bion 1984) at the possibility of total psychological disintegration in the face of European domination.

After all, what is really in play when discussing the European question? Is this genuinely a debate about the Northern Irish border or the utility of market tariffs? These are clearly surface emanations of underlying psychological dynamics – few individuals are truly animated by these questions, and certainly not thirty three million of them. Although different academic disciplines provide alternative explanations, our anthropological accounts have focused on what might be beneath the surface of these views in terms of mental processing. Yet, their emphasis on *intelligibility* tends to ignore the emotional side of human psychology. This is a deficit which Malinowski somewhat overcomes in his insistence that myth is connected to anxieties about death. It is also what Parsons (2002) means when he notes that both the innovation and the flaw of Malinowskian functionalism is the connection of biology and culture. But there is perhaps one last layer which must be peeled off if we are to understand what many readers will see as the obvious irrationality of Terry's worldview.

In our conversations about Brexit, Terry was preoccupied with death. Writing novels about his family's struggle through apocalyptic European war testified to a sense that the memory of the dead must not be allowed to disintegrate. Indeed, he frequently also visited and posted videos on YouTube featuring war memorials and ceremonies (such as for the Falklands) which honoured those lost in battle. So too had he dedicated much of his personal interests to keeping 20th-century historical figures alive. His claim that he was lucky "not having to be burying the man on the left and the right of me in battle" spoke to the inalienable connection between death and his attitude to Europe. Finally, his lamentation that Britain was "no longer able to commit to a policy of total war" (i.e., complete physical annihilation) in order to defend itself again reflected his extreme emotional concern with both the inescapability of death and the salience that this reality has on his own political life. All of these examples point to a triangulation between myth, psyche and death which arises in the form of his subjective consciousness as a specific orientation towards the European project.

3.5 Threats to the Self

Studying mythic storytelling about Britain (e.g., Reynolds 2019) purely in terms of discourse can take us only so far in trying to explain the cultural context in which people made sense of their own attitudes to the Europe. Lévi-Strauss was certainly correct to see myths as fundamentally cognitive phenomena – the result of a kind of internal structural ordering of the external world. Similarly, Malinowski was right to reject a purely culturalist explanation of myth, and instead link it with unconscious biological drives. Owing much to Freud's influence, he noticed that one of the functions of myth is a psychological palliative for unconscious death anxieties. We are thus not surprised to see them emerge through the process of rationalisation and verbalisation into stories that make up religion and culture (Becker 1973). But it remains ultimately necessary to explain how we can connect internal psychological sensations with narrative storytelling that go beyond the simplistic and reductively functionalist approach.

The relationship between anthropology and psychoanalysis is both generative and curiously underexplored. Much of this may be connected to the dominant paradigm of Clifford Geertz (1973), who underscored "the inaccessibility of the mind with an emphasis that the study of culture rests only within what is visible" (Denham 2014, p. 387). Yet many ethnographers note that unconscious fantasies are themselves universal and open to empirical observation. Indeed, Devereux (1969, 1978, 1980) perceptively argued that cultural fantasies from the world's anthropological record matches anything described by Western psychoanalysis. An analogous framework was most significantly taken up by Carl Jung (1991), whose emic approach to the study of archetypes and the collective unconscious attempted to grapple with culturally replicable psychic patterns across space and time.[13] But rather than take this Jungian approach, fertile as it might be, this chapter adopts as its guiding assumption that "culture is a group fantasy projected from the individual unconscious into the external world and sustained by each person's need to defend against his or her fundamental anxieties" (Paul 1989, p. 186). This will help us link shared myths about fighting Europe with the individual psychology which feels acutely sympathetic to them.

One approach to link these theories more coherently with anthropology is from Sandler and Rosenblatt (1967). Their concept of the 'representational world' sees the unconscious as a kind of theatre in which emotionally charged representations reflect the earlier social universe of that person's youth. These fantasies, however, usually come up against the 'ego-censor' (Freud 2008) which utilises defence mechanisms to keep them out of consciousness. This prevents the otherwise intolerable anxiety from spilling over and generating neurotic symptoms. After all, our day-to-day rationality is geared towards the survival of the biological organism and is thus to a large extent preoccupied with the 'reality principle' (Freud 1991). The mythopoetic faculty, however, is much more directed towards the integration of the whole self. In other words, this capacity "creates out of the total sensorium personal meaning in the form of narratives, images, symbols, and myths which are poetic in the broadest sense" (Paul 1989, p. 184). In short, we observe that cultural fantasies and storytelling (i.e., mythopoetic ordering) around something like Brexit may rest on unconscious libidinal energy directed at controlling the overspilling of anxieties around dependence, fracture, and insecurity.

The overarching point is that cultural symbolisation like myth is concerned not only with managing the individual unconscious, but also in providing "an accessible template or model on the basis of which individuals can organize their own personal fantasies" (Paul 1989, p. 187). Culture is symptomatic of universal anxieties moulded through fantasy narrative. These derive predominantly from fear of threat to the self, whether physical or psychic (deMause 1982; Devereux 1980; Stein 1981, 1983). This may not necessarily have a biological root, such as Malinowski proposed in the intolerable fear of death. It may also take the general form of insecure parental attachment, or the unexpected consequence of a caregiver's unconscious patterns of projecting their own neurotic conflicts onto their children. Culture emerges as a means by which to palliate overwhelming anxieties and, much like in both the Lévi-Straussian and Malinowskian mode, help to categorise and order the external world such that we can better orientate ourselves within it and manage these unconscious feelings.

Let's draw on this to make better sense of the ethnographic context. As I have demonstrated throughout this chapter, Terry's inner life was beset by a great number of existential threats: Russia, China, Islam, and the EU. This last one he experienced as quite literally holding the whip over Britain, threatening to turn us from "citizens" to "subjects". One repeated theme was that Brexit was a "fight for our lives" against "EU oligarchs". Many of these beliefs are widely shared among his colleagues in the Brexit Party. On deeper conversation, he revealed his personal view that unless we left the EU, there would be a catastrophic war between London and Brussels. He also believed that such an apocalyptic outcome was inevitable anyway, as World War Three was on the horizon with the rise of China. In addition, Putin was engaged in a terrifying psychological operation to destroy the West through social media. As if it couldn't get any worse, the UK was also being invaded by Muslim migrants, who wanted to implement Sharia law, kill infidels, and shepherd in a new Caliphate throughout Western Europe.

I hope that these stories do not make Terry seem like a caricature of a reactionary. He is charming and polite, the owner and operator of a successful businesses, a family man, a responsible and reasonable adult who reflects on his own experience with great depth.[14] The point is that we cannot come closer to understanding why he thought such things if he is written off as either mentally unstable or a right-wing fanatic. He is a sane and reasonable person, at least to the extent that I was able to witness and observe. Moreover, perhaps most interestingly, many of his views were commonplace among a large segment of both his age cohort and general position in society. These mostly white and middle-class individuals are the other "children of the Second World War", as he described himself. If we take a sympathetic but critical approach to his belief system, then, we must try to understand how the cultural content of mythic thinking (in his fiction, activism or personal interviews) are shaped by, and secondary too, underlying anxieties – including ones which may be shared by many millions of other people.

My overall view is that it seems reasonable to interpret Terry's various fantasies about European enslavement, Muslim invasion, Chinese annihilation, social disintegration, cultural annihilation, Russian destabilisation, and so on, all fundamentally reflect one underlying psychological dynamic: 'ontological insecurity' (Laing 2010). There are a very wide range of adjacent psychodynamic concepts which broadly point to a feeling of being existentially threatened. This form of 'annihilation anxiety' represents an imminent fear about losing control, shrinking, being destroyed or overwhelmed, in addition to the sense of imminent complete catastrophe (Hurvich 2003). Similar concepts utilised by analysts include (but are not limited to): unthinkable anxiety (Winnicott 1960), doomsday expectation (Krystal 1988), disintegration anxiety (Kohut 1972), nameless dread (Bion 1984), schizoid anxiety (Fairbairn 1952), psychotic anxiety (Klein 1975) or traumatic anxiety (Freud 1926).[15]

All of the above concepts speak to basically the same sense of dread about dissolution of the self. Little would be gained from investigating each of them and trying to understand how they connect to this ethnography in question. For the sake of brevity, I will focus on the equivalent concept as understood and explored by R.D. Laing (2010). His notion of 'ontological insecurity' emphasises the connection between existential dread and a sense that things are dissolving; that boundaries should not be porous (but are), that there are constant external threats to the self, or that one's autonomy is in danger. Laing's concept develops the idea that the loss of self and control emerges out of a general lack of fixed sense of identity or reality. In being unable to take their self-identity for granted, such persons are constantly anxious about being destroyed. The danger of this destruction lurks in the boundaries, where Self and not-Self are at their most volatile and unstable. A major manifestation of this includes the destruction of autonomy and becoming subject to the will of others. For Terry, this is clearly manifest in his perception of the EU. But it also emerges in his perception of Islam, China, and Russia.

Moreover, Laing thought that ontologically insecure persons felt the need to isolate themselves from other individuals and groups, in order to stave off the prospect of dissolution into either the 'Other' or an empty nothingness. As such, the key analytic term is the idea of 'engulfment'. This means that the individual "dreads relatedness as such, with anyone or anything, or indeed even with himself, because his uncertainty about the stability of his autonomy lays open to him the dread lest in any relationship he will lose his autonomy and identity" (Laing 2010, p. 44). Rather than take life as it comes, the man with engulfment anxiety "experiences himself as a man who is only saving himself from drowning by the most constant, strenuous, desperate activity" (ibid.). This epitomises Terry's relationship to the EU: he is relentlessly battling against that process which strives to engulf him, destroy his autonomy, carry him off and dissolve his sense of self. The EU is both a cultural symbol and an *expanding institution* which by its nature involves integration on the level of both political state and personal identity (i.e., as Europeans). This seems to factor into the slow but relentless growth of its potential to menace Terry.

In addition, as Laing (2010, p. 44) notes, "the main manoeuvre used to preserve identity under pressure from the dread of engulfment is isolation". In this case, severing Britain's links with Europe functions to ward off the fear of dread that comes from possible engulfment with an external Other. Pulling away from the danger in order to stave off these threats is a common unconscious reaction to this intolerable anxiety about engulfment. Hence, the myths of 'Britain Alone' once more against a European threat may not emanate from political opportunism, right-wing tabloid brainwashing or a delusional reading of European history. It may simply be the discursive, mythopoetic narrative form in which individuals like Terry rationalise and make sense of these unconscious psychodynamic anxieties around 'engulfment' that are coeval with a deep sense of ontological insecurity.

Finally, it is important to note here is that the winning slogan of the 2016 referendum was 'Take Back Control'. In the eyes of Dominic Cummings

(2017), the mastermind behind the Leave campaign, this short and pithy expression was one of, if not *the*, most profoundly influential weapons in the battle for votes. While the phrase refers ostensibly only to policy issues like immigration or the creation of EU law, the fact is that its resonance was so profound and so deep that it must have at least some connection to the psychodynamic relationships that were in play at the time. 'Take Back Control' is the antithesis of the feeling of impeding dissolution, being overrun, and having no capacity to stem the tide of chaos and disintegration that seems to characterise the embodied experience of many people today. In order to capture such attention from the British public, it had to be inspired by more than simply beyond bread-and-butter political issues. It captured an entire mood (Borneman and Ghassem-Fachandi 2017). Indeed, when I asked Terry once what Brexit all was basically about, he replied: "it was quite simple – taking back control". He was not the only one for whom that sentiment was so meaningful.

3.6 Conclusion

I believe I have proposed a coherent and explanatory approach to understanding the fantasies of Terry and the many Brexiters who shared them. I have shown that narratives about fighting European totalitarians, or a civilisational war with Islam, or a general re-run of 1939, are all examples of thinking in mythic terms which help individuals to make sense of the disconcerting changes in the world around them. But they may also represent psychodynamic mechanisms by which unconscious anxieties about dissolution become rationalised and expressed with those whom they are shared. I am neither capable nor qualified to understand this at a more intimate level. Psychoanalytic anthropologists note that culture as a collective fantasy can manage existential anxieties that emerge from infancy. Terry hinted that his father had to "bury" his friends during the conflict. Moreover, he frequently mentioned that he was a "child of the Second World War". Is this ontological insecurity driven by a neurotic anxiety that he absorbed in childhood? Did the grief and catastrophe of war leave a deep impression on his emotional experience of the world, one which left him anxious about an imminent catastrophic threat in the guise of China, Russia, or Islam? These deeper questions are beyond my remit and authority as an anthropologist, but I believe that they are probable.

While this seems to be a compelling explanation, it leaves out one major question. This study might make sense of Terry: but what about the rest of the population? Without being able to generalise too much from my own fieldwork experience, I think that a great many people feel the same as him. Hostility towards Germany, especially the idea that Berlin is secretly trying to take over and run Europe, runs deep among many Brexiters I spoke to. This was even more marked for the older generations. To a certain degree, then, we could hypothesise that this overall sense of dread of invasion by a continental Other is indeed shared not only by those who fought Germany, but also by the generation beneath them who absorbed their trauma. It is empirically indisputable that one of the two biggest predictors of voting for Brexit was age: the older one was, the more likely the vote to leave the EU (Norris and Inglehart 2019). We might reasonably suggest some psychodynamic connection here without resorting to rather two-dimensional ideas about a Eurosceptic 'nostalgia' for the Second World War (e.g., Eaglestone 2018; Melhuish 2022) which offers little by way of genuine explanation. This inherited legacy of trauma across generations may also have played a role.

The principal conclusion of this chapter is three-fold. Firstly, ethnographic evidence suggests that prevalence and belief in 'myth' is not something which is precluded by modern political life. As both an epiphenomenon of human cognition and a necessary mechanism for ordering and mapping the social world, myths remain central even to the 'disenchanted' (Weber 1971) core of industrial postmodernity. We observe this in the myth-making around fighting European totalitarians that animated many Eurosceptics, of whom Terry represents a kind of archetypal figure. But we must also take the psychodynamic relationship to culture seriously too; something Malinowski was better at than Lévi-Strauss, even if the latter paid sustained attention to the true nature of myth as beneath the surface of empirical phenomenon. For the myths I have discussed in this chapter, psychoanalytic approaches which focus on 'ontological insecurity' and 'engulfment' are compelling explanations for *why* stories of impeding catastrophe, invasion, and totalitarian control by Europe resonate so deeply. They also provide a justification for overwhelming unconscious desire for withdrawal, isolation, and attempts to protect the autonomy of the self by voting to leave the EU.

Notes

1 This often involves a deep cynicism and hostility to Berlin, something the former German Ambassador to the UK noted on his professional exit (Williams 2021).
2 Organised by Claire Fox (a former Brexit Party MEP), the *Battle of Ideas* runs a yearly (and highly enjoyable) pseudo-academic conference for the 'anti-woke' crowd that I explore in this book. Many attendees of these large meetings could be seen in the Gramscian (2011) sense as 'organic intellectuals': their political ideology runs directly counter to pro-European assumptions within the governing elite (Copus 2018).
3 He was referring, I later discovered, to the rise of China – for I had inaccurately assumed that he was referring to Russian influence on the borders of Europe. To his credit, he accurately predicted that Putin would invade Eastern Ukraine several years before the 2022 conflict.
4 Though this is not to suggest that accusations of the 'democracy deficit' in the EU are unfounded. Indeed, as Shore (1993, 2000) notes, the fact that it is at least partly true that the EU Commission is fundamentally undemocratic remains an

open invitation for complaints against national membership by Eurosceptic parties.

5 With the notable exception of The Brexit Party, of which Terry himself was involved. Abolishing the House of Lords was central to their manifesto, despite the somewhat curious turnaround when Claire Fox subsequently accepted a peerage after the election.

6 As a means of overcoming any conceptual confusion, my adoption of the idea of 'myth' may be usefully thought of as that which contains 'mythic elements'. This distinction is honest enough to admit that it remains a highly generative way of thinking about my interlocutors, while also recognising that myth as a decidedly formulaic and repeatable 'sacred narrative' is a much less common occurrence in modern societies. In this sense, despite a profound veneration of the man's work as a whole, I disagree with Malinowski's assumption that "the total field of data under observation of the field-worker must somehow fit together and make sense" (Leach 2002, p. 120).

7 However, our preliminary problem is that Lévi-Strauss himself never fully and unequivocally outlines his mythic schemata. Despite several large volumes, in addition to various papers and essays, there is nothing that can be described as an exposition of a total coherent and explanatory theory (Cohen 1969; Godelier 2018). This obscurantism - while perhaps not unusual among the writings of other 20th-century French luminaries - does little to clear up the inherent ambiguities any scholar finds when trying to work with this otherwise highly generative framework. In line with this opacity, my structuralist account will also consist more of raising questions, drawing connections and suggesting relationships than it can represent a coherent and falsifiable hypothesis.

8 Structuralism therefore does not posit a primitive 'mythical' framework in contrast to a modern scientific one, and it certainly does not agree with Lévy-Bruhl's (2015) schematisation of myth as 'pre-logical' distinct from a scientific 'logical' one. This set of assumptions about a progressive development towards more rational forms of thought was shared by other anthropologists like Frazer (1998) and Tylor (2016), but Lévi-Strauss discards them. This was in part as a rejection of the patronising assumptions that primitive man was a story-telling simpleton, but it was mostly more of an honest reflection of how he conceived the universal workings of the human mind (Cohen 1969). Instead, myth can be thought of as a precursor to science, simply operating with different cultural contents. The mental operation through which myth is constructed by individuals Lévi-Strauss (2021) counts as that of a 'bricoleur' – a kind of handyman who takes bits and pieces from different sources and arranges them into something new. The consequence of this shuffling is the creation of a new and unique narrative; however, its actual contents are of much less importance than the underlying 'structure' of mythic thought: hence the name of the theory.

9 Indeed, our own societies are drenched in mythic binary imagery, such as a civilisational war between a Free West and a revanchist Islamic civilisation (Huntingdon 2002).

10 So too do they justify more mundane customs that modern peoples, themselves also caught up in myths, simply take for granted. The story of Adam and Eve leaving the garden rationalises the wearing of clothes and covering up genitalia, for instance, something which other cultures may find startling and bizarre.

11 One critique, concurrent with broader criticism of psychoanalytic work, is that there is a great leap of faith in the ethnographers' ability to truly divine the 'real' meaning of myths in another culture (Strenski 2006). On what basis can anthropologists support their claims to valid interpretation of another culture's myth? An additional criticism attacks Malinowski's underdeveloped epistemological

understanding of symbolism, something which Durkheim's (2008) approach (however flawed) attempts to do (Cohen 1969). Sahlins (1976) also criticises this functionalist approach for not accounting for the rich tapestry of human culture and dissolving what's left with a crude reductionism. Finally, Leach (2002) roundly criticises the "obsessional empiricism" of Malinowski that is "handicapped by the conviction that all behaviour must have a practical end".

12 We can see this illustrated with the Israel/Palestine conflict, where mythic claims to sacred territory overlap poorly onto both historical and demographic realities (Slater 2020).

13 Although, there has been very little cross-fertilisation between Jung and the anthropological discipline as a whole, despite shared interests in myth and meaning (Godelier 2018).

14 For instance, he writes long and detailed essays on the topic of the EU which he publishes on his website. The quality is often higher than many undergraduates I have taught.

15 I make pains to note here that the sheer array of analogous concepts demonstrate that this sense of existential dread is both a universal and extremely common psychodynamic phenomenon. As such, we perhaps should not be surprised that scholars who work on anxiety over death suggest that culture itself is mostly (if not totally) a psychological palliative to these same anxieties about death and destruction of the self (e.g., Becker 1973).

3

CARNIVAL AND CRITIQUE: TOWARDS A STRUCTURAL-FUNCTIONALIST READING OF BREXIT

6.1 Introduction

A social or cultural cleavage occurs with the segmentation of individuals into divided collectivities or affiliations with different and often competing values and interests such as we've seen with Brexit polarisation (Hooghe and Marks 2018). There is nothing uniquely modern about this process, although the collapse of metanarrative and the increasing *anomie* which defines our contemporary world exacerbates the trend towards social fragmentation (Giddens 1990, 1991). While it is true that almost all societies have cleavages in a general sense, they are always subject to the distinct conditions of historical idiosyncrasy. In the previous centuries, for instance, Western Europe was divided by a very different social-structural architecture. The concepts of centre/periphery, religious/secular, urban/rural, and labour/capital all provide a framework through which we can understand the territorial, economic, and religious divisions that in some cases quite literally tore apart the continent in the Early Modern era (Lipset and Rokkan 1967).[1] This chapter analyses how structural conflict emerges today, through an ethnographic analysis of the 'Brexit Day' celebration of January 2020.

One way of understanding structural conflict is to break down these cleavages into the conceptual divisions I previously labelled in the introduction as 'economic grievance' versus 'cultural backlash'. In the first framing, these fluctuating cleavages represent an antagonism between the 'winners' and 'losers' of globalisation. This is because the benefits of transnational economic and political integration are not shared across occupational lines.[2] Secondly, this *structural* cleavage is further complicated by its convergence with a *values* cleavage: what Inglehart (1977) calls the conflict between

DOI: 10.4324/9781003458517-4

'materialist' and 'postmaterialist' values. These terms represent the divergent priorities of individuals in terms of their attitude towards strong leadership, ethnic homogeneity, and in-group cohesion. Such values are segmented largely by age and tertiary education, which reflect alternative conditions of generational socialisation. Moreover, while both 'structure' and 'values' are conceptually distinct, they have a complex, overlapping and fundamentally overdetermining role in explaining events like Brexit.[3] In line with Hooghe and Mark's (2018) discussion, I use the term 'values-structure' to integrate this complexity into one operative term. Thus, the partisan categories of 'Remainer' and 'Brexiter' emerged from a specific historical occurrence in the 2016 referendum. But as cultural symbols which represent these underlying *structural* cleavages, the voting process can be thought of as a kind of freeze-frame which captures this 'silent revolution' not of class conflict but changing values, political styles, demographic interests, identities, and structured loyalties towards institutions like political parties and the nation-state.[4]

If I have provided a descriptive account of how social-structural tension can be understood in static terms, the subsequent question concerns how those cleavages interact dynamically at the level of social fission and social fusion. For political scientists, this generally seems to take the form of political parties, affiliation to which emerges in consequence of how these social divisions translate into an electoral apparatus. They also provide mechanisms by which leaders can be selected to articulate the direction of the group (Mair 2013; Weber 1958). The critical role of parties is then in stabilising and institutionalising patterns of competition such as partisan commitments and institutional structures which are based on these underlying structural cleavages. This indexes a structural coming-together or 'fusion' in which the mechanisms of democratic elections mediate and resolve the friction between social segments (Ford and Jennings 2020).

But structural conflict clearly has many more manifestations than those expressed in elections. It is perhaps up to anthropologists to examine alternative expressions of them in contexts which are less amiable to replicable analysis. The work of the structural-functionalists of the early 20th century provides a compelling framework for those who see social structure as both existing ontologically and, perhaps more importantly, being accessible to human observation. In other words, it is for those anthropologists who remain sceptical around Geertzian claims that "the inaccessibility of the mind... [leads to] an emphasis that the study of culture rests only within what is visible" (Denham 2014 p. 387). We are capable of deducing the existence of structure despite never seeing it, just as we are able to infer the existence of the unconscious despite its sensory invisibility.[5] Structural-functionalists argue that we should think of society as condition of equilibrium or balance of forces of disruption and cohesion and that its purpose is perpetuating its own existence in a state of stability and balance

(Stocking 1995). I share the Manchester School's suspicion that social equilibrium is not "a simple affair, resulting from the neat integration of groups or norms" but instead "emerges through the balancing of oppositions in a dialectical process" (Kuper 1973, p. 139).

The overall message is that understanding the nature of any institutional relationship is less about satisfying psychological needs, à la Malinowski, than about how it contributes to the stability of overall social structure. Instead of seeing rituals and ceremonies in psychological or cultural terms, for instance, anthropologists were encouraged to interpret them as expressions of sentiments which perpetuate concrete 'relations of association'. For Radcliffe-Brown (1940b), this emphasis on equilibrium within an invisible social system had precedence often over the rest of everything else he found in the ethnographic reality (Stocking 1995). Perhaps structural-functionalists share something of the epistemological reductionism of political scientists who reduce populism to nothing more than structural shifts. But this does not make them wrong. In fact, it demonstrates the complexity of appreciating historical change occurring at a level which is not observable to a Geertzian (1973) 'reading' of cultural text.[6]

How one balances the values-divide from the structural-divide varies considerably among scholars, but it does so within a shared framework which correlates particular institutions to social segmentation. In plain language, then: structure still exists. This is true even if anthropologists – by virtue either of their methodology or ideology – are much less likely to perceive it in the ultra-diverse, disembedded character of industrial postmodernity (Giddens 1990). But that does not render a structural-functionalist analysis impotent. It merely requires more of what Malinowski (1948) thought of as a kind of 'imaginative insight' where ethnographic observation is much more tenuous. We may observe it at a personal level – such as I have done numerous times within individual families – but without access to this kind of knowledge, our cup is half-full of meaning and half-empty of function. Structure has not disappeared, and the tools of symbolic anthropology are as capable as ever for making sense of it. Thus, one objective of this chapter is to partly reconcile the methodological antagonism between an estranged positivism and a shallow interpretivism. It trusts in Weber's (2019) intuition that there remains some potential for epistemological settlement between them.

6.2 Seventeen Million 'Fudge Offs'

The 2019 general election, resulting in a resounding 80-seat majority for the pro-Brexit Conservative Party led by Boris Johnson, took place on 12 December. A brief period of counting and inevitable political tussling followed between the results and the formation of the new government on 16 December, after which the usual Christmas lull marked the end of a period of marked antagonism between the polarised factions created by the referendum result. Only a few weeks later, on 31 January 2020, the United Kingdom was to formally relinquish all relations of membership with the European Union (EU). This day, known to many Brexiters as 'Brexit Day' or even 'Independence Day', was marked by a number of cultural gimmicks, including the circulation of a new 50p coin, a small light display at No. 10 Downing Street, and the public illumination of government buildings in the colours of the Union Jack. A small counter-protest on the South Bank of the river Thames drew a modest crowd of spectators whose primary purpose seemed to be the mourning over such an inauspicious occasion as Brexit.

That evening, I was eager to return to more participant-observation. I had experienced little over the inevitably quiet Christmas period that acted as a stopgap between months of vigorous campaigning and the rejuvenation of life that would follow the New Year. Little did I realise, of course, that the events of the 31st January would be one of the last times that I would be able to attend a popular, public occasion before the first series of coronavirus-induced lockdowns that would define nearly the entirety of the rest of my fieldwork. In full ignorance of what was to come, I travelled down to Parliament Square outside Westminster in order to explore and understand what was termed 'Brexit Day' by the *Leave Means Leave* campaign, an organisation adjacent to the Brexit Party. I knew that there would be celebrations in the evening to mark the UK's final and unequivocal exit from the EU. Given the type of interlocutors that would be heading down there, I had a rough idea of what to expect from the evening. But I found that the overall experience of the 'Brexit Day' celebrations far surpassed what I anticipated and addressed many of the core anthropological issues that I had been exploring from my earlier research.

Upon arriving at Parliament Square, the most immediate quality of the spectacle was the combination of people and colours. Thousands of individuals had filled the square: so much so that roads had to be blocked off in order to accommodate them. Underneath the stage was nothing less than an ocean of British flags. These comprised mostly the Union Jack – symbolising the unity of all four nations – in addition to the various English flags which also peppered the crowd. Such symbols are of course primarily the public representation of each country, but it is unambiguously discernible to any sensitive observer that they also function as a potent cultural artefact. Both the Union Jack and the English flag were employed through the campaigns as the counter-image to the blue and gold star image of the EU. The local and the transnational were symbolised through these powerful symbols. In addition, a number of smaller and lesser-known flags were present: the green and white flag of Devon, the three lions of the Royal Arms of England, and even flags with pictures of the Cenotaph war memorial on them. These were marbled by a number of politically partisan light blue Brexit Party flags were percolated throughout the cold but throbbing crowds of that chilly December night.

Beyond flag displays, another curious feature of this celebration were the many signs – often little more than cardboard cut-outs with black marker on them – that mingled with the colourful displays of nationalist pride. There were a number of different messages written on them, including: 'Let's go, WTO!',[7] 'Our Country Again', 'Sorry from ME to EU', 'Lock Up The Traitors', 'BORIS = BRINO',[8] 'FREXIT',[9] 'Our Own Rules', 'I AM ONE – WE ARE ONE – 17.4 MILLION', 'Corrupt UK Police Cover up Autism Hate Crime', and even 'Q': the letter symbolising the elaborate conspiracy theory that Donald Trump is being persecuted by a cabal of cannibalistic paedophiles. All of these various placards spoke to broader sense that Brexit was, at least among a considerable proportion of voters, derived from a sense of rapid sociocultural change (such that one has lost and now regained 'our country'), authoritarian personality structures (punishing treasonous outgroups), and a sense of wholeness in the 'pure people' that voted for Brexit ('we are one'). It is of course debatable how much one can genuinely gauge from noting down placards at the celebration, but I believe that they do align neatly with a great deal of the high-quality research on this area. In combination with many of the flags that were also on display, they gave a certain public voice to views that had otherwise been hidden, ignored, ridiculed, and suppressed by mainstream opinion. They were a celebration of the local and the national. But they also mingled with the kind of conspiratorialism that often accompanies great distance from the centre of political power (Gray 2020), highlighting the connection between Brexit and the sociocultural periphery.

Another note of interest was the people themselves. The vast majority – although certainly not the entirety – of the people gathered here in central London were ethnically White British. In both talking and observing them, it is obvious that they were clearly less formally educated than the majority of the Remainer activists that I had spent considerable time with. This once again reflected the empirical reality that those with tertiary education were much less likely to have voted for Brexit, at least on straightforward statistical terms (Sobolewska and Ford 2020). A number of individuals even took the time to have dressed up in pantomime gear for the occasion. One man was dressed entirely in a Union Jack suit – including cowboy hat and glasses. Another man had taken the time to find a medieval knight's costume, one draped with the traditional English flag. A small group of four women also dressed in Union Jack themed dresses, topped with classic 19th-century hats. A great many people in the group had dressed in a much less ostentatious way than these particular individuals, but even they had still come dressed quite significantly in the red, white, and blue of the national emblem. The entire atmosphere of the celebration was pervaded by a great sense of festivity and carnival – as if this Westminster space, normally reserved for social elites, had been finally taken over and reconquered by a group motivated and energised by an entirely distinct worldview and accompanying set of cultural symbols.

The first few hours of the celebration involved mostly loitering around the area: people were drinking beers, smoking cigarettes, and generally idling in Parliament Square. At the front of, perpendicular to the Houses of Parliament, hands had already been taken up to build an enormous stage for the performances which were to arrive sometime later on in the evening. On top of it was a gigantic television channel to beam out the speakers who would appear in a short time. Multicoloured forms of smoke would constantly gush out of the general infrastructure, and the stage front itself was covered in an eerie blue light that beamed out in front of the people who wished to be as close to the front of the action as possible. Despite the thousands of people in attendance, there was nothing by way of the kind of mob violence that attends other English demonstrations involving copious drinking of alcohol.

The only sad exception to this was the instance, at one point later on in the evening, when a group of people decided to stamp on and destroy an EU flag. Ground down into the mud, it was a tragic and pointless instance of how curiously zealous people can be about cultural symbols which appear to have such modest impact on their actual day-to-day lives. Such instances necessarily invite and merit a deeper anthropological analysis, although I myself was barely privy to the flag destruction and felt myself in reasonable insecurity among people who certainly would have seen me as some kind of enemy. It remained of genuine interest how such an abstraction like an EU flag could invite such unnecessary hatred and fury that trampling on a flag represents, given how little de facto influence it had on daily life in the UK. Were it not for the fact that it must function as a simulacrum for something else that was emotive enough to stimulate a response of physical desecration of a political symbol, I couldn't quite make sense of why it was so ground up in the Westminster mud.

By later on in the night, the actual Brexit celebrities were ready to make their appearance and began, one by one, to take their place on stage. It began with Richard Tice, head of the *Leave Means Leave* group and then Brexit Party MEP. He gave a eulogy to the power of "democracy" which "prevailed over the establishment... prevailed over big business and *Project Fear*... prevailed over the mainstream media". Announcing the "action-packed" line-up of songs and the welcome of a brand-new future for a nation which would be independent, sovereign, proud, and confident. Shortly following, three women entered the stage for the begging of everyone singings 'Land of Hope and Glory', a fiercely patriotic anthem of the imperial era that sings of the power and majesty of the UK. Indeed, this folksy aesthetic chimed with the rest of the costumes and flag waving of the rest of the evening, and indeed perhaps much of the rest of the campaign as a whole. It seemed an echo that was vaguely reminiscent of what Barnett (2012) calls 'Churchillism': the aesthetic involving jingoistic, flag-waving Britishness that was last seen on mass during the Falklands War in 1982.

Next on stage was Ann Widdecombe, one of the most famous Brexiter candidates who featured prominently in the Chapter 1. She gave a rousing speech in which she extolled the virtues of living in a "free country with a glorious future", and the virtues of the "quiet people and ordinary people" who despised politicians, wanted to live in a state of national liberty, and above all saw "nothing wrong with patriotism". In a similar tone to the many speeches that she had made over the course of campaigning for the Brexit Party a few months earlier, Ann took the public position that the EU represented the danger of a "super state" compared to a "sovereign state", a problem especially nefarious given that Europe was trying to "prop us up" and "tell us what to do". Of course, almost all of the statements she had were verifiably questionable if not downright fabrications of the nature of European power-sharing arrangements. But the audience reaction was predictably profoundly supportive: she received generous applause both at the end and throughout the modest speech that she made to thousands of true believers of the Brexit cause.

The next presenter on stage was Tim Martin, famously a publican landlord who owned a chain of *Wetherspoons*: famously known as the cheapest pub in the UK that had a wildly successful brand as a place that was affordable to near enough everyone. Martin had had little political presence before the Brexit campaign, at which he came out as viscerally pro-Leave and donated hundreds of thousands of pounds to anti-EU organisations. In his speech, he outlined that the vote was not against "European people" but "European institutions", many of whom have worked hard (especially as bartenders for him) in businesses across the UK. His announcements made a special point that Brexiters should be "magnanimous in victory" and should stay friends with Remainers. He also argued that "we know what we voted for", and that this vote was "a vote for democracy… it wasn't a vote for xenophobia". He ended with a plea not to sign away a trade deal based on "500 pages…. that only the Attorney General can understand". This last lament invoked the American Revolutionists, who he claimed: "were not worried about signing a deal at the Boston Tea Party". Such thoughts were iterations of his general suspicion, one I had noted throughout the months of campaigning for the Brexit Party, that legal wrangling and excessive formalisation of legal treaties were a kind of confidence trick – one based fundamentally on mystification – which obscured the nature of elite power by wrapping it up in inscrutable legalese jargon.

Following Widdecombe and Martin was the most significant individual for my interpretation. On stage arrived the popular comedian/author Dominic Frisby, who was famous for penning a series of books mostly about lower taxation, small-state and, more recently, the power of crypto-currencies to challenge the power of the government. He was also selected in the 2019 general election to run for the constituency of Old Bexley and Sidcup, although he and many others were later stood down by Nigel Farage in order not to challenge pro-Brexit Conservative Party dominance. An increasingly famous figure on the libertarian right, he was interviewed before the election as part of Farage's media push, including a video in which he gave his perspective on the civilisational nature of tax-collection, the left-wing proclivities of mainstream comedians, and the rise of the digital nomad. All of this was buttressed by Farage interspersing their shared mission as people who fought against what they termed the "nightmare globalist vision" of Brussels.

On stage, Frisby arrived wearing his characteristic stage outfit of top-hat and purple waistcoat. As with the other speakers, he was surrounded by the other flags that gave the impression of an almost anachronistically jingoistic idea of modern Britain. All of these together certainly gave credence to the theory that populist politics can be greatly defined in folksy aesthetic terms (Moffitt 2016). Announcing that he was going to sing several pieces, he said that "this first song is about how there are two sides to everything". Accompanying his voice was an organ instrument which hit a note each time he made a point or named an individual in each song. His first song that he sang that night ran as such:

> They said he's a misogynist, a liar and a cheat,
> An alt-right sexual predator, uncontrolled and indiscrete,
> Of colluding with the enemy, and reason, he's accused,
> Of sexual misconduct, of distributing fake news,
> A lying, narcissistic, national threat, yet...
> Maybe Donald Trump is not all bad!
> I know the very thought will make you mad... But...
> Markets up, taxes are down, he's talking to North Korea,
> Dealt with Iran, doesn't like Sadiq Khan, is there really all that to fear?
> Maybe Donald Trump is not all bad!
> They said impartial and at times even inspired,
> Its many finest moments, oh so fondly we recall,
> This cherished national treasure, that is loved by one and all,
> It educated, it informed, it entertained,
> All the same,
> Maybe we should rethink the BBC!
> Why do we need state-supplied T.V.?
> It's oh-so pious and riddled with bias,
> Could its programmes be any blander?
> Don't watch it you say? You still gotta pay, for this statist propaganda!
> Why should the licence fee be mandatory?

They said she was a strategist, of judgement sound and true,
Experienced and competent, consistent through and through,
Though lacking in charisma, she is forceful and refined,
A strong and stable leader, for these dark and dangerous times,
This shrewd operator has it so well planned,
On the other hand,
Thank the Lord – Theresa May has gone!
Christ, she went on and on and on!
Her Brexit's insane, incompetence reigns, its chaos unabated,
Never said what she thinks about anything, it's like she's automated…
Thank the Lord – Theresa May has gone!

The response to this first song was tumultuously positive – especially at the criticism of the BBC. (One thread which connected many of my Brexiter interlocutors was a genuine animosity towards the BBC). Next, Frisby announced that the following song involved a lot of "industrial" language, and that he was told not to swear on stage, as it would constitute a public order offense. Instead, he said that he would swap out the word 'fuck' for the word 'fudge' but if the audience wanted to sing the key word, it "was their decision and not [his]". The song began:

On the 21st of June, in 2016, the people of the United Kingdom,
And Gibraltar! Went to vote,
On an issue for some that had been burning for years,
The question in full and unaltered was – and I quote:
"Should the United Kingdom remain a member of the European Union,
Or leave the European Union?",
It was the greatest democratic turnout in British history,
I do not scoff,
And when the time came to speak,
The British said Fudge [Fuck] off,
Fudge [Fuck] off..
Campaigning had gone on for many a month,
With debates and discussion on many a front,
They'd argued, they fought, they'd smeared and pulled stunts,
There was David Cameron, Theresa May, George Osbourne, Tony Blair,
John Major, and the BBC…
The British told them to fudge [fuck] off
17 million fudge [fuck] offs.
"If you vote to leave you'll lose your job",
"If you vote to leave you'll lose your home",
"The ensuing recession will last for years",

Said David Cameron, Theresa May, George Osbourne, and the Treasury,
Tony Blair, John Major,
And the BBC, the Bank of England, Mark Carney, the EU, the IMF,
The US President, Saint Obama – "back of the queue",
Loads of celebrities, Gary Lineker, J.K. Rowling, Benedict Cumbertwit,
Lord Adonis – who the fucks he anyway?
The British told them to fudge [fuck] off,
17 million fudge [fuck] offs.
They called in the experts to tell us what's right,
They gave us the benefit of their foresight,
"To leave is calamitous", that's definite,
Food shortages, planes grounded, no medicine, a house price crash, half a million jobs lost, cost of £4,300 to every home, riots, stock market collapse, no sandwiches..
"There'll be an outbreak of super gonorrhoea" – they seriously said that,
Donald Tusk at the EU said it will be the end of western civilisation as we know it,
And one more thing: if you vote to leave that makes you racist.
The British told them to fudge [fuck] off,
17 million fudge [fuck] offs.
A general election was finally called,
I think you know where we told them to go,
We won't need to hear from them ever again!
From who? I've got a list!
From Tony Blair, John Major, John Bercow…
I can't tell you how much pleasure it gives me to say that,
Jo Swinson – LOL!
All those MPs that switched parties without holding a byelection,
Chuka Umana, Sarah Wollaston, Anna Soubry – not a Nazi!
All the MPs who did the opposite of what they promised in their manifestos,
Dominic Grieve, David Gauke, Philip Hammond, Oliver Letwin, Ed Vaizey – dick!
All those patronising Labour MPs who know so much better than you,
Emily Thornberry, Diane Abbot, Jess Philips, Jeremy Corbyn,
That weird one with glasses, long surname,
Hilary Benn – Hilary is a girl's name, what's that all about?
The Civil Service,
The Bank of England,
The EU, the IMF, half of Hackney, Guy Verhofstadt, Emmanuel Macron, the Commentariat,
Jolyn 'Moron', Andrew Marr, Femi weirdo, Aaron Bastani, Gina Miller,
All the celebrities, Hugh Grant, Gary Lineker, Lilly Allen, Steve Coogan, Nish Kumar,

Lord Adonis – who the fudge [fuck] is he anyway?
The British told you to fudge [fuck] off,
17 million fudge [fuck] offs.

This bawdy singing was followed by another speaker, and then the crowd was encouraged to sing along to the tune of "Rule Britannia": another overtly nationalistic tune that Armitage (2000, p. 173) sees as encapsulating the British Empire with its "mixture of adulterated mercantilism, nationalistic anxiety and libertarian fervour". It certainly continued to have a powerful resonance for the thousands of people who gathered at Parliament Square that evening. Curiously, the anthem itself would also be resurrected some eight months later, when rumours that the BBC would 'cancel' *Rule Britannia* after the *Black Lives Matter* movement and a number of individuals came out to say that it was a racist anthem. Clearly, the song had an influential place as one of the many cultural artefacts that deeply resonated with people's location in the 'culture war' – one that I noticed tended to align with a general disposition towards Britain's colonial past.

A number of other people came on stage following these songs to vocalise a sentiment which had been only somewhat articulated discursively. Michelle Dewberry, just before the clock struck, said that "It's not about the people over there [pointing at No.10]. It's not about the elites. It's not about the establishment. It's about you guys!". A similar notion was echoed by Farage, who announced that the battle against "the establishment" had finally been won after decades of campaigning to get the UK out. He also claimed that:

> "The only reason we're here tonight is because Westminster became utterly detached from ordinary people in this country. And those people started to speak. Those people started to rise. Those people forced a referendum. Those people forced a general election and those people despite all the flaws in our system, for the first time in history, that people have beaten the establishment".

One last observation of this tumultuous event was that many of the speakers clearly desired that the social body would once become whole and no longer fractured and polarised by the results of the referendum. Michelle Dewberry, for instance, celebrated the fact that after midnight "there will be no such thing as Leavers and Remainers". Julia Hartley-Brewer, another right-wing talk show host, also gave a speech in which she said mocked that some people feel ashamed to British, and that this night made her intensely proud to be so:

> "We have been a nation divided since 2016. But it didn't have to be that way. And we can end all of that division tonight at 11pm. Now is the

time for us to all come together. Now whether you voted for Brexit, which I have a funny feeling quite a lot of us did, or whether you didn't vote for Brexit, whether you love Brexit or whether you hate Brexit, that doesn't matter anymore. All we ask of you however you voted is that you will accept the democratic mandate for Brexit to happen. And tonight, we Brexiters hold out the hand of friendship to you and to ask you to join us in celebrating tonight".

The preoccupations of speakers clearly resonate with my argument in Chapter 1, in which I argued that Brexit was in some sense a 'ritual of renewal' in which society could be made whole again. The addition to this suggested by what I have shown here demonstrates not only that leaving the EU was an attempt to refashion social wholeness, but that there was also a conscious awareness that Brexit itself had caused an even deeper sense of division and polarisation in the UK. To an extent, this seemed to an admission that the cure was worse than the disease – especially given the total rejection of the 'reality principle' (Freud 1991) in assuming that deep divisions over Brexit would miraculously be healed after the UK formally left. If anything, hindsight shows that this was simply a lull before another round of proxy conflict – this time involving responses to the coronavirus pandemic – would erupt only a few months later.

6.3 Rabelais in London

The significance of this ethnographic moment made sense only much later than the event itself. If any words could characterise the 'Brexit Day' celebration, I believe that they were: satirising, undermining, ridiculing, perhaps even taking revenge. While my interpretation will always be vulnerable to the distorting tendencies of my own psychological bias, the event truly did feel extraordinary, both in content and form. Much of the symbolic landscape of the evening was a complete inversion of the way things normally are. For instance, the proliferation of waved flags were clearly sending a message in a social context where flag-waving is usually seen as vulgar, low status behaviour. (This is of course unless they belonged to the EU). The jingoism and bawdy placards were coarse signs of what seemed like a genuine sense of anger against the group of people understood as 'the establishment'. The notion that this was somehow a victory against 'them' was palpable in the discussions of people in the crowd. Despite what those on stage said, it was unclear whether this was a moment of reconciliation or togetherness, let alone magnanimity in victory. The fact that the keynote song involved the repeated use of the term 'fuck off' captured this sense of what Brexit was really about far more succinctly than many than many sociological analyses could. It seemed to be *quite literally* about telling a certain group of people to 'fuck off' – a coarse but straightforward way of stating something that some scholars have preferred to label 'anti-politics' (Beveridge and Featherstone 2021). The joyous delight in tension-release felt unmistakeable. But was it real?

While 'anti-politics' may be useful category to political scientists, it is hardly an anthropological or ethnographic term. It thus does not completely help us to make sense of the event in ways that resonate with our own 'moral order' of disciplinary thinking (Lederman 2004). So let us now consider how to contextualise the emotions of our ethnographic moment within a more anthropological framework. In doing so, I hope to situate this event not only as meaningful on its own terms and for those who participated in it, but also as another manifestation of shared patterns in cultural life. It is thus fully open to a Geertzian (1973) interpretation and opens all the opportunities that come with generalisation. This is not to say, of course, that the Brexit Day represents a *universal* aspect of human experience, something contemporary anthropologists tend to be wary of theorising. But it certainly seems to epitomise a process of relating between groups which has clear antecedents in history.

Thus, although descriptive terms like 'vulgarity', 'coarseness', 'folksy', 'bawdy', or similar characterisations undoubtedly resonate to some degree, they can only be made sense of in their cultural context through integration with a broader theoretical perspective. What I wish to utilise in this chapter is Mikhail Bakhtin's idea of the carnival and the *carnivalesque* – most notably development in his most famous works, *Problems of Dostoyevsky's Poetics* (1984a) and *Rabelais and His World* (1984b). Bakhtin's work is remarkably anthropological for a scholar of literature, and there has been a considerable growth in scholarship which adopts his terms in order to apply them to specific ethnographic contexts. Although he has been mostly appreciated as a literary and linguistic figure, his work has resonance for social theory owing to the concepts he derived from medieval history.

Bakhtin believed that the *carnivalesque* is an inescapable component of human psychology and re-emerges cross-culturally. It can be defined in terms of a total expression of ritual and festivity, a kind of speech-genre which manifests diachronically across time. He uses the term in two ways: in a narrow sense of festivities and feasting celebrated throughout the year, and also in the more expansive sense of festive practices which developed during the Medieval and Early Modern Europe. Although its content will necessarily be as contingent and heterogeneous on the context in which it is expressed, the form itself is deeply rooted in the human psyche and can never be totally expunged. For this reason, we are likely to see very similar iterations of carnival behaviour throughout history, such as Rome, Greece, or South America (Testa 2021). All of them can be loosely defined as incorporating ritual spectacles (like shows or pageants), comic compositions (like parodies and satires) and heraldry, oaths, curses, and other genres of popular folk humour.

Beyond the basic fact of a being a popular and mass gathering of people, all of these examples of carnival involve the same basic interplay of cultural forces. One general characteristic of carnival is the use of role-play and dressing up. And as I noted, a great variety of people came to the party dressed up in all manner of fancy costumes: Union Jack suits, Medieval knights, 19th-century gentlemen, dancing girls, and so on. They all speak to the fact that in the public squares of the Renaissance, people would use masks and costumes to create temporary identities and disengage from customary power structures and social boundaries (Castle 1986). As Bakhtin says:

> "these masks take on an extraordinary significance... they grant the right not to understand, the right to confuse, to tease, to hyperbolize life; the right to parody others while talking, the right not to be taken literally, not to be oneself".
>
> *(Bakhtin 1981, p. 163)*

This aesthetic is one of the irreducible components to the quality of the *carnivalesque*, and I argue that we can see it expressed quite conspicuously in this ethnographic context.

In a more holistic sense, though, Bakhtin defines an event as *carnivalesque* based on four key characteristics. The first and perhaps most important component of carnival is *profanation*. This means that the traditional rules of piety and reverence towards the customs and norms of authority are publically denuded. Partly this may refer to the mock crowning and de-crowning of moral authority in the form of the carnival king, something Bakhtin believes represents the playful manipulation of the normal world. He says:

> "crowning/decrowning is a dualistic ambivalent ritual, expressing the inevitability and at the same time the creative power of the shift-and-renewal, the joyful relativity of all structure and order, of all authority and all (hierarchical) position... this act, as it were, opens and sanctifies the inside-outside world of carnival".
>
> *(Bakhtin 1984a, p. 124)*

Piety, an irreplaceable feature of all societies weld together by traditional authority, is diminished in periods of *carnivalesque* revelry in its opposite: the obscene, the debased, and what Bakhtin calls the 'bringing down to earth'. During the carnival, all that is held to be lofty and high becomes inverted and dragged back to everyday world of most people, in which the lofty and transcendent values are rejected in favour of the carnal celebration of that which is earthy and unpretentious. It is a time for the inversion of things.

In our ethnographic context, the songs that were sung and reciprocated were indeed so vulgar that it would have been a public order offense for

Frisby to have actually pronounced them. Line after line of each song, high-status and elite individuals (like Tony Blair, Lord Adonis, David Cameron, Barack Obama) were targeted not only for attack but for direct 'bringing down to earth' in the Rabelaisian style. Andrew Adonis in particular – a former New Labour politician who took on the mantle as one of the most vociferously pro-European spokespeople during and after the campaign – was singled out to be publically pilloried and denuded of his influence ("who the fuck is he anyway?"). Indeed, I believe that he is singled out to be 'brought down to earth' *precisely* because his (seemingly unearned) peerage as a Lord elevates him higher than the others. Barack Obama was referred to as "Saint Obama", too, and most everyone else were referred to as patronising idiots who "think they know so much better than you" (i.e., privy to a kind of superior wisdom). The ridicule and hatred directed against those who the crowd saw as too high, transcendent, or spiritual, characterised the entire evening. These festivities were defined by a collective endeavour to destroy whatever pretentions such individuals had to moral authority in British public life.[10]

A second characteristic of the *carnivalesque* which see here is what Bakhtin calls *eccentricity*. This means that behaviour which is characteristically improper becomes – for one brief moment – acceptable. Gestures, languages, customs, and taboos which are socially off-limits transform and become appropriate and indeed encouraged. For Bakhtin, carnival was a place "for working out, in a concretely sensuous, half-real and half-play acted form a new mode of inter-relationships between individuals, counterposed to the all-powerful socio-hierarchical discourse of non-carnival life" (1984a, p. 123). During the medieval era of carnival, the constricting and exploitive relationships between masters and vassals could be briefly loosened. These moments also opened up a space for people to redefine their relationships to authority – although both then and today it remains questionable whether this actually had any effect on the materiality of power relations. The suspension of hierarchies, conventions and norms necessarily involved a different mode of communication. This would be a language which "permits the latent sides of human nature to reveal and express themselves" (ibid). Carnival would allow for a discourse that was "freed from authority of all hierarchical positions," one which gave space to individuals to truly express how they felt about those in power (ibid).

One of the material ways in which this happened was the excessive use of verbal profanities. Bakhtin saw swearing as integral to the process of carnival, for it represented a new form of open communication. In normal Renaissance life, profanities were "excluded from the sphere of official speech because they broke its norms; [and] they were therefore transferred to the familiar sphere of the marketplace" (Bakhtin 1984b, p. 17). Moreover, styles of speech, discourse, and gesture were all much more frank in the carnival square: "permitting no distance between those who came in contact with each other and liberating from norms of etiquette and decency imposed at other times" (Bakhtin 1984b, p. 10). In places like the medieval square during carnival, then, the cursing, and profanity emerge freely and without the fear of punishment for surpassing moral boundaries of civilised public life.

During the Brexit Day celebration, we can see this process quite clearly in the excessive use of swearing, something which the singer Frisby himself admitted "would be a public order offense" if made more explicit. Indeed, I have personally never in my life – despite the hundreds of rallies, demos, marches, and events that I have participated in – ever seen or heard such a gratuitous use of offensive language in public space. It is difficult to communicate the unreality of thousands of people chanting "fuck off... fuck off... fuck off" in Parliament Square, next to Westminster Abbey. Even by modern cultural standards, this eccentric behaviour would not be acceptable in any real public context – and certainly never in a legitimate political one. Not only was there no resistance to this, it was positively reinforced and adored by the crowd. It seemed to me quite patent that there was a kind of release of pent-up energy in these expressions of gratuitous swearing and abuse directed at the people who were seen to be looking down on Brexiters.

This point dovetails with Bakhtin's insistence that laughter is an irreplaceable component of the characteristic of *eccentricity*. Laughter has the "power of making an object come up close, of drawing it into a zone of crude contact where one can finger it familiarly on all sides, turn it upside down, inside out, and peer at it from above" (Bakhtin 1981, p. 23). The ambivalence towards social and moral order that is played with during carnival is expressed through both grotesque realism and the laughter which accompanies the turning upside down of convention, language, hierarchy. But for Bakhtin, when the higher is degraded and brought down to earth, it is not in order to destroy it. Rather, he claims that "to degrade an object does not imply merely hurling it into the void of nonexistence, into absolute destruction, but to hurl it down to the reproductive lower stratum, the zone in which conception and new birth take place" (1984a, p. 21). The point is that when moral authority is degraded through laughter and profanity – as we see during these crude public jokes – it generates a fertile space for exposing the "popular truth" of the arbitrariness and artificiality of the social order (Bakhtin 1984b, p. 94). This Brexit carnival purposefully and necessarily induced hilarity, mocking and laughter towards those who "think they know so much better than you" as part of its *carnivalesque* theatre and demonstration that the inevitability of economic and political unification was simply an illusion.

Another defining feature of laughter is the freedom which it enjoys. It acts as a celebration of permissiveness, something which is indelibly connected to the speech-controls that are central to the political structures of everyday life.

Laughter represents the freedom during limited feast days in which all the tensions and constrictions of everyday life can be released for even just a brief moment. It emanated out of "the great generic body of the people" as an expression of relief and expansion from a period of painful contraction and exploitation (Bakhtin 1984b, p. 88). In our ethnographic context, the vulgarity and coarseness of both the singing and the general atmosphere stands in contrast to professional-managerial culture, which tends to be distinguished by elaborate speech codes about marginalised social groups (Friedman, 2019). Cases like this represent an unequivocal rejection of the ethos of political correctness which dominates among higher-status groups in the West. We can observe a similar phenomenon happening with Donald Trump. Much of his support was built directly on his blatant rejection of politically correct talk: a kind of release valve and celebration of transgressing speech-codes imposed by the upper-middle classes (Conway et al., 2017).

Furthermore, to a much less extent than the public cursing, I believe that the excessive use of Union Jack, English and regional flags may further index this peculiar characteristic of the *carnivalesque*. I think that we can understand the excessive use of flags as an additional example of what Bakhtin labels *eccentricity*. To do so requires a slightly deeper appreciation of the British cultural context. Many countries proudly and commonly display their national flags around both public and private spaces as a sacred object. The United States is probably the most potent example of this phenomenon (Shanafelt 2008). The UK is not: generally speaking, it is extremely rare to see a flag on any lawn, house, or institutional building except an explicitly political one. One is far more likely to see the LGBTQ+ or Ukrainian flag on churches, houses, schools, libraries, or any other civic buildings. This roughly translates to meaning that excessive displays of local regional flags (including the national one) are indeed displays of *cultural eccentricity*, which invert a commonly accepted custom of not publically displaying the British flag. This was demonstrated quite conclusively in the media episode involving MP Emily Thornberry's tweet of an English flag in 2014.[11] The point is that this moment of cultural inversion, in which British and English flags are everywhere celebrated, indexes a moment of strangeness, inversion, and eccentricity.

Thirdly, Bakhtin identifies *free and familiar interaction* as another integral component of carnival. This means that people who would otherwise have little to no interaction with one another, especially as they are separated by cultural barriers and economic hierarchies, can meet in a socially open space. Such a situation means that the obstacles which prevent individuals from meeting at level of relative social equality. All customary identifications like age, social status, wealth, rank, reputation or gender are disregarded in this sphere, allowing a complete unburdening of the complex social relationships which normally define the social world of obligations, group dialects, and norms about interaction. Given this, we would expect to see the *carnivalesque* occur in spaces which are the pinnacle of openness to the free-flow of individuals.

Indeed, this is what we can observe at the Brexit Day event, too. Parliament Square is perhaps one of the last open, public spaces left in modern Britain. This sad situation is owed in no small part to the extensive privatisation of public space in England, a change that has been noted by a number of scholars working in urban studies (Christophers 2019). It is compounded by the general decline in use of physical spaces of public engagement like churches or town halls, and the general collapse of collective organising which used to occur through these civil and religious institutions. For example, much of the fight against the slave trade in 19th-century England was organised through churches (Turley 1991). These spaces have seen a precipitous decline over the 20th and 21st century, especially due to the exponential rise in digital technology and social media (Turkle 2013).

During my several years of fieldwork, I went to Parliament Square probably close to one hundred times. This was almost always for some kind of Brexit related event: People's Vote, Grassroots for Europe, SODEM, and The European Movement were all various groups which at one point or another had an event in the square. On Wednesday mornings, I would visit SODEM nearly every Wednesday morning in order to participate in their activism. The important point was that their space in Parliament Square was only ever simply one protest among many. Over the years, there were demonstrations for Sri Lanka, Palestine, Ukraine, Hong Kong, animal rights, transgender rights, GMO crops, coronavirus lockdowns, the cost-of-living crisis, environmental damage, racism, *Black Lives Matter*, the legal system, the healthcare system, the housing crisis, the police, staying in Europe, leaving Europe, and many more.

The overall point here is that Parliament Square acts as one of the last public spaces for open, democratic, civil engagement. It is a location where people of all socio-economic stations, identities, beliefs or practices can meet in a safe, accessible and public arena in which to convey their message and debate. Unlike the many election rallies in Chapter 1, or indeed many of the pro-European conferences that required payment for entry, there were no barriers for anyone attending the Brexit Day celebrations that night of January 1st. It is true that there were obviously very few people from the anti-Brexit side that attended this carnival, and this speaks to a major criticism of my argument. Yet there was no real *obstacle* for anyone to participate in this party of they wanted to, and there were many instances in which people of a different class or social identity met on equal terms during the event. Bakhtin notes the importance of this kind of public space: "carnival knows neither stage nor footlights… but the central area could only be the square, for by its very idea carnival belongs to the whole people, it is universal, everyone must participate in its familiar contact" (1984b, p. 7). The importance of public spaces like the market square for carnival, both then and now, was that it provided a kind of unofficial public arena in which the people could feel their own sense of collectivity in an embodied sense (Bakhtin 1984b, p. 154).

Finally, Bakhtin claims that *carnivalistic mésalliances* is the fourth necessary feature of the phenomenon. What this translates to is the basic destruction and dissolution of dualistic categories which otherwise comprise our social world. The consequence is an integration of worldviews and relationships into a single reality: the intelligent and the stupid, the sacred and the profane, the high and low, are all dissolved during these moments of *carnivalesque* effervescence. This uniting of opposites is also that which offers the possibility of dialogue and reconciliation: together antagonistic polarities that characterise the everyday world meet and merge into a (perhaps fleeting) oneness that manages to transcend them both. The key is understanding how transformation can occur through the uniting of symbolic counterparts that produce something altogether new and distinct.

These *mésalliances* are quite evident in the Brexit Day celebration. The Remainer/Brexiter distinction has been by far the most corrosive and divisive split in the social body in living memory. It far surpasses any partisanship around political party or identity affiliation (Sobolewska and Ford 2020). There is no exaggeration in saying that this cleavage overwhelmingly defined democratic life in the UK since 2016, and indeed at the time of writing in 2022 largely still does so. It has transcended the divisions between Labour and Conservative which otherwise formed the principal symbolic contours of political affiliation in the 20th century. And as I have pointed to in Chapter 1, both these sides take as the Durkheimian sacred that which corresponds to their transcendent ideal. For many Remainers, that sacred is Europe; for Leavers, it is Brexit itself.

Let us recall, then, that Michelle Dewberry went on stage to proclaim that from midnight "there will be no such thing as Leavers and Remainers". Following her, Hartley-Brewer proclaimed that "we have been a nation divided" and that "we can end all of that division tonight at 11pm… now is the time for us to all come together". This was followed by the assertion that "whether you voted for Brexit [or not] … we ask of you… that you will accept the democratic mandate for Brexit to happen… and we Brexiters hold out the hand of friendship to you and ask you to join us in celebrating tonight". All of these examples reflect the Bakhtinian notion of *mesalliance* in which the dualistic separations come together to form one united whole. The carnival is that moment in which these divisions no longer define the social fabric but are integrated within a totality and overcome. All the opposites or contrasts which at one time characterised society are encouraged to disintegrate. As Bakhtin claims, carnival was a place "for working out, in a concretely sensuous, half-real and half-play acted form a new mode of inter-relationships between individuals, counterposed to the all-powerful socio-hierarchical discourse of non-carnival life" (1984a, p. 123). Then as now, this space provided the space for the renewal of fragmented social form, and the transforming of enmity and conflict between higher-status groups (Remainers) and lower-status ones (Brexiters).[12]

6.4 Is Carnival A Critique?

I have outlined several key concerns in this chapter so far. The first was understanding how we might apply an anthropological framework to the value-structure divides of modern societies. Second, I have discussed in great detail one example of what Gluckman (1940) would have called a "social situation " in the form of the Brexit Day celebration in Parliament Square. This event was highly symbolic and generatively charged illustration of how one structural segment (Brexiter) expressed itself in a moment of collective effervesce against another (Remainer). And while I would be careful not to generalise too much and claim that this group represented *all* Leave voters, it was clear from my participant-observation that the vast majority of attendants fit the schemata of them as analysed by sociologists like Sobolewska and Ford (2020); that is: less educated, less metropolitan, less cosmopolitan, and less wealthy. This was an empirical observation I made even if I was obviously unable to verify this claim in a replicable sense. The crowd were clearly more peripheral – both geographically and culturally – than any crowd of Remainers I had spent considerable time with since 2019. In other words, this is one half of a structural cleavage that we are analysing.

My ethnographic account of the 'Brexit Day' carnival demonstrates that not all structural tension is mediated through electoral means, as scholarship on the relationship between populism and values-structure divides have tended to emphasise. Instead, I have shown that Bakhtin's notion of the *carnivalesque* can help us make sense of what I witnessed in December 2019. There may be variations across cultures of how structural antagonism manifests: between 'upper' and 'lower' classes, 'masters' and 'serfs', 'winners' and 'losers' of globalisation, or those with 'materialist' and 'post-materialist' values, for example.[13] But in all these cases, the strains between the powerful and the powerless structural segments of a whole society come together in moments of regulation through ritualised subversion, satire, profanation, and a 'bringing down to earth' of overly lofty – i.e. *structurally distant* – groups. And although Bakhtin never explicitly says so – largely because he presents something of an underdeveloped framework for understanding social power – these collective rituals appear to iron out the tensions that have otherwise built up over time. This aligns with Radcliffe-Brown's (1940b) claim that ceremonies can be appreciated less in a nebulously 'cultural' way than as practice expressions of the structural need to regulate and restore a sense of dynamic equilibrium.

Yet, there is considerably more to this problem than meets the eye. For if we accept my basic proposition that this episode is an expression of structural divide, what remains is the basic problem of anthropology: how do we explain social change? If we perceive the *carnivalesque* as an attempt to regulate structural tension, as I indeed argue, the corollary enquiry asks whether or not anything actually changed. Do these irreverent *carnivalesque* events truly express a revolt against the *status quo*? Are they proto-revolutionary, in the sense in which Hobsbawm (2017) defines 'primitive rebels' as antecedent to socialists? To what extent do they merely leave the overall inequality of structure intact? Is laughter a genuine agent for transforming power relations or is it merely, as Scott (1985) might say, a kind of 'hidden transcript' or 'weapon of the weak'? These questions remain tremendously important for political anthropologists who are understand the mechanics of social, and in particular *revolutionary*, change (Cherstich et al. 2020). This is because the extent to which events like carnival can genuinely transform the social structure – rather than merely representing an elaborate means of offsetting inequality – have formidable implications for understanding whether there was anything genuinely counter-hegemonic in Brexit, as many of my socialist interlocutors truly believed.

Perhaps the best way to answer this question is to bring it in line with other ethnographic examples of when tensions between social cleavages are expressed through collective rituals but debates continue about their efficacy for genuine change. We can then link this back to Bakhtin's notion of the *carnivalesque*, and the critics who similarly question its truly subversive potential. The most salient illustration of this is from Gluckman's (1963) famous analysis of the Swazi-Ncwala celebration in his *Rituals of Rebellion in South-East Africa*. Drawing mostly from Kuper's (1947) ethnography, the text details the elaborate customs of *simeno* songs which (among other things) publically dispraise and ritually humiliate the king before his subjects. This was based in the relatively simple Bantu context in which the overarching social-structural cleavage is between the monarch and those under his authority. Genuine rebellions were common, and following Aristotle, one of their principles functions was to maintain the *office* of kingship even if the king as an *individual* was removed (Gluckman 1963, p. 129). This ensured the long-term stability of African kingdoms in the face of dissolution and breakdown.

The ethnographic *ritual* of rebellion is directly related to this *actual* rebellion, according to Gluckman, and he thinks that it maintains the political *status quo* at times of tension and destabilisation. But such 'rituals of rebellion' do not in actual fact alter very much at all. This is despite the otherwise highly irreverent and sacrilegious nature of profaning the king, not dissimilarly to the Bakhtinian observation that carnivals mock the established spiritual elite. Gluckman (1963, p. 112) claims that these ritual rebellions "proceed within an established and sacred traditional system, in which there is dispute about particular distributions of power, and not about the structure of the system itself... [which] allows for instituted protest, and in complex ways renews the unity of the system". In other words, these ceremonies only *seem* to change the existing order. The king himself may be totally subverted, and yet, nothing fundamentally shifts. Although in the Zulu context the cleavage is significantly less complex than in our society – being essentially between singular authority and his subjects – the overall sense is that ritual irreverence unifies and integrates two sides of a structural divide rather than challenging it. In my ethnography, this translates to the idea that the Brexit subversion of high-status and structurally dominant groups ultimately changes nothing at all. Even if the UK is now outside of the EU, the structural conditions which led to the vote underwent no authentic transformation.

We can think of the ineffectuality of carnival in a further two ways. One is that it is sanctioned by political authorities, and thus by definition it cannot thus have any genuinely subversive potential. The former approach is typified by Eagleton (1981), who adopts the view that carnival is little more than blowing off steam between antagonistic social forces. Even if there is extreme profanation and public subversion of moral authority, he argues, the reality is that carnival is fully sanctioned by the ruling class. If it wasn't, it wouldn't have been allowed to be staged at all. He argues that carnival is nothing more than the "permissible rupture of hegemony, a contained popular blow-off as disturbing and relatively ineffectual as a revolutionary work of art" (Eagleton 1981, p. 148). To apply this framework in this context, we could argue *contra* Farage's discourse that Brexit represented a popular rebellion against 'the establishment' that if was to truly change anything, it wouldn't have been allowed. Certainly, the Brexit Day event as a *carnivalesque* celebration of revolutionary transformation of the UK would have been shut down if it had *actually* threatened the *status quo*. Many of my 'Lexiter' informants argued that Brexit was imperative because the EU represented the forces of the transnational capitalist class and leaving would be the first step on the road to socialism. The reality is that nothing of the sort has happened since: suggesting a truth in Eagleton's argument that this type of populism does little to threaten class power which shapes neoliberal globalisation.

The second is that by transgressing public norms, carnival simply reifies their ontological stature, thus cannot midwife any genuine overcoming of them. Both would converge in their scepticism that *carnivalesque* moments like we observed in the Brexit Day celebration can truly reconcile antagonistic structural segments. Eco (1984) concurs in rejecting the subversive potential of carnival by adopting Aristotle's (1996) definition of comedy as an artform which is defined by its representation of low-life and antinomianism. The difference between comedy and tragedy, he argued, was that the latter is explicit about which moral laws are violated while the former presupposes them. Thus, during carnival the very 'rules' which are ostensibly being violated by the subversion of the event already presuppose their continued existence. In subverting authority, the population is once again reminded of the authorities' domination over them. They do not transgress the law but simply reinforce it: "they remind us of the existence of the rule... [and thus] the comic is only an instrument of social control and can never be a form of social criticism" (Eco 1984, p. 6).

In short, rather than offering a solution to the arbitrary domination of the ruling elite, carnival creates a sphere which nullifies any revolutionary potential of popular uprising. As Burke (1978, p. 284) more succinctly noted: "comedies built around situations of reversal and played during carnival frequently end... with a reminder of the audience that is time to set the world right up again". In other words, by ridiculing the loftiness of Remainers, my Brexiter interlocutors were ultimately reinforcing the sense that they were the subordinated strata. Laughing at cultural elites merely reminds them that they are not, and perhaps cannot ever be, cultural elites themselves.

Overall, then, my analysis has tried to evaluate the extent to which Bakhtin's notion of the carnival, something I observe ethnographically in the Brexit Day celebration, acts as a genuine agent of social fission and transformation. Bakhtin seems to think that the carnival process contains a genuine challenge to both official ideology and the domination of the ruling elite. But the evidence here favours the view that, like Gluckman's analysis of Zulu (1963), the *carnivalesque* nature of the celebration is little more than a safety-valve for popular discontent. This carries over to Brexit as a whole: it is indicative of structural *tension* but not structural *change*. The evidence that it has any transformational effect on the social world is weak. Public rituals of subversion or rebellion are therefore simply ways of reifying the political *status quo*. Perhaps our Brexit Day example was nothing more than another iteration of the powerlessness of globalisation's 'losers' to effect real change to their benefit, even if EU membership was a casualty in the process. This would certainly align with the overall framing the vote as a kind of 'cultural backlash' (Norris and Inglehart 2019), and support the overall contention that Brexit has done little to change the material facts of status decline and changing values of an increasing 'post-materialist' British population.

*

One last unconventional reading remains. What if both Gluckman and Bakhtin have made the same exact mistake in radically misinterpreting the role of laughter in this ritualised spectacles of revolt? Recall that in the former's ethnography, Swazi commoners tease, mock, and ridicule the king's impotence. Despite Gluckman's (1963, p. 126) distaste for psychological explanations in place of "sociological setting of the process", one approach could adopt a more Malinowskian (1948) functionalist reading to see the role of laughter as a way of dissipating psychological tension. This framework could also be applied during Renaissance carnival, where an analogous irreverence happens against the overbearingly coercive moral authorities of Church and monarch. In my ethnographic context, Remainers are mocked by Brexiters. Humour here is expressing something otherwise unsayable in normal situations, as my Bakhtinian reading of profanity and eccentricity has already suggested. However, there is another dimension to the role of humour which sees it neither in psychological nor individual terms but in structural and collective ones.

The most generative precedent for an alternative reading of this problem comes from Apter's (1983) argument undermining Gluckman's approach to the Swazi-Ncwala ritual. This view overcomes a reductionist approach by invoking Radcliffe-Brown's (1940a) article 'On Joking Relationships', in which the structural-functionalist details the numerous cross-cultural observations of something called 'permitted disrespect'. Normally these 'joking relationships' involving obscenity, profanity, teasing, ridicule, and public irreverence. They conventionally occur between those related by marriage (affines), those connected via lineal filiation, or between distinct clans or tribal organisation (Fortes 1945; Goody 1962; Rigby 1969). The phenomenon is broken down into two types: symmetrical and asymmetrical. These are contingent on the extent to which one side or the other is allowed to respond. Sometimes joking between individuals is reciprocated, but at others it is seen simply absorbed with good humour.

The point of these mocking and irreverent teasing rituals is that they should not be taken literally: there is only the "pretence of hostility and [instead] a real friendliness" (Radcliffe-Brown 1940a, p. 196). In all these cases of a 'joking relationship', the "structural situation underlying such examples is generically the same... involving both attachment and separation, both social conjunction and social disjunction, between the joking partners" (Apter 1983, p. 528). For example, those who are attached by marriage are separated by descent, and those who are attached by tribal mythology are separated by distinct associations of segmentary opposition. Each partner in these joking relationships must face the risk of antagonism and possible conflict, meaning that there is always the risk of a genuine outbreak of violence. Thus, "the function of the joking relationship is to buffer such potential conflict by expressing a sort of mock hostility that acknowledges both the possibility of conflict and the desire to avoid it" (ibid.). Conflict occurring at a structural level between distinct cleavages can be discerned through this public mocking. It both indexes a real possibility of enmity but also helps to dissipate it.

In Gluckman's (1967) case, the *simemo* songs can be read not as subversions of the king in support of kingship but rather as an *asymmetric joking relationship*. For Apter (1983), these songs are only taken to be reflective of genuine rebellious tendencies if they are interpreted in a *literal* sense. But they simply cannot be taken as such. Rather, they are actually signs of friendship and unity. They "do not mean what they say, but imply something of the opposite" (Apter 1983, p. 529). In fact, it would be *non-participation* in the ritual which would evoke the king's displeasure and risk signalling the growth of revolutionary momentum in the population. The joking relationship is in reality a sign that his subjects wish to keep structural relations on good terms. Laughter is not an act of genuine social subversion but an unconscious *acknowledgment* of the structural forces which always threaten the possibility of a traumatic rupture in the underlying dynamics of social life. The structural antagonism in the context of East Africa contains the potential for a catastrophic unravelling of bonds which connect the king to his subjects.[14] In short, we can see public joking not as a weapon of political subversion, nor as a release-valve for enmity, but as an admission of structural dependence and unity. Like the blood feud (Evans-Pritchard 1969), it is a cultural ceremony which functions to reinforce the delicate and unstable bonds between individuals, and keep the entire society in a state of equilibrium.

This interpretation takes the best from a structural analysis while potentially avoiding its downfalls. For Apter (1983, p. 530), Gluckman's view that "the positive function of ritual rebellion relates to the positive function of real rebellion... finds no support in Radcliffe-Brown's theory of permitted disrespect". Instead, we can take a simpler and more direct functionalist approach by seeing that this mock irreverence does not *subvert* the king's authority but acknowledges the potential for conflict *within* it. In a structural-functionalist sense, then, it works to regulate the underlying patterns of association across social cleavages which have the potential for catastrophic disruption. Indeed, we discern the 'joking relationship' at precisely those joints that are the weakest and most likely to vulnerable to collapse. Indeed, according to Kuper (1947), we see that the mock rituals are played before waging war – a time when the military structure was at its most likely to change.

Now, what I have explored in terms of the 'joking relationship' has clear salience for understanding both my ethnographic example and the Bakhtinian analogue utilised as an interpretative framework. As far as I am aware, however, no scholar has applied Radcliffe-Brown's theory directed to the notion of the *carnivalesque*. But it seems tremendously germane. After all, Bakhtin also frames the carnival through a cleavage model with a sharp delineation between two blocs: the ruling elite and the popular, the official and unofficial, and the serious and the joking, the 'naturalising' and the 'historicising'.[15] This is true even if such interpretations of 'the people' vaguely unhistorical, essentialising, and idealised (Clarke and Holquist 1984). We can see a generative analogue in the structural cleavage I have discussed between Remainers and Brexiters, the 'winners' and 'losers' of globalisation, or the 'post-materialists' and the 'materialists'. In both cases, a structural divide or cleavage running through society emerges in symbolic form as new partisan identities with clearly hostile attitudes towards one another. While this is normally managed at the level of democratic elections, the examples I have shown here suggest that there are other instances in which this underlying antagonism can manifest.

One final point of tremendously generative interest is that Radcliffe-Brown's analysis can further turn our assumptions about what the profanity and eccentricity of this *carnivalesque* moment was actually about. We've seen that it could be viewed as a moment of inversion and what van den Berghe (1963 p.414) characterises as the "blowing-off-steam" interpretation. But in line with Apter's critique of Gluckman, what we can perhaps read is that the profanity is evidence not of structural fission but of structural *fusion*. The Swazi-Zulu *simemo* songs are permitted disrespect precisely because the subjects want to *support* the king: they want to ensure that any cleavage separating the two doesn't break off and cause the whole structure to collapse. In short, the ridicule is indicative of an unconscious desire to fuse the social distance, acknowledge potential conflict, and bring the conflictual segments together again.

Perhaps, then, we can see the same thing in Brexit Day celebration: the profanity against the Remainer segment may be less about genuinely desiring separation than it is trying to smooth over the antagonisms which have torn apart the entire country. This includes almost every family in the UK, as I observed during my research on the matter. After all, most of the speeches at the event involved an invitation or provocation to 'come together' in some way and repair the damage of Brexit before moving on. We cannot help but suspect that an unconscious desire for unity after so much enmity might be the underlying cause. Joking and public mockery might not, in the end, index either genuine subversion or letting off steam. Instead, what they could represent are the unconscious frustrations of a society torn about by a polarising referendum, and a strong desire to acknowledge conflict in order to move past it.

6.5 Conclusion

This chapter has focused on one simple example of a "social situation" (Gluckman 1940) in the Brexit Day celebration on 31 January 2020. But this has been merely as a provocation towards understanding two fundamental points. The first was that our disciplinary toolkit was custom fitted for traditional and small-scale societies. These have been very favourable for the production of theories concerning inter-group conflict and consensus, such as in the works of the early structural-functionalist school (Stocking 1995). But such frameworks are attuned to contexts of ethnographic data-collection which have largely disappeared both from the discipline and from the way in which most human beings live. Urbanisation, modernity, population explosion, secularism, nuclear families, alienation: it is radically different world for any potentially structural-functionalist anthropology. This is particularly problematic when making a comparative effort to understand how social segments operate within the macro-scale structural dynamics of fission and fusion (Evans-Pritchard 1969). Yet anthropological theorising of this type – that which focuses on large-scale structural change – is necessary for understanding a general polarisation within the modern world. This chapter addresses this conundrum by demonstrating that the merit and relevance of structural-functionalist theory remains compelling, even though we must place it in conversation with scholarship from other disciplines.

At the beginning of my chapter, I opened this pathway by drawing from the 'neo-cleavage' school of political sociology (Hooghe and Marks 2018). This theoretical framework articulates how the modern social divisions of Europe interact in terms of group cohesion and conflict. However, its methodology is somewhat distant to anthropology: examples include large-scale surveys and more quantitatively focused research instruments. Yet, I consider this not a barrier but an invitation to borrow from the empirical research of other disciplines. We may be comparatively unable to observe cleavages in society directly today, at least when we consider that scholars like Evans-Pritchard (1969) could personally witness battles between competing segments of a clan, or Gluckman (1963) the cleavage between king and his subjects. But that does not mean that structure does not exist anymore: it simply requires a scale of insight that other disciplines are more capable at obtaining. Understanding how social structure works in the contemporary world encourages us to develop cultural and symbolic observations about it, such as the role of 'joking relationships' (Radcliffe-Brown 1940) that I discussed towards the end of the chapter. 'Neo-cleavage' theory can be placed in conversation with the ideas and observations of structural-functionalism that open pathways towards a revitalised anthropology, one which speaks directly to the endemic social friction within the Western world.

Having set out this theoretical context, I then moved on to present my ethnographic material. I focused almost completely on one particular event – the Brexit Day celebration of the 31 January 2020. On this cold winter evening, thousands of people met up in London's Parliament Square to celebrate the legal beginning of Brexit and the termination of half a century of EU membership. The most compelling feature of this bizarre event was its carnivalesque character. In its eccentricity, its strangeness, its profanity and its colour, it was almost totally unlike almost any other moment of my fieldwork – or perhaps my entire life. The most generative theoretical interpretation that I brought to understanding it comes from Bakhtin (1981, 1984a, 1984b), whose work on the *carnivalesque* so wonderfully elucidates this ethnographic experience. It also makes overtures towards understanding what exactly Brexit was truly about. I therefore dedicated a substantial component of the chapter to putting them in dialogue with one another. One point to note is simply the ongoing salience of Bakhtin's theoretical work to anthropology, as it has done for a number of other scholars (Hill 1986; Knauft 1996).

Next, I combined this theoretical approach with my ethnographic material in a discussion about how the Brexit carnival might represent a ritual of fission between two polarised social segments: what neo-cleavage theorists think of as the 'winners' and 'losers' of globalisation (Goodhart 2017; Hobolt 2016; O'Rourke 2019). This I did by analogously drawing out a comparison with Max Gluckman's (1963) famous discussion of the Zulu 'rituals of rebellion'. Carefully likening Bakhtinian carnival to Gluckmanesque revolt, I explored whether these events can be said to act as genuinely subversive processes. To what extent can we understand Brexit or its celebration as an upheaval directed not at Europe per se but against a more privileged and liberal class? This question asks whether events like the carnival (or Brexit as a whole) merely reify and revitalise a *status quo*, one which allows those belonging to a structurally subordinated cleavage to figuratively 'blow off steam' in a brief moment of (perhaps pyrrhic) victory at the dismemberment of European co-operation. I concluded by suggesting that like the withdrawal itself, the *carnivalesque* performance of the Brexit Day celebration is indicative not of change but of stasis. It accomplishes almost nothing towards reversing the trends that have led increasing members of the population to feel ignored or forgotten, or whose values have been essentially undermined. It does, however, symbolically represent what social conflict in modern Britain looks like at a cultural level, rather than simply an electoral one.

This analysis can be taken one step further when we consider not only the negative but also the positive functions of laughter and profanity – two features of both the carnival and the rebellion. I agree with other scholars that humour has the functional effect of promoting subversive or counter-hegemonic behaviour (Bhungalia 2019), but I do not find this a compelling explanation in our case. Following Radcliffe-Brown's (1940) work on joking relationships, we see that it can also be interpreted as a way of unconsciously acknowledging and solidifying relationships which are in danger of collapse. From a structural-functionalist perspective, public satire may therefore emerge as a feature of this underlying tension and risk of disintegration. It arises principally when there is genuine risk that polarised social segments (such as between affines or descent-groups) could lead to violence or collapse. In this case, then, we might suggest that these kind of *carnivalesque* performances of Brexiters against Remainers are not genuine strategies of social fission – leading to the literal break-off of increasing alienated halves of the country – but rather a movement towards holism and unity. Certainly, many of the speeches from Brexiters that I observed during that night seemed to point in this direction. 'Coming together', 'moving on', 'putting the past five years behind us' – these discourses all emerged repeatedly alongside an inexplicable juxtaposition to chants of "fuck off... fuck off... fuck off" against Remainers. I argue that we can only make sense of these bizarre affinities with this unique epistemological framework, one which brings structural-functionalist analysis into conversation Bakhtinian interpretations of *carnivalesque* behaviour.

One of my key contributions is that not all important social antagonism emerges through the party systems and the ballot box. This is certainly the principal way in which competing social bases interact with one another from the perspective of political science (Marks et al. 2021). Of course, such an overall perspective is not wrong; if we understand populism as a resentful backlash to both globalisation and changing values-divides, it makes sense to centre our analysis on democratic electoral trends. But anthropology can bring its own unique contribution to the table by showing that the tension between structural segments has many more possible manifestations than this. It also emerges in ritual, play, dress, carnival, food, and family. We should not cede all the ground in 'populism studies' to theoretical orientations which ignore the totality of human culture in favour of niche fixations on general elections or leadership candidates. If European and American society is coming apart from relentless social-structural transformation, it must be happening at levels other than voting once every four years. Polarisation requires a much more holistic analysis than simply how preferences translate into political parties. The frustrations as well as the benefits of transnationalism have been disproportionately spread across the UK, and we are correct to see them emerge in a variety of ways that are amiable to our disciplinary expertise.

Notes

1 Later on, mass emancipation and the growth of the electoral franchise caused these divisions to essentially 'structure' political conflict and competition. The consequence was the traditional mass political party which defined the previous two centuries. Each was overtly tied to the interests of one cleavage or another; for instance, in the UK the Conservative Party represented the landed (and later bourgeois) interest, and the Labour Party represented the interests of the industrial working class.

2 The growing inequalities between prosperous and mobile graduates and economically redundant and peripheral school leavers produces acute tension, something more or less synonymous with the 'culture wars' (Lasch 1994). As a source of deep polarisation, it also results in the growth of national populism (Eatwell and Goodwin 2018). This is a phenomenon which we can view sociologically not in

terms of its conceptual or aesthetic character but as a backlash to this material and cultural subordination of large demographic segments of the national population (Kriesi et al. 2006).

3 All of these cleavages in some sense speak to the tripartite descriptions of later scholars: that each cleavage has a social-structural component, a psychological component, and an organisational component (Ford and Jennings 2020).

4 In the content of modern Britain, then, scholars have seen the role of these cleavages as central to understanding the vote to leave the EU. Although it is demonstrably not true that Brexit was a vote 'against London' (Calhoun 2002), this post-referendum sentiment is broadly correct in the assessment that the vote was against what London represents in many people's minds: diverse, wealthy, young, globalised, and educated. In short, we can generalise about Britain today and argue that, broadly, 'Remainers' are a category who are younger, more diverse, more educated, more mobile, and more metropolitan. Conversely, 'Brexiters' a cultural category which represents those who are older, less diverse, less educated, less mobile, and more peripheral. The former have values which reflect openness, elasticity, diversity, and mobility. Conversely, the social attitudes of the latter tend to more closed, protective, traditional, and authoritarian.

5 Indeed, early scholars might well have turned Geertz's (1973) formula on its head, arguing not that anthropology was an interpretive project in search of meaning but that it was an experimental science in search of law. For these functionalists, the discipline was an inherently empirical one which would take as its object the study of "relations of association between individual organisms" (Radcliffe-Brown 1940b, p. 2). This is in contrast to culture, which he saw as little more than a "vague abstraction", unworthy of reification and analysis (ibid). He thought that we should look to social phenomena as a reflection of 'structural form': morality, law, religion, etc. are merely components of the machinery which keeps these underlying relationships concrete and meaningful.

6 An ethnographic example will provide an illustration of what structural-functionalists mean when they talk about maintaining dynamic equilibrium in social association. Evans-Pritchard's (1969) study of The *Nuer* is famous for its description of warring Sudanese groups, whose tribal affiliations are broken down into distinct segments. Each subdivision is further crystallised around the lineages of clan affiliation. If a segment is small, that means the kinship relation is more intimate. Intra-clan cohesion thus depends not only on political distance but on *structural* distance between these associations. Naturally, such segments are vulnerable to processes of fission and fusion. Equilibrium between them is regulated by unique social institutions like the blood feud and individual authorities like the leopard-skin chief. Both operate in distinctive ways to regulate the relationship between otherwise antagonistic social groups. Their existence in the social-structure thus has a function in relationship to the overall stability and reproduction of such concrete patterns of association between individuals. From this perspective, cultural form should be seen less in terms of what it *means* than what it *does*.

7 Many Brexit supporters were happy to pursue a 'No Deal' exit if even if that meant that all customs arrangements would revert to the standard means by which foreign countries trade with each other in line with World Trade Organisation policy.

8 In this case, BRINO stands for 'Brexit In Name Only'. The guiding assumption here is that Boris could not have really delivered an 'authentic' Brexit, being as he is still largely a member of the liberal, urban classes and thus instinctually unaffiliated to the pro-Brexit masses. This of course does have a great deal of reality to it: it was always debateable the extent to which Boris really believed in Brexit or whether he was using it purely for his own gain.

9 Meaning a French Exit from the EU. The actual support for Euroscepticism in France is significantly lower than in the UK, for a variety of historical and sociological reasons.

10 Instances of hierarchical tension came up repeatedly during my own dialogue with Brexiters. Once this occurred during one moment of interviewing one of my informants called John: – a Brexit Party candidate who was a businessman. In one peculiar slip of the tongue looked at me and said: "if I had a PhD in Sociology or whatever, I'm therefore meant to be more valuable, *and my opinion is more valuable*, than someone who mends my telephone". While I obviously disagreed that there was basically no difference in opinions between these two hypothetical people – one of which was clearly me – I sensed the frustration that the public sphere crowded out people like John and only really gave the highly educated any room to talk. There was clearly a sense among my interlocutors that those who had prestigious qualifications were the only ones allowed to speak with moral authority. This clearly infuriated many of those who felt that their opinions were just as valuable to public discussions, and seemed to feed a kind of resentment towards an Oxbridge-educated elite that by weight of its education and network carries disproportionate political influence.

11 For non-British readers, this may require more clarification. In 2014, Labour MP Emily Thornberry travelled to the working-class area of Rochester, Kent. Noting a house with an English flag and a white van, she tweeted: "Image from #Rochester". The media immediately picked this up as an instance of metropolitan snobbery. English flags are coded as lower-class in the UK, and the clearly patronising tweet was symptomatic of a cultural disorientation that highly educated and wealthy liberal people feel when visiting these areas of the UK. Another Labour MP, Chris Bryant, said that the tweet showed that Labour have been "hijacked by the north London liberal elite".

12 For further discussion on the exact relationship between status and Brexit see Chan et al. (2020). This literature could ignite an entirely supplementary conversation: if we define status in the Weberian (1958) sense, of *commensality* and *connubium*, then are necessarily much more reliant on the kind of research and methodology favoured by cultural anthropologists. Ethnographies of food, kinship and social status are one such example of this. But positivist sociologists are also able to capture status hierarchies in ways not altogether dissimilar to those working on populism in relationship to both Inglehart's (1977) theory of values and wider discussions on globalisation and economic segmentation. Once again, we can see the positive results of a holistic and Weberian paradigm for the social sciences, which integrates both these epistemological frameworks.

13 To be clear, I am not re-hashing Marx and Engel's vision of history as a relentless class-war. Class is simply one of many different categories which separate human groups, as Weber pointed out. But I do believe that Marx was right to note that economic exploiter/exploited is probably the best historically significant example of a cleavage in which two collectivities are segmented within a social whole. As Lipset and Rokkan (1967) point out, the labour/capital divide is just one of four other cleavages that defined Early Modern Europe.

14 This includes even the queen mother, who could technically challenge his authority. She too joins in with the public mocking of the king during the songs.

15 Hirschktop 1986 (p. 104) in fact criticises Bakhtin for seeing carnival in naturalising/historicising terms, arguing that he reifies the carnivalesque as having its own active agency. As Bakhtin (1984b, p. 11) himself claims: carnival celebrated the "gay relativity of prevailing truths and authorities", but whether this had any real power remains a topic of contention.

4

POPULIST MAN AS PHILOSOPHER: HOW MAGICAL CONSCIOUSNESS SHAPES CONSPIRACY FANTASY

"Society everywhere is in conspiracy against the manhood of every one of its members"

Ralph Waldo Emerson, Self-Reliance *(1883)*

5.1 Introduction

Populism and conspiracy theories seem to go hand in hand. For anyone observing the last days of Donald Trump's 2016 presidency, for instance, it since became impossible to ignore the dynamic between the two. In the previous chapters of this book, I demonstrated that many of my Brexiter interlocutors also engaged with this way of viewing the world. I addressed this theoretically in terms of a particular disposition towards seeing "liberal elites" act in a nefarious manner, and interpreted my interlocutors beliefs as the attribution of a kind of group-based collusion, one which tends to filter reality in terms of occult machinations by powerful bourgeois elites. But I also showed how tricky it can be at times to delineate between legitimate sociological explanations of power and the cruder forms of conspiratorialising that we see in populist worldviews. I also suggest that there might be a cognitive layer to this puzzle: evolutionary psychologists suggest that there could be something about the 'coalitional mentality' in humans which tends to perceive hidden plots and secretive co-ordination (Tooby and Cosmides 2010). The implications are striking: the very epistemological tools we use to understand conspiracies may themselves not be fit for the job.

DOI: 10.4324/9781003458517-5

This chapter thus represents a continuation and development of the previous themes. I place the life and worldview of a central interlocutor, Ajay, in order more fully flesh out the relationship between Brexit and conspiracy theories. What is striking about our relationship is that, more than simply reel off conspiracies about the *World Economic Forum* or Davos, he had developed an elaborate personal cosmology that was so colourful and rich that I am still feel grateful that I met anyone like him. Certainly, he in no way represents the vast majority of characters I met over the course of my ethnographic research. Ajay is truly a unique character – but one whose idiosyncrasies and eccentric beliefs spell out an elaborate, complex, and fascinating philosophy about the world which invites deeper investigation. When we first met, he had just finished off an unsuccessful electoral run for MP of the Brexit Party in a constituency in England. By the last time we spoke, he was living in a motel somewhere in Central America. In between these two moments, our intimate relationship provided me with some of the most interesting ethnographic information that I ever discovered. This chapter represents an attempt not only to present Ajay's view of the world, which I believe is tremendously interesting on its own terms, but also to weave it into academic literature which tries to make sense of why conspiracy theories have emerged as a defining feature of our populist moment.

I first present the life of my interlocutor, and describe his overall cosmology – something he refers to as the endless struggle between the forces of *Yin* and *Yang*. Elaborating upon the richness of his metaphysics, I apply Bion's (1984) paradigm of the alpha-function to make sense of how this bizarre and idiosyncratic worldview may represent a unique process of sorting mythic contents into stable narratives and discourses. I suggest that Ajay intuits the process of what Inglehart (1977) thought of as the post-materialist values revolution in Western societies. But not being trained academically, Ajay's perspective can only be cognisable in terms of stories which make sense to him using the vocabulary of his own life. Mixed up within this dynamic concoction of 'beta elements' (Bion 1984) comes his own unique psychological predilections, much of which are defined by a deep suspicion of "feminism" and a general disgust with modern culture.

In the latter section of this chapter, I analyse specific features of his worldview which are more overtly conspiratorial: his deep suspicion of "experts", "the media", "the scientists", and those in charge of the financial system. I frame his views in terms of what anthropologists might call 'symbolist' versus 'functionalist' approaches to conspiracy theories, drawing attention both to how they *explain* things and *do* things for people like him. But I conclude by aligning my analysis with Greenwood's (2022) idea of 'magical consciousness' – itself influenced by the early work of Lévy-Bruhl (2015) – and argue that we need to understand 'mythopoeic' thought as an integral component of cognition, rather than a hang-up from a pre-enlightened era. By decentring the role of 'logical' thought when we try to understand conspiracy theories, we are able to see that they service an indisputable human need not only to make sense of the world in terms of meaningful and predictable patterns in culture, but to *participate* in them, too.

5.2 Ajay's Life and Background

I knew that Ajay would be worth getting to know simply because of the number of other Brexit Party candidates who told me about him. It was only a modest way through my fieldwork when his name began coming up with startling frequency. The insinuation from my other interlocutors, often more overt than not, was that he had something to say of exceptional interest. By then I had already spoken to several dozen other Brexit Party MPs, and I believed that I was already well on my way to understanding with greater clarity what this ethnographic research might contribute to the literature on populism. Many of those I spoke to were distinguished by nothing more ominous than a nostalgic sense of a lost England. It was clear by this point that a large percentage of them had an inclination for conspiratorialising, but their individual perspectives were idiosyncratic and often fractured. Ideas about what had happened with both Brexit and the pandemic certainly overlapped, but in emotive and mostly incoherent ways. With Ajay, I was fortunate enough to encounter someone for whom many distinctive thematic strands might come together in one person.

My meeting with him was thus formidably serendipitous. It was also uniquely enriching, both personally and ethnographically. As a result, I have chosen to centre this entire chapter simply on a description and exploration of his general worldview. Much more, indeed, could be written about him and his life: but I have had to be selective in my description simply for lack of space. Moreover, as an exceptional (and therefore highly recognisable) figure among my Brexiter interlocutors, keeping him anonymous has been a real challenge. Few people have the idiosyncrasies – and perhaps even the charisma – of a man who has essentially developed his own personal anthropology of Brexit entirely outside the academic ecosystem. This itself has many implications for the contemporary fieldwork experience, but I shall leave them for late on in this chapter. The significant point is simply to note that the fecundity of Ajay's cosmological vision for what is happening in Britain has been without parallel in my fieldwork. Other interlocutors may have had interesting (and perhaps problematic) perspectives on the overall process, but few have been able to fully articulate a total worldview from their experience. Like Radin's (1945) ethnography of the Winnebago Indians, I had to do little to do but build the relationship and simply transcribe his thoughts onto paper. It is after Radin's (2015) other key work, *Primitive Man as Philosopher*, that this chapter is thus named.

I first met Ajay in person during the summer period of the 2020 lockdowns. At that time, things remained 'liminal' (Turner 1970) in the anthropological sense of the term – neither completely back to normal nor altogether frozen in place. A set of contacts had put me in touch with him, and we finally managed to meet up at a pub in East London. What interested at the first moment of our encounter was that he was of Indian descent: I later learnt that his parents had arrived from Gujarat to live in the United Kingdom before he was born. Of course, this does not preclude his support of Brexit; like many other of my interlocutors it further problematised the many critiques which frame the vote as fundamentally about race, racism, or 'Whiteness' in general (Beliso-De Jesús and Pierre 2020; Bhambra 2017; Botterill and Burrell 2019; Bowler 2017; De Genova 2020; Maskovsky 2017). In fact, one the very first things he asked of me was whether I consider myself "white" or not. Given that this was our first meeting, I found such a point-blank question both curious and somewhat uncomfortable. In the end, he claimed he was merely "testing me". His other off the cuff remarks about the profundity of his worldviews ("my ideas are so deep") struck me as lacking in self-awareness, but it was nothing I hadn't heard before. I later retracted my less positive observations of our first encounter on the grounds that a generous interpretation would give more weight to his simple excitement about being able to explain his ideas to a real anthropologist. He was clearly frustrated that, despite their political commonality, many of his fellow Brexiters simply did not appreciate the distinctiveness of his overall metaphysics.

A key recollection of our meetings concerned his vocation: he told me he used to work as an NHS doctor. This was something I had little reason to doubt, although asking why he was not working there anymore still elicited a modestly defensive reaction. The reason, he claimed was that he decided to "go his own way" and create a consultancy that works on "emotional intelligence", or "EQ". Ajay felt that this was something sorely lacking in contemporary medical services. To illustrate, he told me a hypothetical story about a victim of domestic abuse walking into the doctor's office complaining of routine problems:

> "Say the doctor noticed something was wrong, and felt that she wasn't telling the truth. Think about that split second of the doctor looking at her raising her eyes as if to scream that she was in pain but couldn't announce it… that is the kind of emotional intelligence that our medical establishment needs more of".

I felt myself agreeing with him, of course, although quite how he thought he could train this skill for medical professionals still elided me. Curiously, I immediately found myself recalling a similar ethnographic vignette of when Geertz (1973) discussed the 'wink' at the Balinese cockfight. It was my first intuition that Ajay himself had something of an amateur anthropologist to him, although I continually suspected that his pursuit of "emotional intelligence" better reflected his own struggles with reading the inner life of other adult human beings.

Our relationship continued to develop over the years, and we would meet on occasion to go to the pub and catch up. Further on in time, Ajay encouraged me to go for a walk with him a forest near the city. I was unsurprisingly nervous to take a walk through the deep woods with someone who was still relatively unknown. But the fact that he requested this type of meeting itself held ethnographic value. He clearly was comfortable being in uncomfortable social situations, even if I was not. He also insisted on bringing a small hip flask filled with whiskey: I didn't mind drinking some with him, although the act of drinking of alcohol in cold and largely vacant woodland with a stranger was undoubtedly peculiar. We discussed many things, including the lack of spirituality in modern politics and his experience drinking *ayahuasca*. He also told me about the various meditation theses that he had read, some of which included elaborate breathing exercises to "shut off the rational mind". Having some experience in this world already, it was both curious and enriching to find someone who was able to combine yoga and Brexit into a single psychocultural paradigm.

In the end, the harmlessness of our walk was palpably there from the beginning. I sensed that Ajay was simply unaware of some of the general behavioural norms that would have prevented someone else from ever suggesting an activity like this. He clearly relished what he saw as the risky element in trekking through overgrown forest with a stranger. Moreover, he continually dared both himself and me to walk over unstable ice that had collected on top of the small ponds scattered throughout the woodland. I saw a kind of eagerness to behave in a such way that distinguished him from other people: his desire to appear as a risk taker was palpable. It is perhaps what Goffman (2022) might have thought of as a dramatic presentation of the self; one which emphasised daring, adventure, and pushing the boundaries of socially anticipated norms. This would be something which continued to crop up during our later discussions: a topic I will discuss when I detail the specific content of his general outlook. The point is that he relished showing me that he was totally committed to a lifestyle that involved taking risks, even if they were of no demonstrable value.

Our continued meetings impressed upon me a liking for the man, despite some of my earlier misgivings about his general worldview. The following year, our conversations became less frequent as it happened that Ajay was travelling much more often. Initially, he had simply said that he went to Florida – the state being both a possible base for his business and one of the few areas in the United States to avoid the stringent lockdown rules of countries like Britain. Although he spoke in very hushed terms about this move, it became apparent that he wanted to stay across the Atlantic for a long time. As time passed, I grew more curious: where had he ended up? In the end, Ajay somehow found himself in Belize – a tiny poverty-stricken country in Central America. It was almost the total opposite of the life he had enjoyed in London. I questioned him on what he was doing in so curious and far-flung a location – a voyage which ended up turning from months into years as he refused to come back to the UK for any substantial amount of time. How this once zealous Brexiter had ended up going from campaigning against immigration to now living semi-permanently in Belize was, quite frankly, odd.

Ajay's peppered his praising of how wonderful the place was to live with the occasional photo of his Caribbean island paradise. He often said that what he liked about the country was that it reminded him of England in the 1950s and 1960s – stoic and unassuming, with a reluctance to make a fuss. Strangely, however, and despite proclaiming the wonderful ocean views of his apartment, every photo he initially sent me was from *Google Images*. Once, when his webcam wasn't working properly, I could see what was outside his balcony – it looked like a car park in a semi-rural industrial zone of a major city. He remained cagey when I asked him for more information about where he was staying – a kind of dynamic mixture of occlusion and defensiveness coloured all of his responses. When I tried to find out more information about these eccentric and somewhat suspicious living arrangements, he changed the subject.

What was so ethnographically peculiar about this whole charade were the reasons he gave for why he had packed up from a professional life in London in order to live in perhaps one of the most peripheral areas of the planet. Something was clearly not right about the story he told me, but I couldn't ever quite work out what it was. One of the primary explanations he gave was heavily inflected with his increasingly conspiratorial narrative. When we first met, he was extremely suspicious of what was happening with the virus lockdowns – something which he shared in particular with other Brexiters. But as time went on, these fantasies magnified in intensity. He began justifying his refusal to come back to the UK the grounds that something terrible was happening. Totalitarianism, expressed through coerced vaccinations and lockdown policy, was once again raising its ugly head.

Ajay was particularly prone to identifying with the worldview of "The Great Reset": a pseudo-mythical conspiracy theory that the *World Economic Forum* are engineering a quasi-communist revolution in which property will be abolished and all of humanity will be tracked and turned into slaves. He had fully bought into the idea that this was the root of an enormous conspiracy afoot during the coronavirus pandemic. This is a topic I shall return to in the following section of the chapter: the point here is simply to note that his full participation in this ongoing mythic conflict – in this case by leaving the UK – reflected a *personal* participation in a semi-mystical battle between the forces of light and freedom and the forces of darkness and submission. Perhaps the true reason for his decision to hive off and live away from where the nefarious forces had 'won' (via lockdowns and forced vaccinations) might have been for purely personal or financial reasons. But he at least professed this to me in terms of his own personal resistance to perverse occult forces which were profiting from the crisis.

A greater part even than escaping totalitarian lockdowns was Ajay's commitment to avoid the contamination of "woke culture". In the previous chapter, I made some preliminary steps towards a more conceptually satisfying account of what this term actually means. Broadly speaking, we might see it as the preliminary movement towards a kind of nascent "world culture": a cosmological vision in which sacred ethnic categories come together to explain the increasing hyper-diversity of urban centres like London and Birmingham (De Wilde et al. 2019). But although the term may seem desirable to many; to others it remains profoundly unappealing. As Christopher Lasch (1994) argued: this ostensibly "world culture" is little more than of a tourist's view of things. It may be desirable for international elites, but it does not function well at the local level. As Goodhart (2017) also noted, nearly half of the British population still remains within a few miles of where they grew up: their emotional attachment to the local over the global remains more central to their civic identity. For those with this kind of disposition that I got to know over my fieldwork, elaborate new cultural norms involving gender and ethnicity appear as little more than the irrelevant and frivolous nonsense of "liberal elites", wholly detached from their daily lives in much less prestigious vocations.

This was particularly true for Ajay, despite the fact that as a doctor and political candidate he was fairly representative example of a cultural elite. Indeed, his hatred of "wokeness" was statistically rather surprising. So too was his desire to escape from the culture of "woke" by crossing the Atlantic. The very choice of Central America itself was, he claimed, predicated on the fact that "there is no wokeness there". In particular, this was because there was much less of what he called a "safetyist culture" than in his native England. There are no signs to "mind the gap" or "hold the handrail" in Belize, he often said to me, let alone do people expect you to wear a facemask to protect against coronavirus. Even wearing a motorcycle helmet is not something which anyone generally warns against. This is because individuals in that part of the world have *real* problems to worry about, he thought, so expect everyone else to be responsible for their own choices. Moreover, Ajay believed that the root of "wokeness" is clearly in part connected to changes in the use of digital technology. He loved that there was so much "raw nature" in Belize, something he contrasted unfavourably to the "Facebook addictions" of (especially younger) individuals in cities like London and New York.

At the time of writing, Ajay remains holed up somewhere thousands of miles away from where he grew up. Our meetings have become increasingly infrequent, and I have grown personally more concerned about where his adventure has taken him. It is curious quite how this study began simply with an interviewing of a Brexit Party candidate over the 2019 election. My worries for where this anti-establishment journey had taken him increased with time, however. One reason was because he started telling me that he has been systematically removed from the various WhatsApp groups that he was in from both university and business school. This he chalks up to the fact that his former friends "don't want to know the truth" about how "wokeness" and "globalism" have taken over British culture. His old acquaintances have cultivated plush salaries from professional careers and second-homes, he thought, and their desire "not to rock the boat" or wake up (ironically) to "woke" is driven more by fear than anything else. They simply refuse to see that the entire Western world is coming under the grip of a *New World Order* via authoritarian lockdown policies via the elite power of the *World Economic Forum*. Ajay is making a personal stand against this social transformation, he believed, while others choose to bury their heads in the sand. "They don't approve of me, and I don't approve of them" he once retorted, in a peculiarly defensive mode. "My friends from university would rather squark woke crap", he added, than actually engage with these serious issues.

One cannot help imagining that his own obsessive attempts to "debate" every single point of socially accepted reality, before inflecting it with a personal version of what is happening, probably led to his expulsion from these digital mobile groups. It is easy to see how this kind of lecturing on WhatsApp could show his personality to be both highly disagreeable and borderline mentally unstable. Yet I noticed that his isolation from the reality shared by his friends in Britain was reinforced by the new acquaintances that he made in the Brexit Party – "people that aren't afraid to debate and question things". It was particularly salient quality of Leavers that they were always ready to stand up to authority, he thought, something which he didn't realise he liked as much as he did after the pandemic. The last time we spoke, he told me how much happier he was socialising with a group of people that seemed to have as little trust in government, media, academia, business and education as he does. Certainly, this example speaks to the conversations around the increasingly siloed quality of political interactions. But not merely do people chose in which ideological reality to live; to a large extent, others also have the power to choose for them.

Ajay and I had countless conversations, most of which pertained in some way to the state of contemporary British life. As many of these happened over Zoom as well as in-person, writing an ideational history of his thought makes little descriptive sense. The truth is that different content emerged at different times; often we would circle around the same theme repeatedly, while in other situations we would not talk about an issue for many months before it came up again. As a relatively headstrong man, the principal variable for understanding *why* certain topics came up at different times and not others can be largely chalked up to his volatile emotional life. Ajay clearly enjoyed talking, even when our conversations were not structured along the lines of an interview.

Another major factor was that he made his own personal media in order to "spread the word" about what was going so wrong. Ajay certainly wanted more people to see things from his point of view, and he cultivated his public message assiduously. His worldview was rarely presented with any all-round ideological coherence, but his YouTube videos gave deep insight into how he tied everything together. One wonders whether his media production resembled what psychologist Carl Rogers (1961, 1980) thought of as working through emotional tension through speech. In other words, the often bizarre and eccentric videos that Ajay insisted on crafting – locked up in a small room in Central America long after the pandemic had subsided – were perhaps more like a psychological attempt to work through his mental contents than they were a genuine attempt to convince anyone else of anything.

As a result, this chapter is unlike the rest of my book in that it breaks down the content into thematic sections, rather than chronological ones. Ajay's vision of life is much closer to what anthropologists have traditionally thought of as a 'cosmology' than simply a political viewpoint. His elaborate metaphysics, theory of human origins, and interweaving between contemporary cultural phenomena are both much more holistic and much more interesting phenomena than other interlocutorsI spoke to had. The following section of the chapter thus breaks them down in the following order: his theory of human origins, followed by the development of matriarchies and patriarchies, and finally how that fits in with the eternal relationship between *Yin* and *Yang*, and Brexit.

5.3 Yin/Yang: Matriarchy/Patriarchy

By far the most interesting component of Ajay's broader worldview is his very own 'anthropology' both of humanity and, strangely, Brexit itself. In the beginning, he told me at our first meeting, there was matriarchy. There were no father roles in the extended family, for women and men shared all the child-rearing together. All men were uncles and they looked after the children without any sense of individual possession over their collective progeny. This worked well for a while. However, at some point there was a problem. Some men – probably the better-looking and athletic sort – got much more sex than the ones at the bottom of hierarchy. Those men then "realised that these alpha-men spent all day in the hammock and still got sex, while they got nothing". This made them upset. One day, a man of unusual bravery decided to leave the matriarchy and go out alone. He saw that the system was unfair and took the risk of being eaten by a bear to find a new group which would give him a better deal. This man's decision represents the genesis of a *Yang* society, in contrast to the *Yin* of primordial human matriarchy.

In this new system, men – and not women – would have the power. This would be called "patriarchy", and its values would radically diverge from the communal, egalitarian, suffocating ones of the ancient matriarchies. In this new system, men would be allowed to know who their children are, so that they may invest in them. It also coincided with the knowledge that the alpha men in the matriarchy would "spray their seed everywhere" and have more genetic offspring. In the patriarchy, the women would be slightly subordinate to men: their job would be to raise who they knew to be their actual genetic offspring. This would prevent the recurrence of the old system in which the childrearing was shared by all, but only the most desirable men were allowed to be the ones to actually reproduce. This means that patriarchy is a better deal for men overall, he thought, even though it may be more competitive and involve significant risks.

Ajay imagined that the effects of this were two-fold. One was that with patriarchy, came the birth of territory. Women were now seen as much more valuable, and thus needed to be controlled. After all, each one has a womb which allows for the production of new sons. Protecting these wombs thus became the most important issue for men in the patriarchy. It was much more necessary for men to be tough and strong, in order to defend the wombs from other men. Moreover, it also incentivised the production of many more children – so that the wombs can be defended from other violent male-dominated societies. Ajay said that the consequence of this was that patriarchal societies tended to be matrilineal, as they are "womb-focused".

The unique historical occurrence of a society in which there were much more strong men was the death-knell for matriarchies. All over the world, this matriarchy-patriarchy transformation slowly transformed human societies. The latter would easily destroy the former, he thought, given both the aggression and physical superiority of patriarchal groups. Ajay thought that "patriarchal societies must have been very tough and warlike, whist matriarchal ones are softer, given that they are centred around the power of women and focused mostly on communal child rearing". Ajay believed that patriarchal societies are not particularly concerned with child rearing: the emphasis is on *descent* of the children rather than a culture in which the expansive inclusiveness tries to hold the entire group together. Women would also largely be kept outside of the political sphere. He thought that this is why Plato said that women should be kept out of politics: "they have a tendency to make everything about sex". He suggested that this might explain why the "gender" or "trans" ideology is such a common feature of public life today: the vast increase of women in the public sphere has shifted discourse to topics that focus on sexuality at the expense of more traditional "manlike" pursuits.

Thus, at some undefined point in human history, the patriarchy took over the world and destroyed almost every single matriarchy. The soft men created by matriarchy simply cannot compete with the tough, warlike men created by patriarchy – even if this is a worse deal for many women or indeed many of the men who cannot compete. Historical change was an endless pendulum between matriarchies and patriarchies, he believed, as even though the latter has been destroyed by stronger patriarchal societies, they tended to remerge whenever men had become soft, complacent and effeminate as a result of their physical security. Even as recently as a hundred years ago, he believed that Western society was extremely patriarchal. The examples he used to illustrate his idea focused on how little attention children and child-rearing were given in Victorian Britain. Abandoned children, orphan chimney sweeps and traumatic boarding schools for affluent young boys were a social norm. This was because, Ajay claimed, in a patriarchal system, people do not care so much about children other than their own. Women – who he thought by nature *do* care about child-rearing in general – were politically mute. These problems did therefore not appear in public until society would once again tilt towards matriarchy after the Second World War.

This beginning moment for these modern transformations emerged, Ajay thought, during the suffragette movement in the early 20th century. Laudable attempts to give women the right to vote, however, have suffered from a kind of "mission creep", such that women have since then been reshaping the very boundaries of human life itself. What began in the 1920s with the vote has now ended up with an almost 50:50 split of women in high positions of power. Moreover, women now dominate many opinion-shaping institutions (media, education, publishing) rather than simply participate in them. Ajay thought that the feminist movement – with attendant representation of female needs, desires and concerns – has now fully permeated a once-patriarchal culture. He believed that this is having a predictable but destabilising effect on political life in Britain today. Such a change has accelerated greatly because of the safety and affluence of the post-war world, a situation which necessarily tilted the system back towards matriarchy. Institutionally, this is what the welfare state represents – a tribal shift towards helping everyone, regardless of whether they are your own or not. The matriarchal system, exemplified by the dominance of feminism, has returned to define modern human society.

Much of this quasi-anthropology Ajay had revealed to me during our earlier meetings together. He was obviously excited to be talking to an anthropologist about these topics, and they demonstrated a breadth of reading about human origins that far exceeded an average person's. While his theories were obviously eccentric, unverifiable and often empirically and demonstrably untrue, what was interesting about them was not the extent to which it was a historically accurate *qua* anthropology, but rather the fact that they existed at all. The fact that it developed much further into a narrative which explains Brexit is a fascinating example of how our interlocutors can still surprises us with the depth of how the human mind can work through mythic contents to order and shape reality in a meaningful way.

*

After Ajay gave me his take on history over a number of sessions, and he elaborated his terms to link the origins of mankind link with our contemporary moment via the forces of *Yin* and *Yang*. The system he adopts is based on ancient Chinese philosophy of the *Tao*. The whole universe, in Taoist thought, reflects the eternal interplay between these two opposing metaphysical forces. The whole is represented by these dualistic energies in eternal dialogue – life involves both, and each cannot exist without the other. Duality is the core feature of creation, but it is only a seeming conflict. The reality is that both forces not only need each other for balance, they also contain small amounts of each other's quality. Together, the dance between them generates the patterns and order that constitute the intelligible world.

Ajay believed that *Yin* represents the negative, dark, and feminine principal. This is characterised by disintegration, passivity, cold and wetness. *Yang*, for its part, represents the forces of dryness, light and warmth. It is by nature the more masculine force, and is characterised by activity, risk, strength and energy. *Yin* is generally associated with women, and for Ajay with matriarchy in general. *Yang* is associated with men, and patriarchy. *Yin* intelligence is cunning, *Yang* intelligence is aggressive. *Yin* has a tendency towards Machiavellianism, he thought, *Yang* towards bullying. In his own words: "*Yang* describes traits associated with going forward – adventure, courage, and exploring the unknown – but *Yin* describes the opposite traits: to yield, nurture, empathize and avoid risk". He pointed out that we can manifest any of these traits as we move through the circumstances of life, but each person has a kind of sweet spot at the central node of harmonious integration.

Although the two forces are by nature 'gendered', they do not exactly map onto one another in such straightforward terms. Approximately two-thirds of men and one-third of women are more attuned to the *Yang*. Approximately two-thirds of women and one-third of men are more attuned to the *Yin*. Ajay thought that this proportion explained why *most* women emphasise "*Yin* values" like togetherness, inclusion and avoiding conflict, and *most* men emphasise *Yang* values of action, risk, and stoicism. This is also why "woke" values like Equity and Inclusion can be attributed to the growth of the feminist movement and the general dominance of the *Yin* principle, according to

Ajay, as a higher percentage of women in the political sphere have tilted the whole culture in that direction. However, there are still many examples in which this the individual's gender does not always fit the principal: many men will emphasise *Yin* values (like togetherness and inclusion) and many women emphasise *Yang* values (like action and endurance). Margaret Thatcher is an example of the latter; Jeremy Corbyn an example of the former. Both are statistically unlike the other people of their sex in that they emphasise values contrary to the norm of either passivity or competition.

The *Yin* energy he in particular associated with what he called "smothering mother". This was something which has traditionally been called the "nanny state" in Britain by conservative leaning commentators who argue that state directives pose a risk to personal freedoms. Ajay was particularly obsessed with the idea that Britain had become such a "smothering mother" to its citizens: a reality which increased exponentially with excessive coronavirus lockdowns. He saw these as totally inappropriate and overblown responses to a natural immunity problem which did not warrant such authoritarian measures. A culture which is focused on health and safety, inclusion, diversity of form but not content, cautionary policies, high welfare spending and a culture imbued with injunctions about the 'right' forms of gender and sexuality – Ajay thought that these all reflected the presence of *Yin* energy, and by extension the dominance of more "feminine" values. Whether or not he was right in his assessment of the validity of lockdowns remains a topic for scientists to continue debating (Mellone et al. 2021). Ajay, for his part, remained totally convinced. He explains:

> "Take the British stiff upper-lip tradition. School kids were once taught to withstand teasing with rhymes like: 'sticks and stones may break my bones, but words will never hurt me'. Be tough! That's a *Yang* trait. It's the opposite of today's uber sensitive, pour-your-heart-out culture which is *Yin*. Victorian Britain used to be excessively *Yang*, but now many feel Britain has swung too far towards *Yin* as a politically correct, overprotective soft nanny state says that even the word 'blackboard' is deemed hurtful to ethnic groups".

How does this cosmological vision connect to leaving the European Union (EU)? The nature of *Yin* and *Yang* is in perpetual flux. Ajay thought that what has happened since 2016 is that the creeping dominance of "woke" or politically correct "soft *Yin* values" reached its peak through the EU and provoked a major backlash. What both Brexit and the election of Trump represent, according to Ajay, is the return of *Yang* energy in world history. They epitomise the independent, risk-taking adventurousness which has otherwise been smothered by *Yin* for many decades. This is the desire to "make our own way in the world", to pushback against political correctness, to adopt an entrepreneurial culture of risk-taking, self-reliance, and pride. For him, then, 'populism' is just an academic word to describe the *Yang* fightback in a culture which has turned hopelessly *Yin* over the past century. The pendulum has swung once again. He said:

> "Britain has lately been ebbing in retreat – but wants to flow forth, be bold and confident! To take chances and ensure prideful work for our people. It's a case of *attitude*... the typical attitudes of *Yin* with its risk aversion and *Yang's* courage, confidence and self-belief in Britain... Brexiteers feel the pendulum swung too far toward *Yin* and now want to rebalance leaning towards *Yang* – for the UK to reshape its economy with self-belief and stand on her own legs".

Perhaps most curiously, Ajay saw the EU itself as being "the epicentre of all the *Yin* in the world". One evening late in the summer months, he was particularly enthusiastic to show me a video on YouTube that he found. In it, the President of the EU at the time, Donald Tusk, was giving a speech to celebrate the swearing in Ursula von der Leyen. At one point during his long speech, he turned to crowd and announced: "after all, Europe is a woman". I assume that most people would have written off this slightly bizarre metaphor as a case of Tusk's eccentric political vocabulary, or perhaps as an example of liberal moral posturing. But for Ajay it meant much more: it was demonstrable proof of his *Yin*/*Yang*: Matriarchy/Patriarchy cosmology. It represented a moment in which the veil fell from the political charade to reveal that these patterns in social reality were more than an occult cosmology: they were truly the way things were. Europe was the centre of *Yin* ideology: deeply feminised, smothering, contracted, and risk-averse.

In short, as he himself pronounced: "Brexit is a battle for preserving culture, heritage and identity versus preserving the current economic structure". The difference between Brexiters and Remainers, he repeatedly said, comes down to a kind of mythological conflict in which competing visions about the nation's history intertwine with their respective *Yin*/*Yang* energy. At its base is a conflict between Leavers who want to preserve "enshrined cultural heritage" and "self-belief in British adventurousness, invention and discovery". Remainers, for their part, "want to play safe with the single market economy while risking cultural identity dilution". *Yang*-inspired Brexiters "want to be bold and confident to go into an unknown future of economic chance with self-belief", while the *Yin*-inflected Remainers "see chance as risk to be avoided", preferring instead to stay comfortably within the EU. This context overlaps with the nature of political vocabulary. Ajay argues that the words 'sovereignty', 'nationalism' and 'Britishness' were recognised in completely different ways. For Brexiters, they meant reclaiming laws, culture and values. For Remainers, they were seen as isolationist, supremacist, and ultimately racist. The latter view he thought was particularly pernicious in that everything that Leavers were trying to do was ultimately considered morally polluting by Remainers.

As I got to know Ajay much better, I discovered that he developed this cosmology even further. This I gleaned both from personal communication and the acceleration of public media output during further lockdowns, such as his blog and his YouTube videos, which continued to absorb much of his personal time. Rather than seeing the world simply as a *Yin/Yang* phenomenon, he thought that the two could be split even further: into Light and Dark. That way, there is a *Light Yin* and a *Dark Yin,* a *Light Yang* and a *Dark Yang*. The lighter ones are both productive, and work with each other to the benefit of mankind and the universe. The latter, darker ones represent a spiritual degeneration of these principles and end up destroying the collective culture.

So *Light Yang*, for instance, "captures the virtuous energies of coming forth, stepping up, pushing forward, expansionism, adventure, drive, risk-embracing courage and orderliness" but *Dark* or *Extreme Yang* can manifest as "bullying, oppression, fool-hardy aggression and gung-ho risk taking". These dark manifestations "characterize a dearth of good spirit towards fellow human being, which can result in dictatorship". This kind of *Yang* reaches pivotal moments in examples like the slave-trade and the two World Wars, which began a backlash towards *Yin*. More recently, Ajay thought, the 2008 financial crisis was caused by "gung-ho risk taking" of bankers using complex financial products. The austerity which resulted has fuelled a "*Yin* sentiment lurching away from systematic risk" as a consequence of the fall-out. Good capitalism permits risk-taking, he thought, and can involve a semblance of fair-play and equilibrium. However, when *Dark Yang* takes over, chaos and catastrophe results, especially as the risk-takers themselves are not punished.

Conversely, *Light Yin* "captures the virtuous energies of being flexible, accommodating, yielding, emphatic and nurturing and nourishing". However, it took can turn *Dark*, involving "unwarranted risk aversion, stifling smothering, 'poor me' victim-playing, whimpering, and staying aloof to induce guilt in others, by which to manipulate and dictate". These "unholy methods of manipulation" in particular represent the "lowliest of spirit – truly insidious and pernicious" can also result in disorder. *Dark Yin* can be epitomised as crying wolf and playing the victim. This is why, he thought, they gravitate towards left-wing political parties which fixate on victimised groups. Indeed, he thought that Tony Blair's Labour Party enabled this shadowy side of *Yin* to emerge and let this energy gain a powerful foothold in modern Britain, something which seeded the division and wokeism we face today.

Indeed, most nefariously for Ajay, "today's woke mania is *Dark Yin*". Britain has been pushed towards:

> "A culture of precautionary principle (extreme risk aversion), gratuitous offence taking (victim-hood), cancel culture (aloofness), feigned empathy (virtue signalling) and calls for lengthy lockdowns (smothering)... Woke is a form of *Dark Yin*, very dark, pernicious and insidious".

"Wokeness" for Ajay is thus much less an example of a nascent 'world culture' (De Wilde et al. 2019) nor a new hegemonic form of the professional middle class, as other scholars have claimed. Instead, it can be understood as an epiphenomenon of eternal mystical energies undergoing their perpetual transformation. This force of *Dark Yin* has been slowly devouring the patriarchal *Yang* values that built Britain as a powerful nation. This includes getting rid of competition and meritocracy. It indoctrinates students at school, "resulting in today's snowflake generation". Woke aligns with communism and anarchy, rooted in the various waves of the feminist movement, always siding with the underdog in order to cynically gain more advantage for itself. Finally, his disgust at *Dark Yin* (he later also started calling it "dark softness") manifest in his extreme aversion to the coronavirus lockdowns, which he viewed as pointless and harmful examples of government overreach. The extreme risk aversion which characterised the period was "a form of selfishness, not high mindedness" which indexed a crippling softening of the nation's collective spirit. Contrasting this to the *Yang* energy of fighting to defend the country in war, what he saw in 2020 was the pathetic softness of the entire population cowering in fear at a relatively harmless infection. This epitomised the now hegemonic domination of *Dark Yin*. Ajay believed that preventing the immune system from being exposed to danger ultimately weakened it: the system works along a use-it-or-lose-it pathway, and the lockdowns were contributing negatively to this. Much like "safe spaces" or inclusivity initiatives, the act of retreating from risk only served to create more anxiety and, in the end, more vulnerability.

The cosmology I have discussed represents the metaphysical base of his entire system. It was highly serendipitous that I was able to meet anyone quite like Ajay. Indeed, I can think of very few people in my personal network that have ever worked to develop such an elaborate way of connecting so many facets of modern life together. Of course, whether these connections are purely arbitrary fantasies will concern the rest of this chapter. But before then, it is worth noting several other characteristics of Ajay's thought that can distinguished as thematic bundles.

5.4 Indigenous Philosophy and the Alpha-Function

There are many facets to Ajay's vision of the world. On a disciplinary level, one reflection is that his ideas seem to dissolve the hard boundary between fieldwork and academia. The distinction between the two has been a defining feature of the anthropological venture at least since Malinowski. But the distinction between the 'here' (of home) and the 'there' (of the field) has collapsed over the past few decades as the discipline itself changed in line with globalisation (Cole 1977). In its classical period, anthropology sharply delineated the epistemic distinction between self and other in a multiplicity of ways: language, location, subject, ethnicity, even temperature. The archetype of a lonely ethnographer working in the bush – almost always in a hotter and poorer country – still linger today. But even when anthropologists can 'take a subway to the field' (Passaro 1977), there remains something of an epistemological boundary between the researcher and the researched. On one level, this manifests simply as the fact that even when working 'at home', many of our interlocutors have little idea about what our vocation entails – nor what we are writing about them.

This situation was not true for Ajay. In previous eras, anthropologists might spend time with a local witchdoctor in order to understand the tribal group's cosmological ordering of their world. Radin (1945), for instance, took down the descriptions for the Winnebago Medicine Dance from one single individual. Anthropologists used the material on myth, politics, kinship, language and custom in order to understand the interwoven strands that constitute social organisation. But unlike the traditional context, here it is anthropology (or pseudo-anthropology) *itself* which forms the mythic content of our own shaman's storytelling. There is no clear distinction or impermeable boundary between the myths discovered in fieldwork and the academic anthropology used to decipher them. Ajay's theory of patriarchy and matriarchy was clearly influenced by the many theses and articles he had accessed from public sources: the kind of information which is freely available in libraries or the internet to almost any citizen of the global North. His adoption of academic anthropological terminology to suit his own cosmology is of historical salience. In other words, it is not that I am bringing an anthropological epistemology to a wholly indigenous and 'other' way of experiencing the world. The language of anthropology *itself* is shared and contested between ethnographer and interlocutor.

Now, it is true that near-enough all tribal mythologies contain cosmogonic myths of human origin (Abramson and Holbraad 2014). In that sense it is not unique. But the idiosyncratic nature of these contents emerge not because it is simply *another* origin myth, but because this cosmogony is interwoven with the anthropological concepts developed in order to make sense of it. The central point is that as an epistemological language to make sense of the modern, then, anthropological terminology is surprisingly amiable to integration in non-academic 'folk theories' (Gelman and Legare 2011). Such an observation raises interesting questions about the extent to which the social sciences themselves are a kind of 'folk theory' of their own. The overall observation is that anthropological concepts are themselves elastic and, under the right historical conditions, curiously malleable cultural contents for integration in non-academic discourses. Indeed, Ajay's theories resemble a kind of syncretic religion which has incorporated a variety of narrative contents into a wholly novel (and indigenous) framework for understanding what academic scholars think of as 'populism'.

Beyond this disciplinary insight, let us now try to make sense of Ajay's colourful vision of the world in the terms available to us from social science. To begin with, it is worth restating we cannot make any claims as to the generalisability of his cosmology. It is by definition unique and personal to him; on one level, it tells us little about the vast majority of other Brexiters think. There is only an infinitesimally small chance that anyone else made sense of the referendum in terms of the metaphysics that Ajay elaborated upon. This can be productively contrasted to other themes in the literature, such as immigration or authoritarianism, which can be clearly extrapolated across distinct demographic segments and measured in etic and positivistic terms. Ajay's theory of *Yin/Yang* energy, meanwhile, clearly has little resonance outside of his own mental universe. It is example of demonstrable cultural uniqueness, perhaps never to be repeated again.

Nevertheless, if we limit ourselves merely to describing his thought and writing it off as of little historical value, then we may end up missing something special about the underlying dynamics at play. The disparate emotional contents that he has integrated into a coherent verbal framework were clearly shared by the other populist activists. Even though it was only him that was able to linguistically articulate these contents in his mythic *Yin/Yang* system, he did not exactly make them up. He merely re-arranged what psychoanalyst Bion (1998) thought of as the 'basic assumptions' of his social group – such as that mainstream media cannot be trusted or that the EU is too liberal about immigration – and articulated them using his own self-generated vocabulary. From this perspective, what distinguishes Ajay from his colleagues – and makes him closer to his group's philosopher or witchdoctor – was his ability to transform 'beta elements' of mentally undigested affective experience into 'alpha elements'; that is, something which can be *thought* by others. In this sense, his mental process is clearly engaged with what Bion (1984) calls the 'alpha-function': the cognitive activity in which raw experience is transformed into something which can be mentalisable. Like a shaman or psychoanalyst, Ajay's Brexit mythmaking was doing the hard psychological work of crafting unconscious sense impressions into a cognisable narrative flow.

This observation makes for an interesting comparison with Chapter 2. In both cases, I presented an ethnographic record of two individual characters – Terry and Ajay – who engage with the Brexit debate on a level altogether distinct from much of the political discourse of the past decade. They were relucent to fight the battle for Brexit on the grounds of economic trade-offs –

something which has generally been to the strength of Remainers. Rather, their understanding of Britain leaving the EU has been mostly centred on its significance in *mythical* terms. The justification for leaving was never experienced in terms of instrumental or transactional rationality, such as a cost/benefit analysis. Infrequent were any examples in which my interlocutors tried to argue about the benefits of Brexit by incorporating economic models into their analysis.

Instead, Brexit from their perspective seems to have been something more like an expression in mythopoetic terms of the underlying 'basic assumptions' (Bion 1998) of the group – characterised by a deep suspicion of the continent and a sense that Britain is being held down (or even threatened) by something external. Both of these ideas themselves reflect an intermingling of history and myth, either of an ominous European 'Other' (Colley 1992) or an entrepreneurial and industrious Victorian Britain. In both cases, these individuals are engaging discursively with mythic content in order to both shape public narratives and resolve conflicting internal emotional contents. It serves to create a certain sensibility among the confusing (and often quite vicious) arguments around the referendum. For these two men, underlying (but not necessarily *just* personal) affects and emotions are integrated into a cultural framework. It speaks to Paul's (1989) argument that culture is itself a kind of group fantasy, which is projected outwards via the mythopoetic faculty.

Finally, one of the more curious facts about Ajay's vision is that is not wholly unlike many of the mainstream views in the sociological literature. This point perhaps requires greater generosity of interpretation, but I believe that is worth outlining. We can see Ajay's vision touching on the idea of 'economic grievance' explanation of Brexit when we consider that he sees the white working class as bereft of meaning, work, and usefulness as a result of globalisation. While Ajay clearly chalks this up to "secular-feminism" rather than more abstract socio-economic processes, there is a clear elective affinity between the two. Whether this is truly confirmed by the empirical data is something of another question. But the shared observation that globalisation has reshaped Britain to detriment of many groups at the expense of others is worth noting, and is certainly widely shared among scholars working on the topic.

The most interesting comparison, however, is the 'cultural backlash' framework epitomised by both Sobolewska and Ford (2020) and Norris and Inglehart (2019). Let us briefly reconsider what exactly this overall theory represents. The framework derives mostly from Inglehart's (1977) cultural sociology, whose core claim is that the collective value systems which prioritise security and identity strengthen in periods of insecurity, and erode in periods of affluence. This is because the values themselves emerge as the consequence of adaptions to physical survival, a notion which follows from Maslow's (1943) idea of the 'hierarchy of needs'. In periods of austerity or danger, survival is prioritised. This is linked to 'authoritarian' behavioural values, which emphasise group cohesion and the expulsion of threats. Alternatively, when increasing generations of people feel safe and secure, they unconsciously replace such values with 'liberal' ones. This binary Inglehart (1977) thinks of as the defeat of 'materialist' values (i.e., concerned with problems of survival and co-ordination of the collective) by 'post-materialist' ones (i.e., unconcerned with problems of material survival and focused on freedom for the individual).

In the post-war context – despite the immediate problem of austerity and threat of nuclear attack – an unprecedented material and existential abundance in the West transformed generational attitudes towards previously superfluous issues like the environment, gender, sexuality, diversity, and human rights. With slow but relentless change through generational replacement, the once hegemonic 'materialist values' of powerful leadership, emphasis on tradition over novelty, religious belief, ethnocultural homogeneity, and controlled borders, gave way to the 'post-materialist' (or liberal) values of the 1960s. The openness, cosmopolitanism, diversity, emphasis on equality, and desire for technocratic rather than autocratic governance, all represent the triumph of post-materialist values. A society characterised by an ever-increasing percentage of university graduates – instead of one dominated by school-leavers – helped to solidify a now hegemonic set of cultural values favouring them and their 'taste' (Bourdieu 2010) for novelty and diversity. This new class is so dominant in political, cultural, and economic terms that they set the agenda in ways that make older generations – socialised under very different circumstances – feel uncomfortable. Brexit can be largely explained as a 'backlash' against these social changes in favour of more authoritarian – conservative values predominantly by older individuals (Norris and Inglehart 2019).

If we consider, then, the historical transformation of materialist to post-materialist values, we are more able to see how Ajay's cosmology fits into it. In much the same way – although perhaps with less poetry – Inglehart's (1977) theory also posits the continual interplay between two dynamic (but ontologically static) principles in human life: the materialist and the post-materialist. They too are defined in largely abstract ways, as representing intellectual-emotional 'ideal types' (Weber 2019) within which are embedded distinct attitudes and behavioural dispositions. They in some sense depend on one another for meaning, and oscillate in accordance with external conditions that impinge upon collective self-understanding and self-expression.

Consider, once again, how Ajay's own cosmology fits into this pattern. His view was that before roughly the beginning-early middle of the 20th century, Britain was mostly *Yang*. After the war, the tremendous growth of *Yin* has overtaken that *Yang*. This means that society has become more associated with *Yin* values – something he associates with "feminism" and "secularism".

This quite reasonably aligns with the idea of post-materialist values overtaking materialist ones. *Yang*, like "materialist" values, emphasise security, attachment to (and pride of) place, risk-taking, law and order, and strong leadership. *Yin*, like "post-materialist" values, emphasise liberal attitudes towards cultural, ethnic or gender differences, index a concern for the environment, and downplay authoritarian control in favour of social equality. It also tends to be much more secular than the materialist values, given Inglehart's (1977) functionalist contention that religion is part of the authoritarian social infrastructure in its capacity to bind groups to tradition and social solidarity.

Ajay is thus correct to note that the rise of post-materialist values – *Yin* in his terminology – necessarily involve the decline of religious belief in conjunction with the increase in cultural emphasis on cosmopolitanism, feminism, and environmentalism. His claim the EU represents the "epicentre of world *Yin*" aligns with the post-materialist values which are clearly embedded in the constitution of the EU – civic, democratic, and liberal values which quite consciously reject the ethnonational ones of the continents recent history (Shore 1993, 2000). Recall, too, that he sees Brexit/Trump as the stunning return of *Yang* back into a world dominated by *Yin*. This aligns with the scholarly contention that these populist victories are the 'cultural backlash' of materialist values in a world increasingly dominated by post-materialist ones. "Wokeness" for Ajay is the manifestation of the forces of *Dark Yin*, but scholars in the social science might simply call it the hegemony of post-materialist values among a generation which no longer feels indebted to the more conservative and ethnocentric values of their parents and grandparents.

Of course, the idea that Ajay has in some sense intuited the same basic structural processes as sociologists themselves requires a generous reading of his interpretation. Clearly, much of how he explains what is going on involves an elaborate use of his own invented and often quite eccentric mythological vocabulary. I am not saying that Ajay's perspective has the same epistemological value as the works of scholarship I have adopted in this book. But there is a compelling enough claim here that a substantial correlation exists between the two. The concepts do not perfectly correlate, but a sufficiently functional similarity suggests that he is observing, commenting upon, and reacting to the same processes as professional scholars. Even disregarding some of the more problematic components of his cosmology, a reasonable case is to be made that Ajay's worldview represents something like an unrefined emic (rather than etic) perspective. Nobody during the course of my fieldwork came close to articulating anything as close to the academic literature than he had. This is true, even though he had clearly never heard of Inglehart's work and was often hostile "woke academics" who – he wasn't wrong to intuit – are vastly more pro-Remain the rest of the general population.

Of what value, though, is the observation that Ajay created a unique, personal cosmology which more or less fits alongside the same social-structural trends that are outlined by political sociologists? First, they speak to both Lévi-Strauss's (1974) and Radin's (2015) overall point that intellectual sophistication is a hallmark of all human beings everywhere – even if it emerges to different degrees between individuals – rather than the unique possession of any one group. Speculation for its own sake can be found among our interlocutors as much as the academics that study them: theorising Brexit can emerge as an activity indigenous to populists as much as it is to scholars. As Radin says, an occupation with intellectual pursuits is not split between the primitive and the civilised – or today between the 'populist' Brexiters and the 'sophisticated' Remainers – but rather between reflective and unreflective persons who are found in all times and places. It makes little sense, as Boas (1966) did with the Kwakiutl tribe, to speak of groups 'acting' or a 'thinking' in a certain manner. Just as it is claiming that all Inuit 'dance this way' or 'think this way', so too is it debatable whether there are any replicable thought processes to Brexiters or Remainers – despite the literature arguing for a shared beliefs about things like the Empire or national greatness (Dorling and Tomlinson 2019). Radin (1945) refused to say that the Winnebago Indian believe this or that, rather, he would say that a Winnebago man gave him this particular myth. Similarly, while it may be true that populist voters are united in some sense by their shared materialist values, within this subpopulation exist distinct intellectuals who make sense of these same social processes in idiosyncratic ways.

Thus, any attempt to speak in general terms of 'Leavers' or 'Brexiters' may make for compelling narratives, but it makes the same Boasian mistake of imputing some generalised notion (or set of notions) to a highly diverse group. The truth, according to Radin (2015), is that the world has always been split between two classes of people, with one reflective group providing the speculative and religious thinkers and seekers compared to the general mass who are indifferent towards contemplation of this kind. As with ethnographic descriptions of primitive people, much of academic scholarship on populists has been based on what Radin (2015) calls 'the non-intellectual class'. It is true that we cannot generalise about an entire stratum based on the musings of the philosopher minority, as he rightly admits. But it does give us space to see that many of our most broad generalisations misconstrue the extent to which the contents of social reality are themselves refashioned by 'populists' in service of their own aims.

In other words, we must attend to the reality that the Brexit debate was not one of unreasonable populists against contemplative and thoughtful Remainers. This was a wide assumption shared by almost all my Remainer colleagues, acquaintances and friends, in addition to a demonstrably high percentage of academics themselves. Wodak (2015), for instance, argues that populists endorse the ignorance which "marks a return to pre-modernist or pre-Enlightenment thinking". This is just one example of a prevailing cultural assumption which downgrades populist voters to the status of barely sentient. It ignores the reality that there may be just as many contemplative and thoughtful philosophical Brexiters as there are Remainers. In Bion's (1984) terms, the alpha-function belongs to all human beings; and is perhaps most refined among a small class of individuals – shamans, psychoanalysts, philosophers, anthropologists, historians, artists – who feel that irresistible urge to draw together, articulate, and reshape impersonal emotional contents into a coherent and meaningful narrative for everyone else.

5.5 The Joyous Cosmology

Ajay's overall theory being clearer now, it is valuable to continue the discussion on the various other characteristics of his thought. The *Yin/Yang* system can be conceptualised as something like the foundational base of his intellectuology – it forms the meta-framework for how he thinks the world works. But within that cultural system are a number of other thematic strands, all of which I have observed either from our personal conversations or from his video clips, podcast appearances, and personal blog. They all add another layer of richness and sophistication to his cosmological musings, but they also clearly index a thought process which is conspiratorial in nature. Before examining what this means, let us consider his various pronouncements on more specific features of modern Britain.

Science and Spirit

Criticism of what Ajay understood as 'the science' during the coronavirus pandemic formed much of the bedrock of his gripes with modern Western culture. First, he associated it with a profound sense of being let down. "Science has many failed promises" he often said, listing a set of arbitrary historical moments as when people thought the Titanic was unsinkable, that "the world's longest suspension bridge" wouldn't fall down, that aerosols were safe, that the Ozone caused cancer, that online data is safe, that certain drugs were safe for pregnant women, and many other examples. All of these pointed to the truth in his general sense that "science is not some all-powerful dependable force in which to place faith and spirit". We perpetually argued that "we place too much faith in objectivity" and allow "evidence" and "numbers" to dominate how we see things. Rather than appreciating science as a useful tool, modern Westerners have started treating it like a kind of idol. Indeed, the sense of oppressiveness that this has put on us means that, in his words, "scientific objectivity is like a dictator now".

Part of what made Ajay's thought a kind of metaphysics in its own right was his insistence on the reality of "spirit" that permeated all human life. His

Yin/Yang theory certainly contained the seeds of this, but his paradigm developed further in that he believed that secularism (in conjunction with feminism) was another part of the puzzle. He said:

> "Spirit has huge relevance in the Brexit debate. The British people are in very low spirits right now, who would deny that? But has science invented a device to detect human spirit? The trouble is that secularism is exterminating spirit. No one ever says that objective evidence-based science is a God but boy do these secular-brigade worship evidence and demand that we all do. Other wisdoms are disregarded, even *Yin* and *Yang*. This is a mistake, and it's coming home to roost. Evidence is not proof!"

His overall point, one which I confirmed with him over the years, was that "culture can't be measured". For today's people, the secular world was so totally dominant that they are completely unable to grasp that there are qualities to the human experience which do not fit the epistemological paradigm of "metrics mania" – something a social scientist might refer to as Comtian (2017 [1830]) positivism. Ultimately, he said, science cannot answer "a fundamental spiritual question: Who am I? What's my heritage? What's our flag? Our dance? Who is one of us? Where do I come from?". He thought that "even orphans yearn for these answers". In other words, these subjects respond to a primordial human need for attachment and identity, and he felt that science was fundamentally incapable of answering them. The hegemony of what he called "secularism" continued to wreak havoc on our ability to generate true understanding and meaning from our own lives. "Science is not a God", he often exclaimed, and although he was not preaching an alternative religion, his anger with "progressive-secularism" was palpable in the words he used to convey his perspective.

How he ties this up with Brexit once again demonstrates a certain creativity with his metaphysics. For him, "the 2016 referendum gave people a chance to pull the emergency brake". We should listen closely to his vote, he said, rather than "rubbishing them for being racist and stupid", even if it means "getting over our worship attitude to science and rationality" which "misses spirit and emotion". As he crisply remarked:

> "Science is not all enlightenment: it brings *endarkenmen*t too… There is nothing enlightened about subordinating emotional intelligence and spiritual intelligence beneath rational intelligence. That creates imbalance! Men and women both got addicted to rational objectivity and sacrificed the subjective intuitive radar and emotional intelligence".

Ajay invoked a number of apocalyptic examples to illustrate why he thought that science hasn't got nature under control: asteroids, pandemics, killer bugs, antibiotic resistance, war, earthquakes, and many more. The "take-home message" of these lectures was always the same: that humans are extremely vulnerable, and that science creates a false sense of security. We must therefore stop thinking that it can solve all of our problems, which in turn means that we must stop listening to scientists demands for political control. It is imperative to break the chain of dependence upon what he saw as a secular, deluded, and irrational clique of scientific experts who were responsible for the damaging coronavirus policies of 2020–21.

Feminism

Another particularly curious feature of Ajay's ideas was his extreme antipathy towards what he called "the feminist movement". Now, his vision for what this term meant is clearly distinguishable from the consensus of feminists themselves. For Ajay, feminism was not a movement for either personal or collective liberation. Rather, it was a profoundly nefarious force, one which has been "assaulting culture, causing unhappiness and driving Brexit". At other times he labelled it "a force for progressive secularism", breeding political correctness and "suppressing the right to free speech", a heritage "for which the people of Britain fought hard for 800 years". Feminism "has steered schools towards secular liberalism, encouraging atheism", in addition to having "eroded cultural values for good spirit" and filling this void with "materialism". It has "perverted university students", "diluted marriage laws", and "contributed to trampling British culture heritage". Feminist influence has "turned the UK into an overprotective nanny state" because of its "excessive *Yin*" that "defies pragmatic common sense" and traditional British values for individual freedom.

Ajay never explicitly laid out a coherent philosophy of what he means by "feminism". It is of course tempting to identify his worldview as a reflection of deep underlying issues with women. It is certainly true that he never married or had children, and it is possible that his anti-feminist cosmology is a manifestation of deeper unresolved emotional issues. Certainly, the vigour with which he protested both the "feminists" in general and the overbearing "smothering mother" indicated an unconscious relationship to his primary caregiver which is likely to have complex and conflicted roots. However, I was largely unable to delve much deeper into this possibility: whenever he did talk about it, he seemed to have quite positive things to say about his own mother and women in general. It was unclear how much of his theory could be chalked up to personal developmental issues with female caregivers.

What exactly was it about feminism which so frustrated Ajay? One major reason was that he thought it had a powerful effect in emasculating men. The "secular-progressive-feminist" axis involved, he thought, the electoral ganging up on working-class white men in order to call them "privileged". This occurred late towards the end of the 20th century, when Blair's New Labour abandoned them in favour of a more advantageous coalition, one based on the pursuit of political power via changing demographics. These new electoral alliances involved a novel combination of ethnic minorities, the disabled and women; all essentially ganging up, he thought, on the old structure of white working-class males. Ajay saw evidence of this in various polls which recorded the lower two-thirds of social classes voting to Leave, a statistic which he thought also reflects a higher proportion of men voting for Brexit than women. According to him, around 80 per cent of young women voted to Remain – "the most extreme group of progressive feminists" – because they wanted to "avoid" risk and "stay within the European family". (It is important to note that such a statistic is empirically incorrect). This led to a catastrophic decline in the political power of the white working class, who saw their demographic unrepresented and their "common sense, traditional and socialist values diluted".

Finally, Ajay was angry that this movement unfairly target the true victims of modernity. He says that "feminism thinks [men] privileged – but they're not". When we look back in history, he thought, our vision of a world of men dominating women ignores the fact that propertyless men received the right to vote around the same time. Feminism is a "lie" for retroactively ignoring this fact in order to benefit from a narrative which privileges their influence, even though "80 per cent of divorces are triggered by wives", "80 per cent of child custody goes to wives", and "70 per cent of the homeless are male". Men need to feel needed too, said Ajay, and once declared that it was a travesty that men have been reduced to "desk monkeys" who feel betrayed, anxious and angry. The fact that science has not found a quantifiable way to measure "pride of purpose" speaks much more to our epistemological assumptions, he thought, than it does on any kind of objective reality. Globalisation and modernity have wreaked havoc on men, he repeatedly argued, driving them into the arms of *Yang* politics like Brexit or Trump.

Money, Finance, Expertise

Another significant issue he had concerned the relationship between GDP and national wealth. His critique centred on the idea that the "metrics mania" cannot by definition capture our emotional or spiritual lives. He said that "GDP must be abandoned to achieve true welfare" as the figure ignores factors like the benefits of a loving home or the moral evils arising out of the black market. (An opinion shared by many social scientists and anthropologists, including Hickel (2017, 2020) among many others). Ajay believed that the fact that compassion, trust, dignity, culture and loyalty cannot be measured is an example of this cultural folly. The Bank of England in particular has a problem in that they "are addicted to GDP growth" despite having no real evidence that it makes the lives of anyone in England necessarily better. The reason why we are so enchanted by the figure, he thought, is because in our culture of "metrics mania" anything which can be measured, will be. This turns all of our institutions into "fact-checking operations". We are unable to understand things like confidence in the markets very well, he thought, because we are unable to perceive with "emotional intelligence" that value is connected to spirit much more than it is simply with abstract financial reasoning.

Criticism of financial experts dovetailed with a general cynicism and loathing for experts in general. Ajay thought that "elite experts" simply got most it wrong, most of the time. He said:

> "We've normally been in the habit of turning to experts for guidance and advice, but it's even harder now. Because experts have so obviously been getting so many things wrong and we all instinctively know that. *The Financial Times* reported that experts predicted the economy would be damaged instantly after the Brexit vote. But soon after that, *The Guardian* reported that those bad predictions didn't happen. So the experts were wrong. And here, the Bank of England experts were good enough to admit that they got it wrong on Brexit. Most experts even failed to predict the biggest financial crisis of 2008 and one of the few experts who did see it coming says the experts need to change their methods".

Finally, Ajay was convinced that the epistemological problem of not-knowingness collides with an emotional disposition towards novelty and risk. Given that we simply don't know what will happen after leaving the EU, the way in which experts predicted that the UK would fail are ultimately as false as the narratives they used to justify the movement to Remain. Ajay said:

> "And that includes being outside of the EU. People adapt, especially us Brits. So the expert's forecasts based on current behaviour patterns are useless. And that's why they keep getting it wrong with pessimism. And we'd do well to not obsess over their forecasts at this time. The elites and experts have been getting it wrong for decades. Now a moment has come to disregard those elites and get rid of that breed of politicians".

Finally, and perhaps most interesting, Ajay had what I considered an unusually perceptive critique of the relationship between the British Empire and the campaign to stay within the EU. Broadly speaking, most of the academic literature associates the vote to Leave with a nostalgia for Britain's imperial possessions (Dorling and Tomlinson 2019). In this reading, Brexit represented a dynamic (although eccentric) mixture between Little-Englanders and rapacious capitalists who look to break free from the social-democratic limits imposed on capital by the EU. The longing for empire is, ostensibly, also a longing for recreating a network of imperial power. Although many of these authors offer little by way of empirical evidence for these claims, the general sense that there is a connection between Brexit and pro-imperial nostalgia is a powerful assumption for many of the Remainers that I had spoken to over these year of fieldwork.

According to Ajay, however, the reverse is the case. Despite being a fervent Brexiter, he thinks that the financial sector has deeply (and negatively) impacted British culture and identity – such that "progressive mainstream media" is aware that Britain wants to keep its identity so "relentlessly mocks Leavers for clinging to heritage by shaming Empire for plundering the world". He points out that the greatest legacy of the British Empire is not the Commonwealth but London's global hegemony as a financial centre. Those in the City want "silky access to Europe" and it is the greatest share of the economy that the Remainers try to protect. They are thus wrong to accuse Brexiters of clinging to the fruits of Empire when they are the ones who desire to keep financial supremacy in Europe. There is of course room for a great deal of debate on the financial impacts of Brexit, but generally speaking Ajay's intuition that business interests wanted to stay within the EU in order to maintain financial access privileges is correct.

Much of Ajay's attempts at creating epistemic autonomy away from such "experts" led him to pursue his own independent research. This obviously included all the many videos and lectures that he presented in his free time. One particular way this manifested was in his insistence that Britain need polymaths (like himself) over expert knowledge. This is because, he thought, experts see the world in siloed unilinear ways, while polymaths tend to see the complexity and interconnectedness of things. He took great pride in the fact that he read news article from "all sides: left-wing, right-wing, what educated people read and what non-educated people read, progressive, liberal, traditional – even what foreign media says". He delighted in knowing more than one side of the story, something which allows him to remain "balanced in outlook". His degree of trust in mainstream British media elites was exceedingly low, something he hedged against by informing himself of various news media opportunities that were available to him, even in Belize.

His cynicism and suspicion of these "experts" was largely rationalised in terms of their inability to predict the future. Given that their "humility is rare", it is no coincidence that they failed to predict the Brexit vote – just like "they also predicted that the stock market would fall after the result of Brexit, even though it actually went up". Ajay was constantly castigating anyone who would listen that "experts are not priests to believe blindly". His spirited support of Michael Gove's quote that "people have had enough of experts" is right given that they become "elite insider groups all thinking the same way with their jargon". Ajay saw this as another example of the risks of groupthink, which leads to "incorrect expert consensus" on major issues. "Don't treat experts like priests", he often warned, clearly deeply concerned that those who were advising both the British government and the general public were in some sense up to no good. Although he didn't necessarily attribute this to bad faith on their part, his critique rested on the more abstract theoretical ground that scientific paradigms are much worse at predicting outcomes than they are believed to be.

Media

Finally, one central aspect to Ajay's general view of the world was a deep cynicism towards "mainstream media". The term itself tends to be associated with conspiratorial types, for whom nothing generally accepted can be taken at face value. But there was more than something simply reactive about Ajay's stance. Like Terry's attempts to change Brussels Law in Chapter 2, Ajay himself had an uncharacteristically authentic relationship to the issues he was concerned about.

What this means more specifically is that during the coronavirus, he took the time to personally investigate was happening throughout the country. During the height of the pandemic, he (and many others) was called back in to work as emergency doctors, given that the *National Health Service* was at a deficit of medical professionals. Not only did he volunteer to work on the wards, he also went down to the Nightingale Hospital – a rapidly constructed medical site to handle the new wave – with his iPhone in hand in order to film what was going on. Asking people questions, investigating the hospital, depending only on himself for "the truth" – much of his search demonstrated to him (accurately or not) that the mainstream media was not communicating the true figures around how many people were infected. This he told to his MBA and university friends who, as I discussed earlier in the chapter, were appalled that he questioned the accepted narrative concerning the depth of the nation's tragedy. This is because, he thought, they were too sacred to disbelieve the institutions that they trust to deliver them an accurate portrait of reality.

Ajay's former colleagues and friends were, he said, too busy with family and career to give any of this time of day. Their inability to then go and find new sources to trust were simply too much hard work, he thought, in addition to the more salient fact of being so emotionally destabilising. When I asked him about how this affected his relationship with close friends, which it obviously did, Ajay's response was simply that "they were too comfortable". They prefer to stay within the walls of the "comfort zone" rather than hear the "truth" about how mainstream media is manipulating them. He reminisced that his university friends now "had successful careers and fancy cars", satisfied and proud of themselves and how far they'd come in life. This isn't something that they want to risk, he said, as it is a kind of "existential threat" to accept the truth when it puts their promotions in jeopardy. Of course, this narrative put Ajay himself in the hotseat as a renegade Sherlock Holmes figure, who was willing to go the extra mile to find out the truth. Few people were ready to pushback against the lies of the mainstream media, especially those that had carved out plush lifestyles for themselves. In a world dominated by *Yin*, only exceptional individuals like himself were ready to embody the *Yang* attitude that might save the West from its own degeneracy.

5.6 Conspiracy as Critique

How can we tie in these last thematic points to Ajay's general worldview, and what are the implications for psychological and cognitive anthropology? One salient framework is known colloquially as 'conspiracy theory': a label with both a generative potential and a remarkable set of limitations. One immediate problem is one of definition; like the concept of populism, scholars are still divided on how to define what 'conspiracy theory' actually means. The expression itself is relatively novel, traceable in large part to those trying to make sense of 20th-century totalitarianisms (Thalmann 2019). But others might argue that the term is simply a repackaging of what German psychologist Klaus Conrad (1958) called 'apophenia' – the habitual discernment of meaningful patterns in social reality which index an occult controller. While initially correlated with schizophrenic disorders, the term recognises the natural proclivity of humans towards perceiving connection and co-ordination behind random events, possibly as a consequence of evolution (Tooby and Cosmides 2010). Scholars have drawn attention, for instance, to the affinity between witchcraft beliefs and conspiracy theories (Rabo 2021). Both posit that hidden forces determine and explain the mystery of events, although the "disenchanted" (Weber 1971) character of modernity precludes such answers from involving supernatural elements. Indeed, Popper (2011, p. 459) sees conspiracy theories in their modern form as "the typical result of the secularization of religious superstitions".

Nevertheless, a good working definition comes from Cubitt (1989), who argues that conspiracy theories are "a way of making sense of current events and the grand sweep of history that is characterised by intentionalism, dualism, and occultism" (Butter and Knight 2021, p. 1). Conspiratorialists think that there are no real 'accidents' nor 'coincidences' in politics; that the world is Manichean in its division between malicious conspirators and innocent victims, and that the conspiracy itself is hidden until it achieves its objective. Yet part of why this definition remains inadequate is because real conspiracies do actually happen. The suspicion around nefarious plots can in many cases be proven to be true: illustrations included American government funding of mind-control experiments (Ranelagh 1986) or Big Tobacco knowing that cigarettes caused cancer (Proctor 2012). These events necessarily preclude defining 'conspiracy' in ways which stress their empirical inaccuracy. And as I previously noted, Fassin (2021, p. 128) also makes the compelling argument that conspiracies are more than simply delusions, but also "indexes of social relations, political tensions, cultural disquietude, and moral uneasiness". In that sense, conspiracies might be seen as indexing social control – perhaps not dissimilar from Abu-Lughod's (1990) Foucauldian argument that resistance is a 'diagnostic' of power.

A truly in-depth sweep of this literature would be too broad of an undertaking for this chapter. Instead, I suggest that we can begin to understand conspiracy theories better when we frame them alongside the two epistemological building blocks of anthropology: symbolism and functionalism. Despite its drawbacks for "losing sight of the hard surfaces of life" (Geertz 1973, p. 30), we can take the symbolist approach to understand conspiracies as narratives which help us make sense of what the world means. As Jameson (1988, p. 356) says, they can be seen as the "poor person's cognitive mapping in the postmodern age". In other words, the globalised world is so enormous and unmanageable that conspiracies provide a simplistic enough symbolic mapping that life is not overwhelming in its complexity. Like myth and religion, they provide an interpretive framework for making sense of a complex social reality (Geertz 1973; Malinowski 1948).

Yet one of the problems with this approach is that it doesn't help us make sense of why each unique conspiracy theory emerges precisely as it does. How are such theories socially constructed, where, and by whom? For instance, much scholarship has endeavoured to try and understand where the boundary lies when determining the nature of social deviance, whether in behaviour and thought (Becker 1963; Durkheim 2002). Similar problems emerge with conspiracy theories: it is not quite clear why some people are attracted to these alternative forms of meaning-making, while others remain content trusting in the mainstream. Certainly, research suggests that the increase in conspiracies correlates with an overall distrust of mainstream authorities (Renard 2015). Others have argued for a correlation between believing in conspiracy theories when they feel involved in a group, exonerated from crime, or that implicate their enemies (Giry and Tika 2020). Some have even argued that modernity itself is defined by a 'culture of suspicion' (Carroll 1977; Remmling 1969), although anyone familiar with classic ethnographies of witchcraft will see that mistrust is a universal feature of social relations.

One solution is to see conspiracies not as monolithic, but rather part of diverse networks of beliefs and worldviews (Harambam and Aupers 2017). We can perhaps think, then, that both rationality and irrationality coexist in an unstable balance (Boudon 1996). This is particularly interesting when we consider how disputed the relationship is between education and conspiracies: preconceived notions that they are based on ignorance or eccentricity do not seem to stand up to wide empirical scrutiny (Giry and Tika 2020). Conspiracy theories do not map onto a lack of knowledge about the situation, although that context may be a precondition for their attractiveness. Instead, they seem to give a kind of cognitive stability to a world which is seemingly unmanageable. In this sense, the symbolist approach is an important way of understanding how conspiracies can become so embedded in diverse modern cultures.

A functionalist reading of conspiracy theories, on the other hand, focuses more on what that worldview *does* for individuals or for the social order more generally. This approach tends to focus on the political consequences of believing in conspiracies. More concretely, the utility of such beliefs comes from their value as a means of rejecting the power of epistemic authorities like the state. Their attractiveness is located in the role they play in co-opting or 'hiving off' individuals and groups from hegemonic collectivities and directing them towards alternative ones. A major proponent of this view is Cassam (2019), who argues that understanding conspiracy theories requires understanding their *function*; that is, to advance a political or ideological objective. They do so by providing seductive explanations which, although unlikely to be true, manage to yet influence public opinion in a different direction. They can thus be thought of as a form of political propaganda which operates to ease people's rejection of authority. Fringe movements which individuals may otherwise rebuff become much more enticing; for instance, if a culture is broadly critical of nationalism, conspiracy theories can soften the boundaries that allow co-option into movements which promote it. Indeed, Harris (2022) argues that for those who feel that the cultural landscape is shaped by alien perspectives, conspiracy theories are consciously adopted as a strategy of resistance. Embracing contrarian narratives against the mainstream perspective on what's fundamentally going on, adherents can thus reassert their 'epistemic autonomy' in the face of an unfriendly (or even hostile) socio-political context.

These two frameworks are not necessarily antithetical or mutually exclusive, and we can observe situations in which they both contribute a compelling perspective. In ancient Rome, for instance, citizens looking for answers to war, famine and disease would blame disaster on the machinations of a nefarious political elite. Partly this was because citizens were neither able nor interested in understanding how "crowded slums, a disregard for safety or building codes, [or] a dysfunctional senate ruled by fear" contributed to social degradation (Pagán 2020, p. 538). In this context, a symbolist approach will emphasise that conspiracies hedge against what Keeley (1999) calls 'absurdism': the terrifying notion that we live in a world in which nobody, even the emperor Nero, is truly in control. What a functionalist might bring to the conversation, however, is the notion that conspiracies serve as alternatives to authentic (but largely impossible) political engagement in an ancient militaristic dictatorship. This is mirrored among the proliferation of conspiracy theories in the modern Middle East, which Gray (2020) argues are the consequences of arrested economic development, social instability, and political oppression. Clearly, both sides of this argument have a great deal of merit.

Another more recent illustration of this tension comes from 20th-century America. Realist-functionalist scholars like Rogin (1987) analysed the rise of McCarthyism in terms of "the political and material vested interests of elite factions in the Republican party" (Blanuša and Hristov 2020. p. 67). Persecution of communists should be seen in this light by virtue of the functional political advantage which accrued to the perpetrators. Such a framework contrasts with Hofstadter's (1996) symbolist approach to the era, one which emphasised the "long tradition of American countersubversive demonology, marked out by anxieties, unconscious frustrations, intolerance, and anti-democratic potential" (Blanuša and Hristov 2020, p. 68). Where one focused on the cultural and psychological dimensions of politics, the other emphasised how conspiracies functioned to change the political structure in desired ways. Rogin (1987) later revised this debate and took the approach that both sides provided a coherent explanation: a perspective this chapter extrapolates to the broader literature. It is also important to note, finally, that this perspective does not preclude the function being itself a kind of meaning. If we take Malinowski's (1948) theory of myth as an illustration, we can see that often the purpose of a story is the way it provides a cognitive charter or map of the social world. The two sides may only be mutually exclusive at a conceptual level.

Now, both of these approaches could be generatively applied to the worldview of Ajay. We have seen, for instance, in his *Yin/Yang* theory of social change a meaningful explanation for cultural transformation. While this is not particularly conspiratorial on its own, the tendency towards theorising a "woke" agenda behind these changes – especially as they centre on the nefarious power of the EU – certainly fits the general schema. So too does his attitude towards "elites" and "scientists" – both of whom he sees as being involved in nefarious plots to misrepresent the reality of what is going on in order to benefit themselves.

Drawing on this literature, then, we could say that Ajay's view seems to demonstrate the truth behind the convergence of both symbolist and functionalist approaches to conspiracy theories. On the one hand, there is clearly an issue of meaning-making occurring here. His narrative of untrustworthy "woke experts" who are consciously changing Britain for the worse fits well within the literature which approaches them as generative of models for understanding the world. In a similar vein to my previous chapter, such an approach sees these eccentric stories as cognitive models which can organise complex, unstable, and sometimes only arbitrarily related fragments of the social world into a holistic and digestible form. As bizarre as some of Ajay's views might seem, we must admit that they do at least cushion the overwhelmingly intricate patterns of social reality into a seamless whole. It comes as no surprise that his views evoke quasi-theological imagery and metaphor, given Popper's (2011) argument that conspiracies represent secularised superstitions. Both help humans create a broader sense of meaning out of the chaos of existence, especially in times of great social polarisation and instability.

But so too can we read in this ethnography another example of the strength to functionalist approaches to the topic. Much in line with the work of Cassam (2019) and Harris (2022), it is clear that Ajay's view of the world is not simply a way of understanding it, but of organising his life in a particular direction. Ajay clearly felts alienated from mainstream political affiliation, and in consequence devoted much of his life to vigorously defending the Brexit cause. The ideological prism through which he observes and understands Brexit is not simply as a kind of intellectual framework, although it is partly that. Rather, his alternative way of seeing things advances a particular objective. His rejection of state authority (whether over the economy or health policy) is not simply because he feels that it isn't discursively authentic or correct, but also because he is deeply involved in a quasi-revolutionary project to overturn the established order. Brexit was many things, and a form of 'anti-politics' against the way things are must figure prominently among them. Functionally speaking, then, the conspiratorialism that Ajay presents can also be understood as a rejection of the 'epistemic authority' (Harris 2022) of established power, whether in the form of globalising institutions, technocratic state coercion, or political elites themselves.

What these theories *do* for him rather than simply what they *mean* is paramount to understanding how they are so powerful. Believing in them provides a real cognitive escape from the established narratives about what has been happening in Britain since 2016. Ajay's ability to quite literally hive off and join an entirely different group of people – all of whom had quite distinct political objectives compared to the mainstream – was possible only through the adoption of a set of myths about the world which justified these actions. This is of course commonly noted among scholars, who see populism itself as inevitably tied in with conspiracy theories (Eberl et al. 2020). But understanding quite why this situation occurs is slightly more complicated in that we need to ask what these theories *do* for people rather than simply how they use them to make sense of things. For Ajay, conspiracies about science, the economy, the pandemic, and the EU all softened the boundary between the more hegemonic attitudes of the professionals in his personal network and the subversive ones of those who wish to overturn the status quo. Beliefs quite easily become justifications, and his intellectual orientation clearly allowed him to sever reliance from mainstream opinions.

Beyond The Functionalist–Symbolist Debate

One last insight remains. I have argued that both symbolist and functionalist approaches to conspiracy theories are generative paradigms for understanding Ajay's cosmological vision for modern Britain. Yet when we examine his life, there is something missing to an approach which posits such an abstract and instrumental relationship between his beliefs and his actions. It certainly true that he perceives the world through a conspiratorial language that both helps him make sense of things and which gives him a sense of relative political independence from a culture to which he feels alienated. But the key is recognising that narratives of fighting "wokeness" or the domination of *Dark Yin* are *participatory* relationships in which Ajay is himself completely enmeshed. While not conceptually dissimilar from a general functionalist perspective, what we observe here is an alignment between conspiracy and social action which shares a common thread with previous chapter's analysis of myth.

This perspective draws heavily from the work of Greenwood (2022, p. 3), who posits the concept of 'magical consciousness' as the "spectrum of beliefs [and] ritual practices based on participatory, analogical – rather than analytical or logical – thought". Observing the bizarrely pagan aesthetic of the 6 January 2021 riots on Capitol Hill, Greenwood applies anthropological literature on pre-modern and indigenous societies to the study of conspiracy theories. Noting that the latter are usually heavily inflected the same type of mythical imagery that we see in Ajay's cosmology, she builds on Parmigiani's (2021) idea of "conspiracy-believing" (rather than "belief in conspiracies") pagan groups in Italy to emphasise that conspiracies align with a dissent from the status quo. What makes this more complex – and not simply another illustration of a functionalist reading – is the role of the *participation* that is central to these neo-animist practices. It is not merely a question of *meaning* (symbolism) nor *doing* (functionalism) but of *being*: the magical emotional identification with thought and practice.

Much of this can be framed in relationship to the early anthropological work of Lévy-Bruhl (2015). Although he is largely criticised today for making the ostensibly neo-colonial argument that primitive people had a 'pre-logical mentality' – one which is necessarily inferior to modern Europeans – his overall ideas actually open up a highly generative paradigm to understanding conspiracy theories. His actual observation was not a pejorative judgement on the non-Western ability to think clearly, but rather that all human groups have the propensity for two broad types of cognition: the logical and the mythopoeic. The former is analytic and rational, one focused on abstract problem solving. The latter, however, was participatory, mystical and magical. It works by drawing out connections between (often arbitrary) things through storytelling, communicated in an analogic way rather than a logical one (Greenwood 2022). By doing so, the stories we tell ourselves about ourselves shape the cultural meanings that we encounter in the world. In other words, it is indispensable not only for organising individuals into groups, but in feeling ourselves a part of reality as a whole. This may map onto the left-right brain divergence, too, although a neuroscientific approach adds little to the current argument (Greenwood and Goodwyn 2015). The point is that the magical story-telling half of human cognition plays an important role in the formation and maintenance of social groups and the way they each understand the world. In that sense, we can think of it as both uniting and transcending the symbolist/functionalist split in our conceptual frameworks for conspiracy theorising.

Lévy-Bruhl (2015) argued not that primitive man lacked the analytical or logical ability to reason, but rather than this side was fully immersed and dominated by mythopoeic thought. Indigenous, non-modern peoples were simply unbothered by the kind of rationalising mental activity which the moderns assume to be of central importance. Conversely, in our own society, the opposite tendency towards hegemony of the logical cognition drowns out the mythopoeic process of magical storytelling: just the kind we see re-emerge in contemporary conspiracy theories. It is impossible to ignore the colourful vividness of conspiracy theories that currently exist: whether about Jews, 9/11, the JFK assassination, Trump, Jeffrey Epstein, chemtrails, the moon landings, or Barack Obama's birth certificate. All of them illustrate the role of mythopoeic thinking in the disenchanted modern context.

Once again, perhaps the most interesting of all such conspiracy theories is Ajay's own cosmology. Here too can we find 'magical consciousness' as a generative explanation for his own work. For what we find when we consider his beliefs about the world is not simply an explanation nor a general orientation. What we observe is a fully participatory, immersive experience in which he lives his life according to the same magical narratives that he espouses in public. It is not simply that he believes in a mystical, *Yin/Yang* nature of reality. Nor is that these metaphysical forces express themselves in empirically observable political behaviour and action. Rather, he experiences *himself* very much in this great mythological battle for the soul of the modern West.

I met Ajay, after all, during his campaign as a Brexit Party candidate for his local area. He had, at that point, relinquished much of his full-time work in order to campaign to fight against *Dark Yin* and the pernicious forces of "wokeness". Although he believed that the *Yin/Yang* forces must be balanced, he saw in the contemporary West a terrible imbalance in favour of the former. By fighting to defend the referendum result, he was personally participating in the rebalance of *Yang* in the observable social world. Moreover, his decision to investigate the COVID-19 pandemic first-hand – before jetting off to Central America to continue the fight via a kind of digital guerrilla warfare – also testifies to his desire for full-on emotional participation. In short, there is no discernible distinction between the mystical, mythopoeic cosmology and his personal actions as an individual human being.

5.7 Conclusion

This chapter has examined the life and beliefs of Ajay, an ardent Brexiter who developed an entire cosmology around the populist moment since 2016. Uniquely among my interlocutors, Ajay was not content merely to have an opinion about Brexit, but rather to develop a holistic theory about what is going on and broadcast it to the world. This he did through various blogs, radio shows, YouTube videos and talking to researchers like myself. I found in his perspective not merely a uniquely eccentric set of myths about our contemporary situation, but an opportunity to understand what Bion (1984) called the alpha-function mode of cognition: that mental process by which disparate sensory elements can form into a distinct and coherent narrative. Understanding how Ajay made sense of the changing values of Western societies in his own terms gives cognitive anthropologists another opportunity to understand the relationship between sense impressions, political activism, and the narrative content which shape how people orientate themselves in moments of cultural transition.

Moreover, this framing helps us transcend the symbolist/functionalist dichotomy which has been a strong current in both this book and anthropology as a whole. The emotionally participatory quality of 'magical consciousness' (Greenwood 2022) provides an enriching and sophisticated framework for understanding both conspiracy theories and the elaborately mythical narratives which transcend them. Ajay's metaphysical cosmology is one example of this process, but so are the many others we see in more traditionally religious contexts. In both cases, what we observe is the convergence of a symbolic mapping of social reality interlinked with a sense of communal *being* within it. Myth is not something to be merely thought, but something which is *lived*. As both Radin (2015) and Lévy-Bruhl (2015) point out, this emotional, physical, sensational way of being is what is so important to 'primitive' man – not his inability to think logically. A similar point can be made towards Ajay: his *personal* involvement with his own cosmology is just as important as the discursive content that defines it. In consequence, rather than reducing our comparisons between populism and conspiracies to either a symbolic or a functionalist framework, then, this chapter has built upon classic anthropology to demonstrate that there is a kind of unity in the diverse cultural variety of human myth-making. Emotional participation in social reality – engaged through mythopoeic cognition – remains a central part of the modern experience of populism. We would do well not to ignore it.

CONCLUSION

Finishing this book in early 2024, and it feels like Brexit will never end. The sense that the repercussions of leaving the European Union (EU) remain one of the biggest problems in the economy are unavoidable. Even more historically pro-Brexit newspapers like *The Daily Telegraph* have published articles about why it was a bad idea. At the time of writing, a recent poll demonstrated that around 60 per cent of the British public would have wanted to stay or re-join. The confusion and hysteria of the past several years has become slowly more muted, as new 'moral panics' (Cohen 2011) about illegal boat crossings, energy prices, and Prince Harry have since dominated the headlines. From one angle, whatever Brexit truly meant, the debate about the UK's integration with Europe hasn't been finally and irrevocably settled.

For a great deal of the population, however, it is an unavoidable reality that high food prices, customs barriers, and an internationally isolated and weakened UK have at least as much to do with Brexit as they do with the war in Ukraine or energy prices. Whether or not there truly were genuine benefits to leaving the EU, another perspective on what Brexit means is a decline in living standards, strained relationships with continental neighbours, economic difficulties, and a lingering sense of confusion about what the UK is and where it's going. As Dean Acheson once quipped: "Great Britain has lost an empire but not yet found a role". For many post-war politicians, leadership in Europe *was* that new role. After Brexit, a mood of confusion and despondency defines a political context in which nobody really knows what the future of the country might begin to look like.

This book has sought to make sense of the social transformations that the UK faces by conducting an ethnographic investigation into some of its protagonists. These several years have provided an almost uncountable amount

DOI: 10.4324/9781003458517-6

of ethnographic data, and it is thus only natural that what I presented is merely a sliver of what could be written about the era. Yet, I hope that what I did present in this book is more than enough to give the reader a sense of what many of the social, emotional, political, and intellectual themes were of this time. Although I have chosen to discuss sometimes very specific people, the windows on their life have (I hope) been an elucidating experience. A very great deal of other research on Brexit in the social sciences tends naturally to explain it in vast sweeping narratives: about the nation, the economy, or continental unification. I have chosen instead to focus on much smaller examples, such as the life and beliefs of unique individuals, in addition to unique but illuminating social events, in order to provide another set of perspectives on this problem. I did not meet a single Brexiter who was really like any of the others: each one had their own idiosyncratic reasons for wanting to leave the EU. Yet, it was also true that many of such reasons merged in a kind of emotional haze with one another: anxiety about the dissolution of boundaries, for instance, or a sense that things were running out of control. Understanding the interplay between the generalisable and the specific has been central not only to my book but to much of the anthropological venture itself.

To summarise this book, then. My introduction laid out some of the key research questions for this manuscript. How do people experience socio-cultural change? Why are certain individuals attracted to populist ideology? How far can we understand these in terms of issues like race and class, as opposed to more traditional anthropological concepts like meaning or social structure? I then examined out much of the extant literature on Brexit from a variety of different social scientific disciplines. These represented the overall theoretical context in which I placed my ethnographic work. There remains contentious debate among scholars about what trends can be said to truly drive the identification with populism across the world, and this is as true for Brexit as for France, the United States, or Brazil. Whether or not we foreground race, economic, or changing values divides, the truth is probably that all of them place important roles in shaping the subjectivity of Leave voters before and since 2016.

In Chapter 1, I began my ethnographic project by analysing one of the most significant moments of the Brexit period: the 2019 election. After several years of delay and equivocation, the election was a moment in which people were people were able to voice their concerns about the direction of the country. Focusing on Brexit Party candidates in particular, I argued that their votes were not merely a form of 'anti-politics' against what they saw as a rotten system, but also a chance to renew the social order. Interlinking theories on sacrifice and the sacred with the nature of national elections, I re-situated ritual as a key component of an anthropology of populism. Renewing the social order necessarily involves some kind of ceremonial practice, but this has been much less theorised today. My contribution highlights just how important an anthropological understanding of ritual is when we try to make sense of long-term sociocultural transformation in modern European societies.

In Chapter 2, I continued my analysis with an ethnography of Terry. A fervent Brexiter, Terry's general worldview was a kind of archetypal illustration of what many of the older British generations felt about where the UK was headed. Concerned with invasion and takeover not only from the EU, but also from Russia and the Islamic world, Terry's apocalyptic anxieties about losing control certainly reveal much of the pro-Leave mindset about immigration and ethnic change. But his constant retelling of stories related to the Second World War suggest not merely a nostalgia for the past as much as they reveal the way in which the human mind works in the present. Myth, whether from a structuralist or a functionalist point of view, is clearly present in these considerations around Brexit. Rather than seeing it as a hallmark of the pre-modern era, my analysis shows that it is as much a component of the contemporary world as it has ever been. Anthropological contributions to the study of myth prove wonderfully generative ways of thinking about the construction of political narratives today.

In Chapter 3, I returned to a more participatory-observational moment of fieldwork. I argued that, although we might be unable to witness social-structural cleavages in the way that we did for small-scale societies, it undoubtedly still exists. What anthropology brings to the table are ways of seeing such structural tensions occur at the level of the *carnivalesque* (Bakhtin 1984a, 1984b). I explore this with my analysis of the *Brexit Party* celebrations when the UK left the EU: a public party held in central London on 31 January 2020. The chapter's debate focuses on whether moments of public profanity and eccentric behaviour can be viewed as acts of political subversion, or whether we should better see it as little more than blowing off steam. I also add a subsequent reading, one which suggests that 'joking relationships' are symbolic demonstrations that structural tension is acknowledged and, in the end, might be overcome. Providing ethnographic examples of this relationship are important contributions to thinking about what anthropology can offer to the scholarship which is undertaking the task of studying polarisation today.

In Chapter 4, I built on many of the themes of the previous chapter to work through my ethnographic material more significantly in terms of how conspiracies work. Many interlocutors took an approach to understanding unwanted social change in terms of occluded human agency: a classically conspiratorial perspective. My informant in this chapter, Ajay, had similar such fantasies of elite 'expert' manipulation of both facts and the social world. However, what remained unique about his experience was the totally idiosyncratic cosmology that he himself built to describe what was going on in terms of *Yin* and *Yang* metaphysics. Much like in Chapter 2's exploration of mythic thinking, I posited that we could think of Bion's (1984) idea of the alpha-function to tease out the relationship between the process of cognition and a narrative which dream thoughts can be known, and communicated. Moreover, by combining this with the Greenwood's (2020) concept of 'magical consciousness', a concept she builds from Lévy-Bruhl's early work, I demonstrated that we could go beyond the symbolist-functionalist split of understanding conspiracy theories and add that *being* – understood as emotional participation in our political narratives – has a key role to play in this understanding of our contemporary moment.

What then, are the overall contributions of this book to the literature on the anthropology of either populism or Brexit? I believe the most important is simply the re-assertion that our discipline can bring tremendous value to these discussions, even if they are largely dominated by other epistemological frameworks. It is clear from this book that I have provided something of a sceptical angle about the relationship between Brexit and, for example, race. This I believe is because I concur with the empirical literature simply cannot justify a significant relationship between the two (Norris and Inglehart 2019). This is true even if some scholars argued that non-white immigration has a central role in the rise of populism today (Kaufmann 2018). Neither can class be put as the central plank on which we balance our analysis. This is because Brexit was more so a vote from the middle-classes than it was for those in lower socioeconomic brackets (Dorling and Tomlinson 2019).

Rather than focusing on these popular categories, then, I chose instead to situate my analysis in the language of classic anthropology: Malinowski, Levi-Strauss, Durkheim, Lévy-Bruhl, Radcliffe-Brown, Frazer, and Bloch. Classical anthropology remains a robust and generative framework for understanding what is going on in today's politics. Ritual, structure, myth, symbol, ceremony – they are all powerful concepts which, sadly, are much less in vogue among my contemporaries. I hope that this book has re-situated them as just as relevant for understanding the modern world as a Foucault, Derrida, or Butler. The strength and reinvigoration of our discipline will come not from adopting the literature of philosophers but from being true to our own intellectual tradition.

But it is also important to note that what anthropology can bring to populism studies is not merely a 'batch of concepts' but rather an entirely different way of looking at this problem. It is true, as other scholars have demonstrated, that generalised ideas like 'postmaterialist' values or 'globalisation' have a role to play in understanding the vote to leave the EU. So too, indeed, do themes like 'post-colonial nostalgia' or a desire to see the UK great again permeate the pro-Brexit discourses. But ultimately, such wide and sweeping generalisations can only take us so far in understanding what Brexit 'means' for each and every person who has been involved in the issue for the debate since (and even much before) 2016. At the level of the individual, Brexit has an irreducibly unique aspect: one which cannot be separated from their own psyche. In emphasising what psychological anthropology can bring to understanding this point, I hope I have provided a compelling enough case for the merits of our disciplinary contributions to an *Anthropology of Now*.

As one of the greatest anthropologists of all time, Clifford Geertz (1973, p. 5) once said: "man is an animal suspended in webs of significance he himself has spun". I hope that this book has made some modest headway towards disentangling our strange cultural moment for the next generation. Whether or not Brexit will forever mean Brexit is a battle for them, and us.

BIBLIOGRAPHY

Abramson, A. and Holbraad, M. (2014). Introduction: The Cosmological Frame in Anthropology. In Abramson, A. and Holbraad, M. (Eds) *Framing Cosmologies: The Anthropology of Worlds*. Manchester: Manchester University Press.

Abu-Lughod, L. (1990). The Romance of Resistance: Tracing Transformations of Power Through Bedouin Women. *American Ethnologist* 17(1): 41–55.

Adorno, T., Frenkel-Brunswick, E., Levinson, D., and Sanford, E.N. (2019). *The Authoritarian Personality*. London: Verso.

Altemeyer, B. (1988). *Enemies of Freedom: Understanding Rightwing Authoritarianism*. San Francisco, CA: Jossey-Bass.

Altemeyer, B. (1996). *The Authoritarian Spectre*. Cambridge, MA: Harvard University Press.

Altemeyer, B. (2020). *Right-Wing Authoritarianism*. Winnipeg, MB: University of Mantioba Press.

Amory, D. (1997). African Studies as American Institution. In Gupta, A. and Ferguson, J. (Eds), *Anthropological Locations: Boundaries and Grounds of a Field Science*. Berkeley, CA: University of California Press.

Anderson, B. (1990b). Further Adventures of Charisma. In *Language and Power; Exploring Political Cultures in Indonesia*. Jakarta: Equinox.

Anderson, B. (2016). *Imagined Communities: Reflections on the Origin and Spread of Nationalism*. London: Verso.

Anderson, M. (2019). Conclusion: Anti-Racism, Liberalism, and Anthropology in the Age of Trump. In, *From Boas to Black Power: Racism, Liberalism, and American Anthropology*. Stanford, CA: Stanford University Press.

Andrew, E. (1983). Class in Itself and Class against Capital: Karl Marx and His Classifiers. *Canadian Journal of Political Science / Revue Canadienne de Science Politique* 16(3): 577–584.

Appadurai, A. (1990). Disjuncture and Difference in the Global Cultural Economy. *Theory, Culture & Society* 7(2–3): 295–310.

Aristotle (1996). Poetics. London: Penguin.

Asad, T. (1993). Ethnography, Literature, and Politics: Some Readings and Uses of Salman Rushdie's Satanic Verses. In *Genealogies of Religion: Discipline and Reasons of Power in Christianity and Islam*. Baltimore, MD: Johns Hopkins University Press.

Autor, D.H., Dorn, D., and Hanson, G.H. (2013). The China Syndrome: Local Labor Market Effects of Import Competition in the United States. *American Economic Review* 103(6): 2121–2168.

Autor, D.H., Dorn, D., Hanson, G.H., and Majlesi, K. (2017). Importing Political Polarization? The Electoral Consequences of Rising Trade Exposure. NBER working paper series 22637.

Auyero, J., Burbano de Lare, A., and Fernanda Berti, M. (2013). "Violence and the State at the Urban Margins". *Journal of Contemporary Ethnography* 43(1): 94–116.

Bakhtin, M. (1981). *The Dialogic Imagination*. Austin, TX: University of Texas Press.

Bakhtin, M. (1984a). *Problems of Dostoevsky's Poetics*. Minneapolis, MN: University of Minnesota Press.

Bakhtin, M. (1984b). *Rabelais and His World*. Bloomington, IN: Indiana University Press.

Balthazar, A.C. (2017) Made in Britain: Brexit, Teacups, and the Materiality of the Nation. *American Ethnologist* 44(2): 220–224.

Banerjee, M. (2007). Sacred Elections. *Economic and Political Weekly*, 42(17): 1556–1562.

Banton, M. (1996). The Cultural Determinants of Xenophobia. *Anthropology Today* 12(2): 8–12.

Barnett, A. (2017). *The Lure of Greatness: England's Brexit and America's Trump*. London: Unbound.

Barthes, R. (2009). *Mythologies*. London: Vintage.

Bataille, G. (1991). *The Accursed Share: Volume One*. New York: Zone Books.

Bauman, Z. (2000). *Liquid Modernity*. Cambridge: Polity Press.

Becker, Alton L. (1995). *Beyond Translation: Essays Toward a Modern Philology*. Ann Arbor, MI: University of Michigan Press.

Becker, E. (1973). *The Denial of Death*. New York: Simon & Schuster.

Becker, H. (1963). *Outsiders: Studies in the Sociology of Deviance*. New York: The Free Press.

Beliso-De Jesús, A. and Pierre, J. (2020). Special Section: Anthropology of White Supremacy. *American Anthropologist* 122: 65–75.

Bendix, R. (1974). Inequality and Social Structure: A Comparison of Marx and Weber. *American Sociological Review* 39(2): 149–161.

Berger, P. (1990). *The Sacred Canopy: Elements of a Sociological Theory of Religion*. New York: Anchor.

Berger, P., Davie, G., and Fokas, E. (2008). *Religious America, Secular Europe? A Theme and Variations*. London: Routledge.

Bergmann, E. (2018). *Conspiracy & Populism: The Politics of Misinformation*. London: Palgrave.

Bergmann, E. and Butter, M. (2021). Conspiracy Theory and Populism. In Butter, M. and Knight, P. (Eds), *Routledge Handbook of Conspiracy Theories*. London: Routledge.

Berliner, D., Lambek, M., Shweder, R., Irvine, R., and Piette, A. (2016). "Anthropology and the Study of Contradictions. *HAU: Journal of Ethnographic Theory* 6 (1): 1–27.

Berreman, G. (1962). *Behind Many Masks: Ethnography and Impression Management in a Himalayan Hill Village*. New York: Society for Applied Anthropology.

Betz, H.G. and Meret, S. (2009). Revisiting Lepanto: The Political Mobilization Against Islam in Contemporary Western Europe. *Patterns of Prejudice* 43(3–4): 313–334.

Beveridge, R. and Featherstone, D. (2021). Introduction: Anti-politics, austerity and spaces of politicisation. *Environment and Planning C: Politics and Space* 39(3): 437–450.

Bhambra, G.K. (2017). Brexit, Trump, and 'Methodological Whiteness': On the Misrecognition of Race and Class. *The British Journal of Sociology* 68(1): 214–232.

Bhungalia, L. (2019). Laughing At Power: Humour, Transgression, and the Politics of Refusal in Palestine. *Environment and Planning C: Politics and Space* 38(3): 387–404.

Biehl, J. (2005). *Vita: Life in a Zone of Social Abandonment*. Berkeley, CA: University of California Press.

Billig, O. (1985). The Lawyer Terrorist and His Comrades. *Political Psychology* 6: 29–46.

Bion, W. (1984). *Learning From Experience*. London: Routledge.

Bion, W. (1998). *Experiences in Groups: And Other Papers*. London: Routledge.

Bishop, D. (2019). How Little We Know: Reflections on Our Ignorance of the EU. *LSE Brexit Blog*. https://blogs.lse.ac.uk/brexit/2019/09/24/how-little-we-know-reflections-on-our-ignorance-of-the-eu. 24September 2019. Accessed 19 May 2022.

Blanuša, N. and Hristov, T. (2020). Psychoanalysis, Critical Theory and Conspiracy Theory. In Butter, M. and Knight, P. (Eds), *Routledge Handbook of Conspiracy Theories*. London: Routledge.

Bloch, M. (1992). *Prey Into Hunter: The Politics of Religious Experience*. Cambridge: Cambridge University Press.

Bloom, A. (2012). *The Closing of the American Mind: How Higher Education Has Failed Democracy and Impoverished the Souls of Today's Students*. New York: Simon & Schuster.

Boas, F. (1966). *Kwakiutl Ethnography*. Chicago, IL: University of Chicago Press.

Bollas, C. (2017). *The Shadow of the Object: Psychoanalysis of the Unthought Known*. London: Routledge.

Boltanski, L. (2012) *Énigmes et Complots: Une Enquête à Propos d'Enquêtes*. Paris: Gallimard.

Bolton, M. (2019). Conceptual Vandalism, Historical Distortion: The Labour Antisemitism Crisis and the Limits of Class Instrumentalism. *Journal of Contemporary Antisemitism* 3(2): 11–30.

Borneman, J. (1991). *After The Wall: East Meets West in the New Berlin*. New York: Basic Books.

Borneman, J. (1992). *Belonging in the Two Berlins: Kin, State, Nation*. Cambridge: Cambridge University Press.

Borneman, J. (2002). Introduction: German Sacrifice Today. In Eghigian, E. and Berg, M. (Eds), *Sacrifice and National Belonging in Twentieth-Century Germany*. College Station, TX: Texas A&M University Press.

Borneman, J. (2010). European Rituals of Initiation and the Production of Men. *Social Anthropology* 18(3): 289–301.

Borneman, J. and Ghassem-Fachandi, P. (2017). The Concept of Stimmung: From Indifference to Xenophobia in Germany's Refugee Crisis. *HAU* 7(3): 105–135.

Borneman, J. and Hammoudi, A. (2009). *Being There: The Fieldwork Encounter and the Making of Truth*. Berkeley, CA: University of California Press.

Bossevain, J. (1970). Fieldworks in Malta. In Spindler, G. (Ed.), *Being an Anthropologist*. New York: Holt, Rinehart and Winston.

Botterill, K. and Burrell, K. (2019). (In)visibility, privilege and the Performance of Whiteness in Brexit Britain: Polish Migrants in Britain's Shifting Migration Regime. *Environment and Planning C: Politics and Space* 37: 23–28.

Boudon, R. (2004). *Pourquoi Les Intellectuels N'aiment Pas Le Liberalism*. Paris: Odile Jacob.

Bourdieu, P. (1990). *In Other Words: Essays Toward a Reflective Sociology*. Stanford, CA: Stanford University Press.

Bourdieu, P. (2001). *Contre-feux 2*. Paris: Raisons d'Agir.

Bourdieu, P. (2010). *Distinction: A Social Critique of the Judgement of Taste*. London: Routledge.

Bourdieu, P. (1977). *Outline of a Theory of Practice*. Cambridge: Cambridge University Press.

Bourgois, P. (2003). *In Search of Respect: Selling Crack in El Barrio*. Cambridge: Cambridge University Press.

Bowler, R. (2017). Whiteness, Britishness and the Racist Reality of Brexit. Centre for Applied Social Science Working Paper. University of Sunderland. Available at: http://sure.sunderland.ac.uk/id/eprint/8463.

Brinkley, D. (1990). Dean Acheson and the "Special Relationship": The West Point Speech of December 1962. *The Historical Journal* 33(3): 599–608.

Brown, W. (2017). *Undoing the Demos: Neoliberalism's Stealth Revolution*. New York: Zone Books.

Browning, C. (2019). Brexit Populism and Fantasies of Fulfilment. *Cambridge Review of International Affairs* 32(3): 222–244.

Buckels, E.E. and Trapnell, P. (2013). Disgust Facilitates Outgroup Dehumanization. *Group Processes & Intergroup Relations* 16(6): 771–780.

Burke, P. (1978). *Popular Culture in Early Modern Europe*. London: Templesmith.

Burnett, J. (2017). Racial Violence and the Brexit State. *Race & Class* 58(4): 85–97.

Burnham, J. (2020). *The Machiavellians: Defenders of Freedom*. New York: Lume Books.

Burnham, J. (2021). *The Managerial Revolution: What is Happening in the World*. New York: Lume Books.

Butler, J. (2004). *Precarious Life: The Powers of Mourning and Violence*. London: Verso.

Butler, J. (2010). *Frames of War: When is Life Grievable?*London: Verso.

Butter, M. and Knight, P. (2020). General Introduction. In Butter, M. and Knight, P. (Eds), *Routledge Handbook of Conspiracy Theories*. London: Routledge.

Calhoun, C. (2016). Brexit Is a Mutiny Against the Cosmopolitan Elite. *New Perspectives Quarterly* 33: 50–58.

Campanella, E. and Dassù, M. (2019). Brexit and Nostalgia. *Survival: Global Politics and Strategy* 61(3): 103–111.

Campion-Vincent, V. (2015). Note Sur les Entrepreneurs en Complots. *Diogène* 249 (50): 99–106.

Cannadine, D. (2013). *The Undivided Past: History Beyond Our Differences*. London: Penguin.

Carey, J. (1992). *The Intellectuals and the Masses: Pride and Prejudice Among the Literary Intelligentsia, 1880–1939*. London: Faber & Faber.

Carl, N., Dennison, J., and Evans, G. (2019). European but not European Enough: An Explanation for Brexit. *European Union Politics* 20(2): 282–304.

Carr J., Clifton-Sprigg J., James J., and Vujić S. (2020). *Love Thy Neighbour? Brexit Hate Crime*. Bonn: Institute of Labor Economics.

Carroll, J. (1977). *Puritan, Paranoid, Remissive: A Sociology of Modern Culture*. London: Routledge.

Cassam, Q. (2019). *Conspiracy Theories*. Cambridge: Polity Press.

Cassirer, E. (2009). *The Myth of the State*. New Haven, CT: Yale University Press.

Cayla, D. (2021). *Populism and Neoliberalism*. London: Routledge.

Chan, T., Henderson, M., Sironi, M., and Kawalerowicz, J. (2020). Understanding the Social and Cultural Bases of Brexit. *British Journal of Sociology* 71(5): 830–851.

Chandra, K. (2004). *Why Ethnic Parties Succeed*. Cambridge: Cambridge University Press.

Chernaik, W. (2016). Victory's Crest: Milton, the English Nation, and Cromwell. In Stevens, P. and Loewenstein, D. (Eds), *Early Modern Nationalism and Milton's England*. Toronto, ON: University of Toronto Press.

Chibnik, M. (2011). *Anthropology, Economics, and Choice*. Austin, TX: University of Texas Press.

Clifford, J. (1988). *The Predicament of Culture: Twentieth-Century Ethnography, Literature, and Art*. Cambridge, MA: Harvard University Press.

Clifford, J. and Marcus, G. (1986). *Writing Culture: The Poetics and Politics of Ethnography*. Berkeley, CA: University of California Press.

Cockbain, E. (2013). Grooming and the 'Asian sex gang predator': The Construction of a Racial Crime Threat. *Race & Class* 54(4): 22–32.

Cohen, P.S. (1969). Theories of Myth. *Man* 4(3): 337–353.

Cohen, S. (2011) [1973]. *Folk Devils and Moral Panics: The Creation of the Mods and Rockers*. New York: Routledge.

Cohn, R. (2008). *Mass Migration Under Sail: European Immigration to the Antebellum United States*. Cambridge: Cambridge University Press.

Colantone, I. and Stanig, P. (2018). Global Competition and Brexit. *American Political Science Review* 112(2): 201–218.

Cole, J.W. (1977). Anthropology Comes Part-Way Home: Community Studies in Europe. *Annual Review of Anthropology* 6: 349–378.

Coles, K. (2004). Election Day: The Construction of Democracy through Technique. *Cultural Anthropology* 19(4): 551–580.

Colley, L. (1992). *Britons: Forging the Nation 1707–1837*. New Haven, CT: Yale University Press.

Colley, L. (2016). Brexiters are nostalgics in search of a lost empire. *The Financial Times*. Available at: www.ft.com/content/63de3610-07b0-11e6-9b51-0fb5e65703ce.

Comte, A. (2017 [1830]). *A General View of Positivism*. London: Routledge.

Conrad, K. (1958). *Die beginnende Schizophrenie: Versuch einer Gestaltanalyse des Wahns*. Stuttgart: Georg Thieme Verlag.

Copsey, N. (2008). *Contemporary British Fascism: The British National Party and the Quest for Legitimacy*. London: Routledge.

Copsey, N. (2011). Introduction: Contemporary Perspectives on the British National Party. In Copsey, N. and Macklin, G. (Eds), *British National Party: Contemporary Perspectives*. London: Routledge.

Copus, C. (2018). The Brexit Referendum: Testing the Support of Elites and their Allies for Democracy; or, Racists, Bigots and Xenophobes, Oh My!. *British Politics* 13: 90–104.

Costello, T.H., Bowes, S.M., Stevens, S.T., Waldman, I.D., Tasimi, A., and Lilienfeld, S.O. (2022). Clarifying the Structure and Nature of Left-wing Authoritarianism. *Journal of Personality and Social Psychology* 122(1): 135–170.

Covington, C. (2018). Populism and the Danger of Illusion. *Contemporary Psychoanalysis* 54(2).

Coyle, D. (2016). Brexit and Globalisation. In Baldwin (R.) (Ed.), *Brexit Beckons: Thinking ahead by leading economists*. London: CEPR Press.

Crim, B. (2002). Was it All Just a Dream. In Eghigian, E. and Berg, M. (Eds), *Sacrifice and National Belonging in Twentieth Century Germany*. College Station, TX: Texas A&M University Press.

Cubitt, G. (1989). Conspiracy Myths and Conspiracy Theories. *Journal of the Anthropological Society of Oxford* 20(1): 12–26.

Cummings, D. (2017). On the Referendum #21: Branching histories of the 2016 referendum and the 'frogs before the storm'. Dominic Cummings's Blog. Available at: https://dominiccummings.com/2017/01/09/on-the-referendum-21-branching-histories-of-the-2016-referendum-and-the-frogs-before-the-storm-2/.

Cummings, R. (2020). Ain't No Black in the (Brexit) Union Jack? Race and Empire in the Era of Brexit and the Windrush Scandal. *Journal of Postcolonial Writing* 56(5): 593–606.

Curtice, J. (2016). Brexit: Behind the Referendum. *Political Insight* 7(2): 4–7.

Curtice, J. (2017). Why Leave Won the UK's EU Referendum. *JCMS: Journal of Common Market Studies* 55: 19–37.

Curtice, J., Hudson, N., and Montagu, I. (2020). *British Social Attitudes: The 37th Report*. London: The National Centre for Social Research.

Damon, F. (2003). What Good Are Elections? An Anthropological Analysis of American Elections. *Taiwan Journal of Anthropology* 1: 39–81.

Darrouzet, C., Wild, H., and Wilkinson, S. (2010). Participatory Ethnography at Work: Practicing in the Puzzle Palaces of a Large, Complex Healthcare Organization. In Cefkin, M. (Ed.), *Ethnography and the Corporate Encounter: Reflections on Research in and of Corporations*New York: Berghahn Books.

Das, V., and Poole, D. (2004). *(eds.) Anthropology in the Margins of the State*. Santa Fe, NM: School of American Research Press.

De Genova, N. (2020). 'Everything is Permitted': Trump, White Supremacy, Fascism. *American Anthropologist* 122(1).

De Heusch, L. (1985). *Sacrifice in Africa: A Structuralist Approach*. Manchester: Manchester University Press.

De Vries, C. and Edwards, E. (2009). Taking Europe to its Extremes: Extremist Parties and Public Euroskepticism. *Party Politics* 15(1): 5–28.

de Mause, L. (1982). *Foundations of Psychohistory*. New York: Creative Roots.

Denham, A. (2014). Psychoanalytic Anthropology. *Clio's Psyche* 20(4): 383–394.

Denham, J. and Devine, D. (2018). England, Englishness and the Labour Party. *The Political Quarterly* 89: 621–630.

Dennison, J. (2020). How Niche Parties React to Losing Their Niche: The Cases of the Brexit Party, the Green Party and Change UK. *Parliamentary Affairs* 73(1): 125–141.

Descola, P. (1998). *The Spears of Twilights: Life and Death in the Amazon Jungle*. London: New Press.

Descola, P. (2005). On Anthropological Knowledge. *Social Anthropology* 13: 65–73.

Detienne, M. (1989). Introduction. In Detienne, M. and Vernant, J.-P. (Eds), *The Cuisine of Sacrifice Among the Greeks*. Chicago, IL: University of Chicago Press.

Devereux, G. (1969). *Reality and Dream: The Psychotherapy of a Plains Indian*. New York: Doubleday.

Devereux, G. (1978). *Ethnopsychoanalysis: Psychoanalysis and Anthropology as Complimentary Frames of Reference*. Berkeley, CA: University of California Press.

Devereux, G. (1980). *Basic Problems of Ethnopsychiatry*. Chicago, IL: University of Chicago Press.

Diamond, N. (1970). Fieldwork in a Complex Society: Taiwan. In Spindler, G. (Ed.), *Being an Anthropologist*. New York: Holt, Rinehart and Winston.

Diez, T. (2004). Europe's Others and the Return of Geopolitics. *Cambridge Review of International Affairs* 17(2): 319–335.

Dinesen, P., Schaeffer, M, and Sønderskov, K. (2020). Ethnic Diversity and Social Trust: A Narrative and Meta-Analytical Review. *Annual Review of Political Science* 23(1): 441–465.

Dorling, D. and Tomlinson, S. (2019). *Rule Britannia: Brexit and the End of Empire*. London: Biteback.

Douglas, J. (2016). *Social Meanings of Suicide*. Princeton, NJ: Princeton University Press.

Douglas, M. (2002). *Purity and Danger: An Analysis of Concepts of Pollution and Taboo*. London: Routledge.

Dundes, A. (2007). Folk Ideas As Units of Worldview. In Bonner, S. (Ed.), *The Meaning of Folklore: The Analytical Essays of Alan Dundes*. Logan, UT: Utah State University Press.

Dunn, J. (1980). *The History of Political Theory and Other Essays*. Cambridge: Cambridge University Press.

Dunn, J. (1991). Paul's Understanding of the Death of Jesus as Sacrifice. In Sykes, S. (Ed.), *Sacrifice and Redemption: Durham Essays in Theology*. Cambridge: Cambridge University Press.

Durkheim, E. (1982). *The Rules of Sociological Method and Selected Texts on Sociology and its Method*. New York: Free Press.

Durkheim, E. (2002). *Suicide: A Study in Sociology*. London: Routledge.

Durkheim, E. (2008). *Elementary Forms of Religious Life*. Oxford: Oxford University Press.

Durkheim, E. (2008). *The Elementary Forms of Religious Life*. Oxford: Oxford University Press.

Durkheim, E. (2013). *The Division of Labour in Society*. London: Red Globe Press.

Eaglestone, R. (2018). Cruel Nostalgia and the Memory of the Second World War. In Eaglestone, R. (Ed.), *Brexit and Literature*. London: Routledge.

Eatwell, R. and Goodwin, M. (2018). *National Populism: The Revolt Against Liberal Democracy*. London: Pelican.

Eberl, J.-M., Huber, R., and Greussing, E. (2020). From Populism to the "Plandemic“: Why Populists Believe in COVID-19 Conspiracies. *Journal of Elections, Public Opinion, and Parties* 31(1): 272–284.

Eco, U. (1984). The Frames of Comic "Freedom". In Sebeok, T.A. (Ed.), *Carnival!*. Berlin: Mouton.

Edwards, J. and Strathern, M. (2000). Including Our Own. In Carsten, J. (Ed.), *Cultures of Relatedness: New Approaches to the Study of Kinship*. Cambridge: Cambridge University Press.

Eghigian, E. (2002). Injury, Fate, Resentment, and Sacrifice in German Political Culture, 1914–1939. In Eghigian, E. and Berg, M. (Eds.), *Sacrifice and National*

Belonging in Twentieth-Century Germany. College Station, TX: Texas A&M University Press.

El-Enany, N. (2021). *Bordering Britain: Law, Race, and Empire*. Manchester: Manchester University Press.

Eliade, M. (1959). *The Sacred and the Profane: The Nature of Religion*. Sydney: Elsevier Australia.

Eliade, M. (1979). *Myths, Dreams and Mysteries*. London: HarperCollins.

Elias, N. (2006). *The Court Society: Volumes One and Two*. Dublin: University College Dublin Press.

Elliott, B. (2021). *The Roots of Populism: Neoliberalism and Working-Class Lives*. Manchester: Manchester University Press.

Engelke, M. (2008). The Objects of Evidence. *Journal of the Royal Anthropological Institute* 14: S1-S2.

Engels, F. (1949). Letter to F. Mehring. In *Karl Marx and Friedrich Engels: Selected Works in Two Volumes*. Moscow: Foreign Languages Publishing House.

Engesser, S., Ernst, N., Esser, F., and Büchel, F. (2017). Populism and Social Media: How Politicians Spread a Fragmented Ideology. *Information, Communication and Society* 20(8): 1109–1126.

Enriquez, E. and Centeno, M. (2016). *War And Society*. Cambridge: Polity Press.

Entman, R. (1989). How the Media Affect What People Think: An Information Processing Approach. *The Journal of Politics* 51(2): 347–370.

Epstein, A. (1967). *(ed.) The Craft of Social Anthropology*. London: Tavistock.

Erikson, E. (1968). *Identity: Youth and Crisis*. London: Faber & Faber.

Escobar, A. (2011). *Encountering Development: The Making and Unmaking of the Third World*. Princeton, NJ: Princeton University Press.

Evans-Pritchard, E.E. (1951). Some Features and Forms of Nuer Sacrifices. *Africa: Journal of the International African Institute*, 21(2): 112–121.

Evans-Pritchard, E.E. (1954). The Meaning of Sacrifice Among the Nuer. *The Journal of the Royal Anthropological Institute of Great Britain and Ireland* 84(1/2): 21–33.

Evans-Pritchard, E.E. (1969). *The Nuer: A Description of the Modes of Livelihood and Political Institutions of a Nilotic People*. Oxford: Oxford University Press.

Evans-Pritchard, E.E. (1976). *Witchcraft, Oracles and Magic Among the Azande*. Oxford: Oxford University Press.

Evans, G. (2020). Brexit is the Graveyard of Post-Industrial Britain: Ethnography as Eulogy for East-London and England. *Ethnologie Française* 50(3): 559–573.

Fabian, J. (1983). *Time and the Other: How Anthropology Makes its Object*. New York: Columbia University Press.

Fairbairn, W.R.D. (1952). *Psychoanalytic Studies of the Personality*. London: Routledge.

Fan, J. (2019). Woke Capital: The Role Of Corporations in Social Movements. *Harvard Business Law Review* 9(2): 441–494.

Fassin, D. (2021). Of Plots and Men: The Heuristics of Conspiracy Theories. *Current Anthropology* 62(2): 128–137.

Fassin, D. and Rechtman, R. (2009). *The Empire of Trauma: An Inquiry into the Condition of Victimhood*. Princeton, NJ: Princeton University Press.

Faulkner, S., Guy, H., and Vis, F. (2021). Right-wing Populism, Visual Disinformation, and Brexit. In Tumber, H. and Waisbord, S. (Eds), *The Routledge Companion to Media Disinformation and Populism*. London: Routledge.

Feldman, S. and Stenner, K. (1997). Perceived Threat and Authoritarianism. *Political Psychology* 18(4): 741–770.

Fenichel, O. (1996). *The Psychoanalytic Theory of Neurosis*. New York: W.W. Norton & Co.

Ferguson, J. and Gupta, A. (2002). Spatializing States: Toward an Ethnography of Neoliberal Governmentality. *American Ethnologist* 29: 981–1002.

Finchelstein, F. (2017). *From Fascism to Populism in History*. Berkeley, CA: University of California Press.

Finchelstein, F. (2020). *A Brief History of Fascist Lies*. Berkeley, CA: University of California Press.

Fisher, D. (1986). Rockefeller Philanthropy: And the Rise of Social Anthropology. *Anthropology Today* 2(1): 5–8.

FitzGibbon, J., Leruth, B., and Startin, N. (2016) *Euroscepticism as a Transnational and Pan-European Phenomenon: The Emergence of a New Sphere of Opposition*. London: Routledge.

Fleming, P. (1973). The Politics of Marriage Among Non-Catholic European Royalty. *Current Anthropology* 14(3): 231–249.

Flinders, M. (2018). The (Anti-)Politics of Brexit. In Diamond, P., Nedergaard, P., and Rosamond, B. (Eds), *The Routledge Handbook of the Politics of Brexit*. London: Routledge.

Follesdal, A. and Hix, S. (2006). Why There Is a Democratic Deficit in the EU: A Response to Majone and Moravcsik. *Journal of Common Market Studies* 44: 533–562.

Ford, R. (2019). Raising the White Flag. *Ethnicities* 20(1): 228–233.

Ford, R. and Goodwin, M. (2014). *Revolt on the Right: Explaining Support for the Radical Right in Britain*. London: Routledge.

Ford, R. and Jennings, W. (2020). The Changing Cleavage Politics of Western Europe. *Annual Review of Political Science* 23(1): 295–314.

Ford, R., Bale, T., Jennings W., and Surridge, P. (2021). *The British General Election of 2019*. London: Palgrave.

Forster, A. (2002). *Euroscepticism in Contemporary British Politics: Opposition to Europe in the Conservative and Labour Parties since 1945*. London: Routledge.

Fortes, M. (1945). *The Dynamics of Clanship Among the Tallensi: Being the First Part of an Analysis of the Social Structure of a Trans-Volta Tribe*. London: Routledge.

Foucault, M. (1980). *Power/Knowledge: Selected Interviews and Other Writings, 1972–1977*. New York: Pantheon Books.

Foucault, M. (2001). *The Order of Things*. London: Routledge.

Foucault, M. (2020). *Discipline and Punish: The Birth of the Prison*. London: Penguin.

Foy, S.L., Schleifer, C., and Tiryakian, E.A. (2018). The Rise of Rational Choice Theory as a Scientific/Intellectual Movement in Sociology. *Am Soc* 49: 16–36.

Frank, T. (2020). *The People, No: A Brief History of Anti-Populism*. New York: Metropolitan Books.

Frazer, J.G. 1998 [1890]. *The Golden Bough: A Study in Magic and Religion*. Oxford: Oxford World Classics.

Freilich, M. (1970). *Marginal Natives: Anthropology at Work*. New York: Harper and Row.

Freud, S. (1926). Inhibitions, Symptoms, and Anxiety. In Strachey, J. and Freud, A. (Eds), *The Standard Edition of the Complete Psychological Works of Sigmund Freud*. London: The Hogarth Press.

Freud, S. (1961) [1930]. *Civilization and Its Discontents*. New York: W.W. Norton & Co.
Freud, S. (1990). *Group Psychology and the Analysis of the Ego*. New York: W.W. Norton & Co.
Freud, S. (1991). *On Metapsychology: Beyond the Pleasure Principle, The Ego and the Id, And Other Works*. London: Penguin.
Freud, S. (2001). *Totem and Taboo*. London: Routledge.
Freud, S. (2008). *The Interpretation of Dreams*. Oxford: Oxford World's Classics.
Freud, S. (2010). *An Outline of Psycho-Analysis*. Eastford: Martino Fine Books.
Friedman, J. (2019). *PC Worlds: Political Correctness and Rising Elites at the End of Hegemony*. New York: Berghahn.
Friedman, J., Green, S., Eriksen, T. H., and Gringrich, A. (2010). Anthropologists Are Talking about the New Right in Europe. *Ethnos* 68(4): 554–572.
Furedi, F. (2014). *Populism and the European Culture Wars: The Conflict of Values Between Hungary and the EU*. London: Routledge.
Furedi, F. (2020). *Democracy Under Siege: Don't Let Them Lock It Down!*London: Zer0 Books.
Galston, W. (2018). The Populist Challenge to Liberal Democracy. *Journal of Democracy* 29(2): 5–19.
Geertz, C. (1974). From the Native's Point of View: On the Nature of Anthropological Understanding. *Bulletin of the American Academy of Arts and Sciences* 28(1): 26–45.
Geertz, C. (1978). Stir Crazy. *The New York Review of Books* 30.
Geertz, C. (1998). Deep Hanging Out. *The New York Review of Books* 45(16): 69–72.
Geertz, C. (2017). *The Interpretation of Cultures*. New York: Basic Books.
Geetz, C. (1980). *Negara: The Theatre State in Nineteenth-Century Bali*. Princeton, NJ: Princeton University Press.
Gellner, E. (1993). The Mightier Pen? Edward Said and the Double Standards of Inside-Out Colonialism. *Times Literary Supplement*: 3–4.
Gellwitzki, C.N.L. and Houde, A.-M. (2022) Feeling the Heat: Emotions, Politicization, and the European Union. *JCMS: Journal of Common Market Studies*: 1–18.
Gelman, S. and Legare, C. (2011). Concepts and Folk Theories. *Annual Review of Anthropology* 40(1): 379–398.
Geurkink, B., Zaslove, A., Sluiter, R., and Jacobs, K. (2020). Populist Attitudes, Political Trust, and External Political Efficacy: Old Wine in New Bottles? *Political Studies* 68(1): 247–267.
Giddens, A. (1990). *The Consequences Of Modernity*. Cambridge: Polity Press.
Giddens, A. (1991). *Modernity and Self-Identity: Self and Society in the Late Modern Age*. Cambridge: Polity Press.
Gildea, R. (2019). *Empires of the Mind: The Colonial Past and the Politics of the Present*. Cambridge: Cambridge University Press.
Gilroy, P. (2020). *Postcolonial Melancholia*. New York: Columbia University Press.
Girard, R. (2013). *Violence and the Sacred*. London: Bloomsbury.
Giry, J. and Tika, P. (2020). Conspiracy Theories in Political Science and Political Theory. In Butter, M. and Knight, P. (Eds), *Routledge Handbook of Conspiracy Theories*. London: Routledge.
Gluckman, M. (1961). Ethnographic Data in British Social Anthropology. *The Sociological Review* 9: 5–17.

Gluckman, M. (1963). Rituals of Rebellion in South-East Africa. In *Order and Rebellion in Tribal Africa*. London: Cohen and West.

Godelier, M. (1986). *The Making of Great Men: Male Domination and Power Among the New Guinea Baruya*. Cambridge: Cambridge University Press.

Godelier, M. (2018). *Claude Lévi-Strauss: A Critical Study of His Thought*. London: Verso.

Goertzel, T. (1994). Belief in Conspiracy Theories. *Political Psychology* 15: 731–742.

Goffman, E. (1961). *Asylums: Essays On the Social Situation of Mental Patients and Other Inmates*. New York: Anchor.

Golec de Zavala, A., Guerra, R., and Simão, C. (2017). The Relationship Between the Brexit Vote and Individual Predictors of Prejudice: Collective Narcissism, Right Wing Authoritarianism, Social Dominance Orientation. *Frontiers in Psychology* 8.

Goodhart, D. (2017). *The Road to Somewhere: The New Tribes Shaping British Politics*. London: Penguin.

Goodwin, M. (2011). *New British Fascism: Rise of the British National Party*. London and New York: Routledge.

Goodwin, M. and Ford, R. (2014). *Revolt on the Right: Explaining Support for the Radical Right in Britain*. London: Routledge.

Goodwin, M. and Milazzo, C. (2015). *UKIP: Inside the Campaign to Redraw the Map of British Politics*. Oxford: Oxford University Press.

Goody, K. (1986). *The Logic of Writing and the Organization of Society*. Cambridge: Cambridge University Press.

Goward, N. (1984). The Fieldwork Experience. In Ellen, R.F. (Ed.), *Ethnographic Research: A Guide to General Conduct*. London: Academic Press.

Graeber, D. (2002). *Toward an Anthropological Theory of Value: The False Coin of Our Own Dreams*. New York: Palgrave.

Graeber, D. (2014). *The Democracy Project: A History, a Crisis, a Movement*. London: Penguin.

Graeber, D. (2017). "At Long Last". In, Turner, T., *The Fire of the Jaguar*. Chicago, IL: HAU.

Gramsci, A. (2011). *Prison Notebooks*: Vols I-III. New York: Columbia University Press.

Gray, M. (2020). Conspiracy Theories in the Middle East. In Butter, M. and Knight, P. (Eds), *Routledge Handbook of Conspiracy Theories*. London: Routledge.

Green, S., Gregory, C., Reeves, M., Cowan, J.K., Demetriou, O., Koch, I., Carrithers, M., Andersson, R., Gingrich, A., Macdonald, S., Açıksöz, S.C., Yildirim, U., Eriksen, T.H., Shore, C., Holmes, D.R., Herzfeld, M., Strathern, M., Jensen, C.B., Martin, K., Dalakoglou, D., Poulimenakos, G., Jansen, S., Brkovič, Č., Wilson, T. M., Besnier, N., Guinness, D., Hann, M., Ballinger, P., and Dzenovska, D. (2016). Brexit Referendum: First Reactions From Anthropology. *Social Anthropology* 24: 478–502.

Greenwood, S. (2022). "A Spectrum of Magical Consciousness: Conspiracy Theories and the Stories We Tell Ourselves". *Anthropology Today* 38: 3–7.

Greenwood, S. and Goodwyn, E. (2015). *Magical Consciousness: An Anthropological and Neurobiological Approach*. London: Routledge.

Grensted, L. (1920). *A Short History of the Atonement*. Manchester: Manchester University Press.

Gupta, A. and Ferguson, J. (1997). Discipline and Practice: 'The Field' as Site, Method, and Location in Anthropology. In, Gupta, A. and Ferguson, J. (Eds),

Anthropological Locations: Boundaries and Grounds of a Field Science. Berkeley, CA: University of California Press.
Gupta, K. (1979). Travails of a Woman Fieldworker: A Small Town in Uttar Pradesh. In Srinivas, M., Shah, A., and Ramaswamy, E. (Eds), *The Fieldworker and the Field*. Delhi: Oxford University Press.
Gusterson, H. (1997). Studying Up Revisited. *PoLAR: Political and Legal Anthropology Review* 20: 114–119.
Gusterton, H. (2017). From Brexit to Trump: Anthropology and the Rise of Nationalist Populism. *American Ethnologist* 44(2): 209–214.
Gutkind, P. (1967). Comment on Colson. *Current Anthropology* 8: 105–106.
Haddon, A.C. (1897). The Saving of Vanishing Knowledge. *Nature* 55: 305–306.
Hafez, F. (2014). Shifting Borders: Islamophobia as Common Ground for Building Pan-European Right-Wing Unity. *Patterns of Prejudice* 48(5): 479–499.
Hall, S. and Massey D (2010). Interpreting The Crisis. *Soundings* 44(44): 57–71.
Hann, C. (2019). Anthropology and Populism. *Anthropology Today* 35: 1–2.
Hannerz, U. (1986). Theory in Anthropology: Small is Beautiful? The Problem of Complex Cultures. *Comparative Studies in Society and History* 28(1):362–367.
Harambam, J. and Aupers, S. (2017). 'I Am Not a Conspiracy Theorist': Relational Identifications in the Dutch Conspiracy Milieu . *Cultural Sociology* 11(1): 113–129.
Harding, S. and Hintikka, M. (2003) *(eds.) Discovering Reality: Feminist Perspectives on Epistemology, Metaphysics, Methodology and Philosophy of Science*. London: Kluwer.
Harris, K. (2022). Conspiracy Theories, Populism, and Epistemic Autonomy. *Journal of the American Philosophical Association*: 1–16.
Hart, C. (1970). Fieldwork among the Tiwi, 1928–1929. In Spindler, G.D. (Ed.), *Being an Anthropologist*. New York: Holt, Rinehart and Winston.
Hart, P., Stern, E.K., and Sundelius, B. (1997). *Beyond Groupthink: Political Group Dynamics and Foreign Policy-Making*. Ann Arbor, MI: University of Michigan Press.
Harvey, D. (2007). *A Brief History of Neoliberalism*. Oxford: Oxford University Press.
Hastrup, K. (2004). Getting It Right: Knowledge and Evidence in Anthropology. *Anthropological Theory* 4(4): 455–472.
Havelock, E. (1988). *The Muse Learns to Write: Reflections on Orality and Literacy from Antiquity to the Present*. New Haven, CT: Yale University Press.
Hawkins, B. (2021). *Deconstructing Brexit Discourses: Embedded Euroscepticism, Fantasy Objects, and the United Kingdom's Vote to Leave the European Union*. London: Routledge.
Hekman, S. (1997). Truth and Method: Feminist Standpoint Theory Revisited. *Signs* 22(2): 341–365.
Heppell, T. (2021). The British Labour Party and the Antisemitism Crisis: Jeremy Corbyn and Image Repair Theory. *The British Journal of Politics and International Relations* 23(4): 645–662.
Herzfeld, M. (1980). Honour and Shame: Problems in the Comparative Analysis of Moral Systems. *Man* 15(2): 339–351.
Herzfeld, M. (1984). The Horns of the Mediterraneanist Dilemma. *American Ethnologist* 11(3): 439–454.
Herzfeld, M. (1992). *The Social Production of Indifference: Exploring the Symbolic Roots of Western Bureaucracy*. Chicago, IL: University of Chicago Press.

Hickel, J. (2017). *The Divide: A Brief Guide to Global Inequality and Its Solutions*. London: Penguin.

Hickel, J. (2020). *Less Is More: How Degrowth Will Save The World*. London: Penguin.

Hill, J. (1986). The Refiguration of the Anthropology of Language. *Cultural Anthropology* 1(1): 89–102.

HM Treasury (2016). HM Treasury Analysis: The Immediate Economic Impact of Leaving the EU. Available at: https://assets.publishing.service.gov.uk/government/uploads/system/uploads/attachment_data/file/524967/hm_treasury_analysis_the_immediate_economic_impact_of_leaving_the_eu_web.pdf.

HM Treasury (2018). EU Exit: Long-Term Economic Analysis. Available at: https://assets.publishing.service.gov.uk/government/uploads/system/uploads/attachment_data/file/760484/28_November_EU_Exit_-_Long-term_economic_analysis__1_.pdf.

Ho, K. (2009). *Liquidated: An Ethnography of Wall Street*. Durham, NC: Duke University Press.

Ho, P. and Jin, C. (2011). La Théorie du Complot Comme un Simulacre de Sciences Sociales?. *Sociétés* 112: 147–161.

Hobolt, S. (2016) The Brexit Vote: A Divided Nation, a Divided Continent. *Journal of European Public Policy* 23(9): 1259–1277.

Hobsbawm, E. (2003). *Interesting Times: A Twentieth-Century Life*. London: Abacus.

Hofstadter, R. (1996 [1965]). *The Paranoid Style in American Politics and Other Essays*. Cambridge, MA: Harvard University Press.

Holland, T. (2020). *Dominion: The Making of the Western Mind*. London: Abacus.

Hooghe, L. and Marks, G. (2018). Cleavage Theory Meets Europe's Crises: Lipset, Rokkan, and the Transnational Cleavage. *Journal of European Public Policy* 25(1): 109–135.

Hubert, H. and Mauss, M. (1964 [1898]). *Sacrifice: Its Nature and Function*. Chicago, IL: University of Chicago Press.

Hudson, R. (1988). Uneven Development in Capitalist Societies: Changing Spatial Divisions of Labour, Forms of Spatial Organization of Production and Service Provision, and Their Impacts on Localities. *Transactions of the Institute of British Geographers* 13(4): 484–496.

Huntingdon, S. (2002). *The Clash of Civilizations: And the Remaking of World Order*. London: Simon & Schuster.

Hurvich, M. (2003). The Place of Annihilation Anxieties in Psychoanalytic Theory. *Journal of the American Psychoanalytic Association* 51: 579–616.

Hutton, W. and Adonis, A. (2018). *Saving Britain: How We Must Change To Prosper In Europe*. Abacus.

Hymer, S. (1979). *The Multinational Corporation: A Radical Approach*. Cambridge: Cambridge University Press.

Hymes, D. (1972). Introduction: The Use of Anthropology: Critical, Political, Personal. In Hymes, D. (1972), *Reinventing Anthropology*. New York: Pantheon.

Inglehart, R. (2016) [1977]. *The Silent Revolution*. Princeton, NJ: Princeton University Press.

Irwin, R. (2007). *For Lust of Knowing: The Orientalists and Their Enemies*. London: Penguin.

Jackson, P.N. (2021). Debate: Donald Trump and Fascism Studies. *Fascism* 10(1): 1–15.

James, W. (2003). *The Ceremonial Animal*. Oxford: Clarendon.

Jennings, W. and Fisher, S. (2016). *Expert Predictions of the 2016 EU Referendum*. London: Political Studies Association.

Johnston, A. (2019). Wokeness as Capital. *LSE Blog*. Available from: https://blogs.lse.ac.uk/researchingsociology/2019/09/03/wokeness-as-capital.

Jones, B. (1975). Max Weber and the Concept of Social Class. *The Sociological Review* 23(4): 729–757.

Jung, C. (1991). *Archetypes and the Collective Unconscious*. London: Routledge.

Kaufmann, E. (2018). *Whiteshift: Populism, Immigration, and the Future of White Majorities*. London: Penguin.

Keefer, P., Scartascini, C., and Vlaicu, R. (2021). Trust, Populism, and the Quality of Government. In Bågenholm, A., Bauhr, M., Grimes, M., and Rothstein, B. (Eds), *The Oxford Handbook of the Quality of Government*. Oxford: Oxford University Press.

Keeley, B. (1999). Of Conspiracy Theories. *Journal of Philosophy* 96(3): 109–126.

Keenan, D. (2005). *The Question of Sacrifice*. Indianapolis, IN: Indian University Press.

Kelsey, D. (2016). Hero Mythology and Right-Wing Populism. *Journalism Studies* 17 (8): 971–988.

Kempny, M. (1992). Malinowski's Theory of Needs and its Relevance for Emerging of the Sociological Functionalism. *The Polish Sociological Bulletin* 97: 45–56.

Kenny, M. (2017). Back to the Populist Future? Understanding Nostalgia in Contemporary Ideological Discourse. *Journal of Political Ideologies* 22(3): 256–273.

Kitcher, P. (2001). *Science, Truth, and Democracy*. Oxford: Oxford University Press.

Klein, M. (1975). *Love, Guilt, and Reparation and Other Works 1921–1945*. New York: Delacorte Press.

Knauft, B.(1996). *Genealogies For the Present in Cultural Anthropology*. New York: Routledge.

Knight, D. (2017). Anxiety and Cosmopolitan Futures: Brexit and Scotland. *American Ethnologist* 44(2): 237–242.

Köbben, A. (1967). Participation and Quantification: Fieldwork among the Djuka (bush negroes of Surinam). In Jongmans, D. and Gutkind, P. (Eds), *Anthropologists in the Field*. Assen: Van Gorcum, Prakke and Prakke.

Koch, I. (2017). What's in a Vote? Brexit Beyond Culture Wars. *American Ethnologist* 44(2): 225–230.

Koegler, C., Malreddy, P.K., and Tronicke, M. (2020). The Colonial Remains of Brexit: Empire Nostalgia and Narcissistic Nationalism. *Journal of Postcolonial Writing* 56: 585–592.

Kohut, H. (1972). Thoughts on Narcissism and Narcissistic Rage. *Psychoanalytic Study of the Child* 27: 360–400.

Koopmans, R. and Zürn, M. (2019). Cosmopolitanism and Communitarianism – How Globalization Is Reshaping Politics in the Twenty-First Century. In De Wilde, P., Koopmans, R., Merkel, W., Strijbis, O., and Zürn, M. (Eds), *The Struggle Over Borders: Cosmopolitanism and Communitarianism*. Cambridge: Cambridge University Press.

Korzybski, A. (1933). Science and Sanity. An Introduction to Non-Aristotelian Systems and General Semantics. *The International Non-Aristotelian Library Publishing Company*: 747–761.

Kotkin, J. (2020). *The Coming of Neo-Feudalism: A Warning to the Global Middle Class*. New York: Encounter Books.

Kriesi, H., Grande, E., Lachat, R., Dolezal, M., Bornschier, S., and Frey, T. (2006). Globalization and the Transformation of the National Political Space: Six European Countries Compared. *European Journal of Political Research* 45: 921–956.

Krystal, H. (1988). *Integration and Self-Healing*. Hillsdale, NJ: Analytic Press.

Kuklick, H. (1991). *The Savage Within: The Social History of British Anthropology, 1885–1945*. Cambridge: Cambridge University Press.

Kulz, C. (2020). British Migrants in Berlin: Negotiating Postcolonial Melancholia and Racialised Nationalism in the Wake of Brexit. *Ethnic and Racial Studies* 45(7): 1326–1346.

Kumar, K. (2006). Empire and English Nationalism. *Nations and Nationalism* 12(1): 1–13.

Kunnath, G. (2013). Anthropology's Ethical Dilemmas: Reflections From the Maoist Fields of India. *Current Anthropology* 54 (6): 740–752.

Kurtz, D. (1996). Hegemony and Anthropology. Gramsci, Exegeses, Reinterpretations. *Critique of Anthropology* 16(2): 103–135.

Laclau, E. (2005). *On Populist Reason*. London: Verso.

Lähdesmäki, T. (2018). Founding Myths of EU Europe and the Workings of Power in the EU Heritage and History Initiatives. *European Journal of Cultural Studies* 22 (5–6): 781–798.

Laing, R.D. (2010). *The Divided Self: An Existential Study in Sanity and Madness*. London: Penguin.

Lambert, H. (2009). Evidentiary Truths? The Evidence of Anthropology Through the Anthropology of Medical Evidence. *Anthropology Today* 25: 16–20.

Lamont, M. and Molnár, V. (2002). The Study of Boundaries in the Social Sciences. *Annual Review of Sociology* 28: 167–195.

Langlois, L. (2021). The Brexit Vote and The Trump Vote: A Comparative Study of the Common Trends and Factors that Led to a Populist Radical Right Vote in Britain and the United States. *Revue LISA* 19(51).

Lapavitsas, C. (2018). *The Left Case Against the EU*. Cambridge: Polity Press.

Laplantine, F. (2014). *Thinking Between Shores: Georges Devereux*. Available at: https://booksandideas.net/Thinking-Between-Shores-Georges.html.

Larner, W. (2003). Neoliberalism? *Environment and Planning D: Society and Space* 21: 509–512.

Lasch, C. (1994). *The Revolt of the Elites: And the Betrayal of Democracy*. New York: W.W. Norton & Co.

Lasch, C. (2018). *The Culture of Narcissism: American Life in An Age of Diminishing Expectations*. New York: W.W. Norton & Co.

Latour, B. and Woolgar, S. (1987). *Laboratory Life: The Construction of Scientific Facts*. Princeton, NJ: Princeton University Press.

Laurence, J., Schmid, K., and Rae, J.R. (2019). Prejudice, Contact, and Threat At the Diversity-Segregation Nexus: A Cross-Sectional and Longitudinal Analysis of How Ethnic Out-Group Size And Segregation Interrelate for Inter-group Relations. *Social Forces* 97(3): 1029–1066.

Leach, E. (2002). The Epistemological Background to Malinowski's Empiricism. In Firth, R. (Ed.), *Man and Culture: An Evaluation of the Work of Bronislaw Malinowski*. London: Routledge.

Leach, E. (2002). The Epistemological Background to Malinowski's Empiricism. In Firth, R. (Ed.), *Man and Culture: An Evaluation of the Work of Bronislaw Malinowski*. London: Routledge.

Lederman, R. (1998). Globalization and the Future of Culture Areas: Melanesianist Anthropology in Transition. *Annual Review of Anthropology* 27: 427–449.
Lederman, R. (2004). Towards an Anthropology of Disciplinarity. *Critical Matrix* 15: 60–68.
Lennon, M. (2018). Revisiting 'The Repugnant Other' in the Era of Trump. *HAU: Journal of Ethnographic Theory* 8(3): 439–454.
Lévi-Strauss, C. (1955). The Structural Study of Myth. *The Journal of American Folklore* 68(270): 428–444.
Lévi-Strauss, C. (1964). *Totemism*. London: Merlin Press.
Lévi-Strauss, C. (1969). *The Elementary Structures of Kinship*. Boston: Beacon Press.
Lévi-Strauss, C. (1974). *Structural Anthropology: Volume One*. New York: Basic Books.
Lévi-Strauss, C. (2011 [1955]). *Tristes Tropiques*. London: Penguin.
Lévi-Strauss, C. (2021). *Wild Thought: A New Translation of 'La Pensee Sauvage'*. Chicago, IL: University of Chicago Press.
Lévy-Bruhl, L. (2015) [1910]. *How Natives Think*. London: Martino Fine Books.
Lewis, D. (1973). Anthropology and Colonialism. *Current Anthropology* 14(5): 581–602.
Lewis, I. (1976). *Social Anthropology in Perspective: The Relevance of Social Anthropology*. London: Penguin.
Lichtenberg, J. (2001). *Psychoanalysis and Motivation*. London: Routledge.
Lind, M. (2021). *The New Class War: Saving Democracy from the Metropolitan Elite*. London: Atlantic Books.
Lipset, S. and Rokkan, S. (1967). Cleavage Structures, Party Systems, and Voter Alignments: An Introduction. In Lipset, S. and Rokkan, S. (Eds), *Party Systems and Voter Alignments: Cross-National Perspectives*. New York: Free Press.
Littoz-Monnet, A. (2020). *Governing through Expertise. The Politics of Bioethics*. Cambridge: Cambridge University Press.
Liu, C. (2021). *Virtue Hoarders: The Case Against the Professional Managerial Class*. Minneapolis, MN: University of Minnesota Press.
Longino, H. (2001). *The Fate of Knowledge*. Princeton, NJ: Princeton University Press.
Low, A. (2016). Brexit is not the will of the British people - it never has been. *LSE Brexit Blog*. Available at: https://blogs.lse.ac.uk/brexit/2016/10/24/brexit-is-not-the-will-of-the-british-people-it-never-has-been.
Low, S.M. (2001). The Edge and the Center: Gated Communities and the Discourse of Urban Fear. *American Anthropologist* 103: 45–58.
Luhmann, N. (1990). *Political Theory in the Welfare State*. New York: Walter de Gruyter.
Lukács, G. (2000). *History and Class Consciousness: Studies in Marxist Dialectics*. Cambridge, MA: The MIT Press.
Lukes, S. (1975). Political Ritual and Social Integration. *Sociology* 9: 289–308.
Lukianoff, G. and Haidt, J. (2019). *The Coddling of the American Mind: How Good Intentions and Bad Ideas are Setting up a Generation For Failure*. London: Penguin.
Luxemburg, R. (2016). *The Complete Works of Rosa Luxemburg, Volume II: Economic Writings*. London: Verso.
Mair, J. (2017). Post-Truth Anthropology. *Anthropology Today* 33(3):3–4.
Mair, P. (2013). *Ruling the Void: The Hollowing of Western Democracy*. London: Verso.
Malinowski, B. (1927). *Sex and Repression in Savage Society*. London: Routledge.

Malinowski, B. (1948). *Magic, Science and Religion*. Glencoe: Free Press.
Malinowski, B. (1979). *Myth in Primitive Psychology*. London: Greenwood Press.
Malinowski, B. (2014). *Argonauts of the Western Pacific: An Account of Native Enterprise and Adventure in the Archipelagos of Melanesian New Guinea*. London: Routledge.
Malinowski, M. (1978). *Argonauts of the Western Pacific: An Account of Native Enterprise and Adventure in the Archipelagos of Melanesian New Guinea*. London: Routledge.
Malkki, L. (1992). National Geographic: The Rooting of Peoples and the Territorialization of National Identity among Scholars and Refugees. *Cultural Anthropology* 7(1): 4–44·.
Mandelbaum, M. (2020). 'Making Our Country Great Again': The Politics of Subjectivity in an Age of National-Populism. *International Journal for the Semiotics of Law* 33: 451–476.
Manley, G. (2021). Temporalities of Emergent Axiomatic Violence in Brexit Scotland. *Anthropological Forum* 31(3): 275–290.
Manners, I. (2018). Political Psychology of European Integration: The (Re)production of Identity and Difference in the Brexit Debate. *Political Psychology* 39(6): 1213–1232.
Mannheim, K. (1952). The Problem of Generations. In Paul, K. (Ed.) *Essays on the Sociology of Knowledge: Collected Works*, Vol. 5. New York: Routledge.
Marcus, G. (1995). Ethnography in/of the World System: The Emergence of Multi-Sited Ethnography. *Annual Review of Anthropology* 24: 85–117.
Marková, I., Linell, P., and Gillespie, A. (2007). "Trust and Distrust in Society". In, Marková, I., and Gillespie, A., *Trust and Distrust: Sociocultural Perspectives*. Charlotte, NC: Information Age Publishing.
Marks, G., Attewell, D., Rovny, J., and Hooghe, L. (2021). Cleavage Theory. In Riddervold, R., Trondal, J., and Newsome, A. (Eds), *The Palgrave Handbook of EU Crises*. London: Palgrave.
Martin, J. (2018). Police and Policing. *Annual Review of Anthropology* 47(1): 133–148.
Marx, K. (1975). A Contribution to the Critique of Hegel's Philosophy of Right: Introduction. *Collected Works*, Vol. 3. London: Lawrence and Wishart.
Marx, K. (1993). *Grundrisse: Foundations of the Critique of Political Economy*. London: Penguin.
Marx, K. (1994). *Selected Writings*. London: Hackett Publishing.
Marx, K. (1998). *The German Ideology: Including Book on Feuerbach*. New York: Prometheus.
Marx, K. (2008). *Capital: An Abridged Edition*. Oxford: Oxford University Press.
Marx, K. and Engels, F. (2002). *The Communist Manifesto*. London: Penguin.
Maskovsky, J. (2017). Toward The Anthropology of White Nationalist Postracialism: Comments Inspired by Hall, Goldstein, and Ingram's 'The Hands of Donald Trump'. *HAU: Journal of Ethnographic Theory* 7(1): 433–440.
Maslow, A. (1943). A Theory of Human Motivation . *Psychological Review* 50(4): 370–396.
Mason, P. (2021). *How To Stop Fascism: History, Ideology, Resistance*. London: Allen Lane.
Mason, R. (1994). The Scottish Reformation and the Origins of Anglo-British Imperialism. In Mason, R. (Ed.), *Scots and Britons: Scottish Political Thought and the Union of 1603*. Cambridge: Cambridge University Press.

Matter, S. (2010). Clashing Claims: Neopatrimonial Governance, Land Tenure Transformation, and Violence at Enoosupukia, Kenya. *PoLAR: Political and Legal Anthropology Review* 33: 67–88.
Mauss, M. (2000). *The Gift: The Form and Reason for Exchange in Archaic Societies*. New York: W.W. Norton & Co.
Mayblin, M. (2014). The Untold Sacrifice: The Monotony and Incompleteness of Self-Sacrifice in Northeast Brazil. *Ethnos* 79(3): 342–364.
Mayblin, M. and Course, M. (2014). The Other Side of Sacrifice: Introduction. *Ethnos* 79(3): 307–319.
Mazzarella, W. (2019). The Anthropology of Populism: Beyond the Liberal Settlement. *Annual Review of Anthropology*, 48(1): 45–60.
Melhuish, F. (2022). Euroscepticism, Anti-Nostalgic Nostalgia, and the Past Perfect Post-Brexit Future. *Journal of Common Market Studies*.
Mellone, A., Gong, Z., and Scarciotti, G. (2021). Modelling, prediction and design of COVID-19 lockdowns by stringency and duration. *Sci Rep* 11.
Meunier-Aitsahalia, S. and Ross, G. (1993). Democratic Deficit or Democratic Surplus? A Reply to Andrew Moravcsik's Comments on the French Referendum. *French Politics and Society* 11(1): 57–69.
Miller, J., Saunders, K., and Farhart, C. (2016). Conspiracy Endorsement as Motivated Reasoning: The Moderating Roles of Political Knowledge and Trust. *American Journal of Political Science* 60(4): 824–844.
Mills, C.W. (2000). *The Power Elite*. Oxford: Oxford University Press.
Mintchev, N. (2021). The Cultural Politics of Racism in the Brexit Conjuncture. *International Journal of Cultural Studies* 24(1): 123–140.
Mintchev, N. and Moore, H.L. (2019). Brexit's Identity Politics and the Question of Subjectivity. *Psychoanalysis, Culture & Society* 24(4): 452–472.
Moffitt, B. (2016). *The Global Rise of Populism: Performance, Political Style, and Representation*. Stanford, CA: Stanford University Press.
Molé, N.J. (2010). Precarious Subjects: Anticipating Neoliberalism in Northern Italy's Workplace. *American Anthropologist* 112(1): 38–53.
Moravcsik, A. (2003). The Myth of the European Democratic Deficit. *Raisons Politiques* 10: 87–105.
Moss, J, Robinson, E, and Watts, J. (2020). Brexit and the Everyday Politics of Emotion: Methodological Lessons from History. *Political Studies* 68(4): 837–856.
Mudde, C. (2004). The Populist Zeitgeist. *Government and Opposition* 39(4): 542–563.
Mudde, C. and Kaltwasser, C.R. (2013). Populism. In Freeden, M., Sargent, L.T. and Stears, M. (Eds), *The Oxford Handbook of Political Ideologies*. Oxford: Oxford University Press.
Müller, J.-W. (2017). *What is Populism?*London: Penguin.
Munslow, A. (2012). *A History of History*. London: Routledge.
Murie, A. (2016). *The Right to Buy? Selling off Public and Social Housing*. London: Policy Press.
Nader, L. (1972). Up the Anthropologist: Perspectives Gained from Studying Up. In Hymes, D. (Ed.), *Reinventing Anthropology*. New York: Vintage.
Namier, L. (1978). *The Structure of Politics at the Accession of George* III. London: Palgrave.
Neilson, B. and Rossiter, N. (2008). Precarity as a political concept, or, Fordism as exception. *Theory, Culture & Society* 25(7–8): 51–72.

Nietzsche, F. (2013). *On The Genealogy of Morals: A Polemic*. London: Penguin.
Nisbet, R. (1969). *Social Change and History: Aspects of the Western Theory of Development*. Oxford: Oxford University Press.
Norris, P. and Inglehart, R. (2019). *Cultural Backlash: Trump, Brexit and Authoritarian Backlash*. Cambridge: Cambridge University Press.
O'Rourke, K. (2019). *A Short History of Brexit: From Brentry to Backstop*. London: Pelican.
Obeid, M. (2011). The "Trials and Errors" of Politics: Municipal Elections at the Lebanese Border. *PoLAR: Political and Legal Anthropology Review* 34: 251–267.
Ortner, S. (1995). Resistance and the Problem of Ethnographic Refusal. *Comparative Studies in Society and History* 37(1): 173–193.
Orwell, G. (2016). *Seeing Things as They Are: Selected Journalism and Other Writings*. London: Penguin.
Otto, R. (1923). *The Idea of the Holy*. Oxford: Oxford University Press.
Oztig, L., Gurkan, T., and Aydin, K. (2021). The Strategic Logic of Islamophobic Populism. *Government and Opposition* 56(3).
Pagán, V. (2020). Conspiracy Theories in the Roman Empire. In Butter, M. and Knight, P. (Eds), *Routledge Handbook of Conspiracy Theories*. London: Routledge.
Pagel, C. and Yates, C. (2022). Role of Mathematical Modelling in Future Pandemic Response Policy. *BMJ* 378.
Paley, J. (2002). Toward An Anthropology of Democracy. *Annual Review of Anthropology* 31: 469–496.
Panoff, M. (1988). Du Mythe A La Propagande: Un Cas Mélanésian. *L'Homme* XXVIII(2–3):252–262.
Pareto, V. (1991). *The Rise and Fall of Elites: An Application of Theoretical Sociology*. Piscataway: Transaction Publishers.
Parmigiani, G. (2021). Magic and Politics: Conspirtuality and Covid-19. *Journal of the American Academy of Religion* 89(2): 506–529.
Parsons, T. (2002). *Malinowski and the Theory of Social Systems*. London: Routledge.
Pasieka, A. (2019). Anthropology of the Far Right: What If We Like Che 'Unlikeable' Others?. *Anthropology Today* 35: 3–6.
Passaro, J. (1977). You Can't Take the Subway to the Field!": "Village" Epistemologies in the Global Village. In Gupta, A. and Ferguson, J. (Eds) *Anthropological Locations: Boundaries and Grounds of a Field Science*. Berkeley, CA: University of California Press.
Paul, R. (1989). Psychoanalytic Anthropology. *Annual Review of Anthropology* 18: 177–202.
Perlman, J.E. (1976). *The Myth of Marginality: Urban Poverty and Politics in Rio de Janeiro*. Berkeley, CA: University of California Press.
Polanyi, K. (2002). *The Great Transformation: The Political and Economic Origins of Our Time*. New York: Beacon.
Popper, K. (2002) [1959]. *The Logic of Scientific Discovery*. London: Routledge.
Popper, K. (2011). *The Open Society and Its Enemies*. London: Routledge.
Proctor, R.N. (2012). The History of the Discovery of the Cigarette–lung Cancer Link: Evidentiary Traditions, Corporate Denial, Global Toll. *Tobacco Control* 21: 87–91.
Rabo, A. (2021). Conspiracy Theory As Occult Cosmology in Anthropology. In Butter, M. and Knight, P. (Eds), *Routledge Handbook of Conspiracy Theories*. London: Routledge.

Radcliffe-Brown, A.R. (1940). On Joking Relationships. *Africa: Journal of the International African Institute* 13(3): 195–210.

Radin, P. (1945). *The Road of Life and Death: A Ritual Drama of the American Indians*. Princeton, NJ: Princeton University Press.

Radin, P. (2015). *Primitive Man as Philosopher*. New York: NYRB Classics.

Ralph, L. (2014). *Renegade Dreams: Living Through Injury in Gangland Chicago*. Chicago, IL: University of Chicago Press.

Ralph, L. (2020). *The Torture Letters: Reckoning with Police Violence*. Chicago, IL: University of Chicago Press.

Ranelagh, J. (1986). *The Agency: The Rise and Decline of the CIA: From Wild Bill Donovan to William Casey*. New York: Simon & Schuster.

Rank, O. (1952). *The Myth of the Birth of the Hero*. New York: Robert Brunner.

Rapport, N. and Overing, J. (2000). *Social and Cultural Anthropology: The Key Concepts*. London: Routledge.

Rawlinson, F. (2020). *How Press Propaganda Paved the Way to Brexit*. London: Palgrave.

Remmling, G. (1969) *Road to Suspicion: A Study of Modern Mentality and the Sociology of Knowledge*. New York: Appleton-Century-Crofts.

Renard, J. (2015). Why do People Adhere to Conspiracy Theories?. *Diogène* 1–2: 107–119.

Reynolds, D. (2019). *Island Stories: Britain and Its History in the Age of Brexit*. London: William Collins.

Rhodes, C. (2022). *Woke Capitalism: How Corporate Mentality is Sabotaging Democracy*. Bristol: Bristol University Press.

Ringel, F. (2020). Brexit as Postindustrial Critique. *HAU* 10(2).

Rivers, W.H.R. (1922) *(ed.) Essays on the Depopulation of Melanesia*. Cambridge: Cambridge University Press.

Robbins, J. (2013). Beyond the Suffering Subject: Toward an Anthropology of the Good. *The Journal of the Royal Anthropological Institute* 19(3): 447–462.

Robinson, W. and Harris, J. (2000). Towards a Global Ruling Class? Globalization and the Transnational Capitalist Class. *Science & Society* 64(1): 11–54.

Rogers, C. (1961). *On Becoming a Person: A Therapist's View of Psychotherapy*. London: Constable.

Rogers, C. (1980). *A Way of Being*. Boston, MA: Houghton Mifflin.

Rogin, M. (1987). *'Ronald Reagan' The Movie: And Other Episodes in Political Demonology*. London: University of California Press.

Rosaldo, R. (1980). *Ilongot Headhunting, 1883–1974: A Study in Society and History*. Stanford, CA: Stanford University Press.

Rutland, P. (2017). Trump, Putin, and the Future of US-Russian Relations. *Slavic Review* 76(1): 41–56.

Saberwal, S. (1969). Rapport and Resistance Among the Embu of Central Kenya (1963–64). In Henry, F. and Saberwal, S. (Eds), *Stress and Response in Fieldwork*. New York: Holt, Rinehart and Winston.

Sahlins, M. (1976). *Culture and Practical Reason*. Chicago, IL: University of Chicago Press.

Sahlins, M. (1987). *Islands of History*. Chicago, IL: University of Chicago Press.

Said, E. (2003). *Orientalism*. London: Penguin.

Sampson, T. (2017). Brexit: The Economics of International Disintegration. *Journal of Economic Perspectives* 31(4): 163–184.

Sandler, J. and Rosenblatt, B. (1967). The Concept of the Representational World. *The Psychoanalytic Study of the Child* 17: 128–145.

Sassen, S. (2014). *Expulsions: Brutality and Complexity in the Global Economy*. Cambridge, MA: Harvard University Press.

Saunders, R. (2020). Brexit and Empire: 'Global Britain' and the Myth of Imperial Nostalgia. *The Journal of Imperial and Commonwealth History* 48(6): 1140–1174.

Savelsberg, J. (1994). Knowledge, Domination and Criminal Punishment. *American Journal of Sociology* 99(4): 911–944.

Schäfer, A. (2021). Cultural Backlash? How (Not) to Explain the Rise of Authoritarian Populism. *British Journal of Political Science*: 1–17.

Schaffer, F. (1997). Political Concepts and the Study of Democracy. The Case of Demokarassi in Senegal. *PoLAR: Political and Legal Anthropology Review* 20(1): 40–49.

Scheff, T. and Retzinger, S. (2003). Hitler's Appeal: Alienation, Shame-rage, and revenge. In Silberman (Ed.), *Violence and Society: A Reader*. London: Pearson.

Scheper-Hughes, N. (1993). *Death Without Weeping: The Violence of Everyday Life in Brazil*. Berkeley, CA: University of California Press.

Schindler, C. (2016). From Zionist to Corbynist: The Evolution of Britain's Labour Left. *Jewish Quarterly* 63(2): 38–41.

Schroeder, R. (2018). Digital Media and the Rise of Right-Wing Populism. In *Social Theory After the Internet: Media, Technology, and Globalization*. London: UCL Press.

Schumpter, J. (2010). *Capitalism, Socialism, and Democracy*. London: Martino Fine Books.

Scott, J. (1985). *Weapons of the Weak: Everyday Forms of Peasant Resistance*. New Haven, CT: Yale University Press.

Scott, J. (2020). *Seeing Like A State: How Certain Schemes To Improve The Human Condition Have Failed*. New Haven, CT: Yale University Press.

Seymour, R. (2017). *Corbyn: The Strange Rebirth of Radical Politics*. London: Verso.

Shaw, M. (2022). *Political Racism: Brexit and its Aftermath*. London: Agenda.

Sheils, D. (1975). Toward a Unified Theory of Ancestor Worship. *Social Forces* 54(2): 427–440.

Shipman, T. (2017). *All Out War: The Full Story of Brexit*. London: William Collins.

Shipman, T. (2018). *Fall Out: A Year of Political Mayhem*. London: William Collins.

Shlaim, A. (2014). *The Iron Wall: Israel and the Arab World*. London: Penguin.

Shore, C. (1993). Inventing the 'People's Europe': Critical Approaches to European Community 'Cultural Policy'. *Man* 28: 779–800.

Shore, C. (2000). *Building Europe: The Cultural Politics of European Integration*. London: Routledge.

Shore, C. (2006). Government without Statehood? Anthropological Perspectives on Governance and Sovereignty in the European Union. *European Law Journal* 12(6): 709–724.

Shore, C. (2021). Britain, Brexit and Euroscepticism: Anthropological Perspectives on Angry Politics, Technopopulism and the UK Referendum. *Anthropological Journal of European Cultures* 30: 1–22.

Sklair, L. (2002). "The Transnational Capitalist Class and Global Politics: Deconstructing the Corporate: State Connection". *International Political Science Review / Revue Internationale de Science Politique* 23(2): 159–174.

Slater, J. (2020). *Mythologies Without End: The US, Israel, and the Arab-Israeli Conflict 1917–2020*. Oxford: Oxford University Press.

Sobolewska, M. and Ford, R. (2020). *Brexitland: Identity, Diversity, and the Reshaping of British Politics*. Cambridge: Cambridge University Press.

Spencer, J. (2012). *Anthropology, Politics, and the State: Democracy and Violence in South Asia*. Cambridge: Cambridge University Press.

Standing, G. (2011). *The Precariat: The New Dangerous Class*. London: Bloomsbury Academic.

Stanley, B. (2008). The Thin Ideology of Populism. *Journal of Political Ideologies* 13 (1): 95–110.

Starn, O. (1991). Missing the Revolution: Anthropologists and the War in Peru. *Cultural Anthropology* 6(1): 63–91.

Stein, H.F. (1983). Psychoanalytic Anthropology and the Meaning of Meaning. In Bain, B. (Ed.), *Sociogenesis of Language and Human Conduct*. New York: Plenum.

Stenner, K. (2005). *The Authoritarian Dynamic*. Cambridge University Press.

Stevens, P. (2022). *Britain Alone: The Path from Suez to Brexit*. London: Faber & Faber.

Stocking, G. (1968). *Race, Culture, and Evolution: Essays in the History of Anthropology*. Chicago, IL: University of Chicago Press.

Stocking, G.W. (1992). *The Ethnographer's Magic And Other Essays in the History of Anthropology*. Madison, WI: Wisconsin University Press.

Stocking, G.W. (1995). *After Tylor: British Social Anthropology, 1888–1951*. Madison, WI: University of Wisconsin Press.

Stoeckel, F., Lyons, B., and Reifler, J. (2021). Public Misperceptions of European Integration in the UK. *Journal of Elections: Public Opinion and Parties*, 1–21.

Streeck, W. (2019). The European Union is a Liberal Empire, and it is About to Fall. *LSE Brexit Blog*. Available at: https://blogs.lse.ac.uk/brexit/2019/03/06/long-read-the-europea n-union-is-a-liberal-empire-and-it-is-about-to-fall (Accessed 20 March 2019).

Strenski, I. (2006). *Malinowski and the Work of Myth*. Princeton, NJ: Princeton University Press.

Tajfel, H. (1974). Social Identity and Intergroup Behaviour. *Social Science Information* 13 (2): 65–93.

Taleb, N. (2019). *Skin in the Game: Hidden Asymmetries in Daily Life*. London: Penguin.

Tamkin, E. (2020). *The Influence of Soros: Politics, Power, and the Struggle for an Open Society*. New York: Harper.

Tooby, J. and Cosmides, L. (2010). Groups in Mind: The Coalitional Roots of War and Morality. In Olesen-Høgh, H. (Ed.), *Human Morality and Sociality: Evolutionary and Comparative Perspectives*. London: Palgrave.

Thalmann, K. (2019). *The Stigmatization of Conspiracy Theory Since the 1950s: 'A Plot to Make us Look Foolish'*. London: Routledge.

Thompson, E.P. (2013). *The Making of the English Working Class*. London: Penguin.

Thompson, S. and Yar, M. (2019) *The Politics of Misrecognition*. London: Routledge.

Tilford, S. (2016). Five Brexit Economic Myths. *Bulletin for the Centre for European Reform*. Available at: www.cer.eu/publications/archive/bulletin-article/2016/five-b rexit-economic-myths.

Times Higher Education (2016). EU referendum: nine out of 10 university staff back Remain. Available at: www.timeshighereducation.com/news/european-union-referendum-nine-out-of-ten-university-staff-back-remain.

Tooby, J. and Cosmides, L. (2010). Groups in Mind: The Coalitional Roots of War and Morality. In Høgh-Olesen, H. (Ed.), *Human Morality & Sociality: Evolutionary & Comparative Perspectives*. New York: Palgrave.

Traverso, E. (2019). *The New Faces of Fascism: Populism and the Far Right*. London: Verso.
Trouillot, M.-R. (2003). *Global Transformations: Anthropology and the Modern World*. London: Palgrave.
Trouillot, M.-R. (1992). The Caribbean Region: An Open Frontier in Anthropological Theory. *Annual Review of Anthropology* 21: 19–42.
Trouillot, M.R. (2003). Anthropology and the Savage Slot: The Poetics and Politics of Otherness. In Trouillot, M.R., *Global Transformations*. New York: Palgrave.
Tsing, A. (2015). *The Mushroom at the End of the World: On the Possibility of Life in Capitalist Ruins*. Princeton, NJ: Princeton University Press.
Tuck, R. (2020). *The Left Case for Brexit: Reflections on the Current Crisis*. Cambridge: Polity Press.
Turley, D. (1991). *The Culture of English Antislavery*. London: Routledge.
Turner, V. (1970). *The Forest of Symbols: Aspects of the Ndembu Ritual*. Ithaca, NY: Cornell University Press.
Tylor, E.B. (1958). *The Origins of Culture*. New York: Harper.
Tylor, E.B. (2016 [1871]) *Primitive Culture: Volume One*. London: Dover.
Urban, G. and Koh, K.-N. (2013). Ethnographic Research on Modern Business Corporations. *Annual Review of Anthropology* 42(1): 139–158.
Valluvan, S. and Kalra, V. (2019) Racial Nationalisms: Brexit, Borders and Little Englander Contradictions. *Ethnic and Racial Studies* 42(14): 2393–2412.
Van Gennep, A. (1961). *The Rites of Passage*. Chicago, IL: University of Chicago Press.
Van Marle, F. and Maruna, S. (2009). 'Ontological Insecurity' and 'Terror Management': Linking Two Free-Floating Anxieties. *Punishment & Society* 12(1): 7–26.
Van Vugt, M. and Schalle, M. (2008). Evolutionary Approaches to Group Dynamics: An Introduction. *Group Dynamics: Theory, Research, and Practice* 12(1): 1–6.
Varoufakis, Y. (2017). *And the Weak Suffer What They Must? Europe, Austerity, and the Threat to Global Stability*. London: Vintage.
Varoufakis, Y. (2018). *Adults in the Room: My Battle with Europe's Deep Establishment*. London: Vintage.
Veblen, T. (2009). *The Theory of the Leisure Class*. Oxford: Oxford University Press.
Verdery, K. (2018). *My Life as a Spy: Investigations in a Secret Police File*. Durham, NC: Duke University Press.
Vines, E. and Marsh, D. (2018). Anti-politics: Beyond Supply-side Versus Demand-side Explanations. *British Politics* 14: 433–453.
Virdee, S. and McGeever, B. (2017). Racism, Crisis, Brexit. *Ethnic and Racial Studies* 41(10): 1802–1819.
Viveiros de Castro, E. (2014). *Cannibal Metaphysics*. Minneapolis, MN: University of Minnesota Press.
von Clausewitz, C. (2008). *On War*. Oxford: Oxford University Press.
Wacquant, L. (2008). *Urban Outcasts: A Comparative Sociology of Advanced Marginality*. Cambridge: Polity Press.
Wallerstein, I. (2000). *The Essential Wallerstein*. New York: New Press.
Ward, S. and Rasch, A. (2019) *Embers of Empire in Brexit Britain*. London: Bloomsbury Academic.
Warren, D. (2022). 'Woke' Corporations and the Stigmatization of Corporate Social Initiatives. *Business Ethics Quarterly* 32(1): 169–198.

Warren, M. (2018). Trust and Democracy. In Uslaner, E. (Ed.), *The Oxford Handbook of Social and Political Trust*. Oxford: Oxford University Press.
Waters, A. (1997). Conspiracy Theories as Ethnosociologies: Explanation and Intention in African American Political Culture. *Journal of Black Studies* 28(1): 112–125.
Weber, M. (1949). *The Methodology of the Social Sciences*. New York: Free Press.
Weber, M. (1958). *The Religion of India. The Sociology of Hinduism and Buddhism*. New York: The Free Press.
Weber, M. (1971). *The Sociology of Religion*. London: Methuen.
Weber, M. (2010) "The Distribution of Power Within the Community: Classes, Stände, Parties. *Journal of Classical Sociology* 10(2): 137–152.
Weber, M. (2019). *Economy and Society: A New Translation*. Cambridge, MA: Harvard University Press.
Wellings, B. (2018). Brexit and English Identity. In Diamond, P., Nedergaard, P., and Rosamond, B. (Eds), *The Routledge Handbook of the Politics of Brexit*. London: Routledge.
Wellings, B. (2020). Brexit, Nationalism and the Disintegration in the European Union and the United Kingdom. *Journal of Contemporary European Studies*, 1–13.
Whittaker, C. (1965). The Delphic Oracle: Belief and Behaviour in Ancient Greece – and Africa. *Harvard Theological Review* 58(1): 21–47.
Wilcox, C. (1992). *God's Warriors: The Christian Right in Twentieth-Century America*. Baltimore, MD: John Hopkins University Press.
Williams, M.H. (2010). Can Leopards Change Their Spots? Between Xenophobia and Trans-Ethnic Populism among West European Far Right Parties. *Nationalism and Ethnic Politics* 16(1): 111–134.
Williams, T. (2021). Mobilizing the Past: Germany and the Second World War in Debates on Brexit. *Revue LISA/LISA E-Journal* 19(51).
Winnicott, D. (1960). *The Maturational Processes and the Facilitating Environment*. London: Hogarth Press.
Wodak, R. (2015). *The Politics of Fear: What Right-Wing Populist Discourses Mean*. London: Sage.
Wolf, E. (1958). The Virgin of Guadalupe: A Mexican National Symbol. *The Journal of American Folklore* 71(279): 34–39.
Zmerli, S. and Newton, K. (2008). Social Trust and Attitudes toward Democracy. *The Public Opinion Quarterly* 72(4): 706–724.

INDEX

Kolibri 360 GmbH
Ferdinand-Jühlke-Straße 7
99095 Erfurt, Deutschland
produktsicherheit@kolibri360.de